RAISING CASH

RAISING CASH

A Guide to Financing and Controlling Your Business

Sol Postyn

Jo Kirschner Postyn

LIFETIME LEARNING PUBLICATIONS
A division of Wadsworth, Inc. Belmont, California

London, Singapore, Sydney
Toronto, Mexico City

Jacket Designer: Ben Wong
Text Designer: Michael Rogondino
Developmental Editor: Sylvia Stein
Photographs: Tom Tracey
Composition: Graphic Typesetting Service

Printed in the United States of America

1 2 3 4 5 6 7 8 9 10—86 85 84 83 82

Library of Congress Cataloging in Publication Data

Postyn, Sol
  Raising cash.

  Bibliography: p.
  Includes index.
  1. Small business—Finance. I. Postyn, Jo Kirschner   II. Title.
HG4027.7.P67   658.1'522   81-13665
ISBN 0-534-97966-1   AACR2

This publication is designed to provide accurate and authoritative information on the subject matter covered. It is sold with the understanding that the publisher is not engaged in rendering legal, accounting, or professional services. If legal advice or other professional assistance is required, the services of a competent professional person should be sought.

Descriptive
Contents

The key factor in getting financing is establishing credibility with your lender or investor. Proving your ability to be in touch with all aspects of your business is a prerequisite to establishing and maintaining credibility.

You must understand the relationship between goals, the amount of financing you need, and the length of time you will need it. There are various ways to determine how much financing you require, how much you are likely to get, and what kind of financing to seek—loan, investment, or a combination of these.

You can't do everything yourself. If you understand the accountant's/bookkeeper's job, you'll be better able to hire effective personnel to provide you and your lender/investor with timely financial communications and to use that information productively in controlling and administering your business.

Chapter 4   Creating Your Accounting System   37

Accounting/bookkeeping functions are interrelated in an accounting system, which is not operative until necessary procedures have been developed and implemented. Of the various types of systems available—manual, semiautomatic, and automatic—you must decide which best meets the needs of your business.

Chapter 5   Should You Computerize Your System?   50

With the advent of the microcomputer and the abundance of commercial data-processing programs, computerized financial information is available to all, not just to giant corporations. Caution is the key in selecting an appropriate system for your needs, and expert counsel is a must.

PART THREE: PLANNING YOUR BUSINESS   75

Chapter 6   Financial Planning   77

Planning is the key to the success of your operation. Some of the essential elements of financial planning are breakeven, the operating and capital budgets, the cash forecast, and projected balance sheet.

Chapter 7   Keeping Cash Flowing and Profits Growing   92

Two major obstacles to cash flow are accounts receivable and inventory. Both are critical areas you must control in order to maximize profits. You should also segment your business by product, service, or geographical area so you may assess each according to its profit contribution.

Chapter 8   Getting Help from Professionals and Peers   106

An advisory team (board of directors) is available to a company of almost any size. It should consist of professionals (attorney, CPA, banker, insurance adviser), members of the business community faced with similar problems, and key members of your staff, if your business is large enough to warrant it.

PART FOUR: DESIGNING YOUR BUSINESS PLAN   117

Chapter 9   How to Write Your Plan—Prose Section   119

Potential lenders or investors will want to know the background of your business, your business philosophy, your goals, the products or services you offer, and your methods of distribution. They will also want to know who makes up your company's organization, including staff, board, and outside consultants, and how the company is administered and controlled.

Chapter 10   How to Write Your Plan—Financial Section   131

The financial section of your business plan consists of three comparative reports, showing the relationship between past accomplishments and future projections of the profit or loss statement, the cash statement, the balance sheet, and a fourth report—the capital budget. The purpose of this part of your plan is to substantiate, with numbers, the points you have made in the prose section.

PART FIVE: CLOSING THE DEAL   153

Chapter 11   Negotiations   155

Before beginning negotiations with a potential lender or investor, it will help to understand the needs of the person or persons about to put up the money. Certain terms are bound to be part of the negotiations and it's to your advantage to understand them.

Chapter 12   Getting Cash from Banks   169

Once you determine how much financing you need and how long you'll need it, you must explore possible sources. Banks are the most traditional and obvious consideration.

Chapter 13   Getting Cash from Uncle Sam   179

The Small Business Administration and small business investment companies are also sources of financing. There are pros and cons to getting cash from a government-affiliated or subsidized agency, and you should be familiar with them.

Chapter 14   Other Options for Raising Cash   190

Other sources of money include the private sector (such as industries and finance companies), offerings to the public through selling stock, limited partnership interests, forming a partnership, a joint venture, customers, suppliers, service people, landlords, and even buying a business.

Appendixes   202

The sample business plan demonstrates for a hypothetical company what is discussed in Part Four. The next four appendixes go into more detail than the text on preparing four important documents. Appendix F provides a handy list of SBA field offices nationwide.

Detailed Contents

Preface

As an entrepreneur, you may have already discovered that cash coming in does not always match cash going out. Thus it's inevitable that you will at some point have to finance your business. But if your background has been in making or marketing a product, rather than in finance, the prospect of raising money may cause you some concern. In today's turbulent economy, the project is even more intimidating. Our purpose, therefore, is to help you obtain and maintain the cash you need to run your business efficiently and profitably.

Raising Cash Covers the Whole Scope of Your Financing Requirements

Whether you need money to get a new business going, to maintain a smooth cash flow, or to buy an essential building or piece of equipment, this book will show you:

- when to look for financing
- what to do before attempting to raise cash
- who to seek out as a source of cash
- where to find alternative sources of money
- how to determine the amount you need
- how to negotiate the best deal for your business

And Emphasizes the Need for Control Over Your Business

Years of working with entrepreneurs like you, as well as with lenders and investors, have convinced us that the key to raising cash is what you do *before* you attempt to get financing. To put it another way, the image you project, of yourself and of your operation, will determine your success in getting your loan or investment. That image hinges on the kind of control you can demonstrate over your business. Regardless of your background, you must show that you have a firm grasp on the financial aspects of your operation.

It Shows You How to Implement the Tools of Control

Thus, we will cover such matters as:

- monitoring your cash flow
- avoiding distortion of your gross profit
- keeping a tight rein on your accounts receivable and inventory
- determining whether you should computerize your accounting system

This is not to say that you have to become a financial expert. On the contrary, you can get help from your staff, your CPA, attorney, insurance people, and others. But as the boss of your business, you are the one who will represent your company to a potential lender or investor so you must know what is going on.

And Helps You Design a Business Plan—Your Financing Tool

After you have understood and applied the procedures we recommend, we will help you design your business plan, the tool with which you approach a potential lender or investor. As an adjunct to these instructions, we've given you a complete *sample business plan* that can serve as a pattern for your own.

It Gives You Essential Techniques for Business Planning

In a special section of our book you will also find step-by-step instructions through which you will learn to:

- forecast your cash requirements so that you may anticipate the amount of financing your company needs
- prepare an operating budget so that you can project your company's earnings for the coming year
- construct a long-term forecast so that you'll anticipate what the future will look like before you get there
- compile a capital budget so that you'll have an idea of what fixed asset expenditures will cost and which will provide the best investments

And Practical Examples and Case Histories

Throughout the book, we've provided dozens of practical examples and techniques to guide you through the steps of controlling your business and raising cash. We've also included many case histories. In them you'll encounter other companies with problems similar to your own. You will find that there are many viable solutions to your company's financial problems and you will learn to control your business with confidence so that you can indeed raise the cash you need.

ACKNOWLEDGMENTS

The efforts of many others have supplemented our own in writing this book. Among them are friends, family members, and colleagues—too numerous to mention individually—who have lent us their interest, encouragement, and support. All of them have our gratitude.

We also acknowledge, with appreciation, the tangible efforts of the following: our editor, Sylvia E. Stein; Edna Ilyin Miller; Serge Chemla; Russell B. Skelton; Raymond Talbot; Brian Boas, C.P.A.; Bernard G. Werth, C.P.A.; Richard Grant; George Sarlow; Donald Friedman; Frank Mulberg, C.P.A., L.L.B.; Berwyn Westra; Theodore Gunkel; Michael Rice; Bruna Fazio; and Barbara Shapiro.

Sol Postyn
Jo Kirschner Postyn

To Sarah and Noah
With our love and appreciation

RAISING CASH

PART ONE

BEGINNING THE SEARCH FOR CASH

1

Establishing Credibility with Lenders/Investors

This chapter will

- Explain how raising cash depends on the credibility you establish with a potential lender/investor

- Define the components of credibility

- Point out the particular areas of concern in your business and how they affect your credibility

The boss of a business typically attaches a certain mystique to the process of raising money, but there's really no mystery involved at all. Your chances of getting financing depend on credibility. Because few persons will put up cash unless they, too, will benefit, your job in seeking financing is to prove that you and your company are a healthy risk and a good investment. You must show that you can run a profitable business. And because every facet of your operation affects your credibility, it's up to you to demonstrate that you're "in touch" with all aspects of your organization. You don't have to be an expert in every area and you certainly must delegate responsibility, but you should be familiar with the overall operation.

BEING BELIEVABLE

You're the boss; so some of the first things a potential lender/investor will want to know about you are your qualifications, your experience, and how they affect your operation. Just be yourself and put your best foot forward. At the same time, plan to show the negative side of the picture—your limitations.

3

> Give the bad with the good, illustrating how you take advantage of your strong suits while keeping your weak points under control.

This honest approach elicits more gratifying responses than a blustery attempt to present yourself as someone incapable of failure or lacking inadequacies. Whether you're making your loan or investment appeal to a single individual (who may be representing a lending institution) or a group, realism will always get you further. To illustrate, let's look at the case of a guy on the verge of bankruptcy who got himself a second chance by leveling with his investors.

Bert Roggi, president of Roggi Wines, excelled in neither marketing nor administration. In fact, he was not adept in any of the procedures of his business except manufacturing the product. Fortunately, in that he was a master.

His shortcomings caught up with him, though, just about the time of an annual stockholder's meeting. Because these investors had provided the funds that helped start the business, we felt they had a right to know all the facts. Thus, as the company's CPA, it was our job to face the disgruntled group and admit to the following deficiencies:

- After several consecutive years, the company continued to show a loss.

- Liquid assets, or cash and **accounts receivable** (money owed to the winery), were inadequate to cover the company's current debts.

- The winery was on a C.O.D. basis with many of its suppliers.

- The company was also in a difficult position with the Internal Revenue Service, having received a warning for not depositing payroll tax funds (thereby supplementing operating cash)—a procedure that might appear an easy source of funds but is taboo in *any* business. Because of this indiscretion, management could no longer expect any indulgence from that quarter.

As we explained the situation, the atmosphere in the room became increasingly heavy and the faces became longer and longer—until we showed the other side of the picture. We reminded the group that a weak marketing program in its earlier years had been responsible for many of the company's current problems. We also described the tremendous acceptance the product was receiving in the marketplace and reported that several of the company's wines had won gold and silver medals in some stiff competition. These wines were being served in the White House and by the mayor of Los Angeles, who had introduced them to some prominent French vintners.

We also announced that the winery's board of directors, which had been aware of the company's woes for some time, had responded by hiring both a marketing and a business manager. In conclusion, we summarized the favorable projections offered by the newly assembled team and presented their suggested alternatives to marketing and financial problems. Gradually, the atmosphere in the room changed. As we proceeded to make the group understand what the problems were and believe they could be corrected, the previously irate stockholders' attitudes changed. By the end of the meeting, there were even offers of additional loans to the company by the people who had been hostile at the onset. Being candid had earned Roggi Wines enormous credibility.

PUTTING YOUR MONEY WHERE YOUR MOUTH IS

Another factor important to credibility is the amount of your **capital,** that is, the amount of money you invest in your business or are able to raise among others, which becomes a permanent investment in your company.* It does not have to be repaid and you don't need to pay any interest on it. Your colleagues who help out with your **capital base** are remunerated in other ways. They may share in the company's profits through dividends or partnership distribution. In other instances, when their investment appreciates, they realize the benefits of that appreciation when you sell the business or when they sell their shares in the company.

Because the amount of capital your business has indicates how much you and your investors are willing and able to risk for the survival of your company, putting your money where your mouth is is an adage you *must* take seriously when you're attempting to establish credibility.

> If you're not willing to take a risk for your business, you can hardly expect anyone else to.

---

*Don't confuse capital with **equity,** which has two components: capital and **retained earnings,** or the money the firm earns that is kept in the business. The amount of capital you have in your company has a major effect on the amount of equity.

The crucial consideration from the lender's or investor's point of view is that there be enough capital to give your business a sufficient base to enable it to flourish.

An equally important factor is the relationship of your equity (which includes capital) to the amount of debt the business carries. This relationship, usually referred to as the **debt-equity ratio,** tells the lender/investor or financial analyst how much the owner or owners have at stake in the business, as compared with the claims of **creditors** (all those owed short-term loans and other costs, like rent, equipment, and labor). If you are laden with debt, your creditors are going to be constantly on your back. But you don't have to pay back capital; so that is one stress with which you won't have to contend. The more equity (including capital) your business has, the larger your cushion. If you have a higher level of equity than debt, you have more time to earn enough money to pay off your creditors. If it's a loan you're after, your debt-equity ratio will be carefully scrutinized.

KNOWING AND MARKETING YOUR PRODUCT

Along with you and your capital base, one of a potential lender/investor's major concerns will be your product or service. Ask yourself these questions:

1.   Do I have a viable product or service?

2.   Will it sell?

3.   If it's a new product, can I create a market for it?

You must show that you are thoroughly familiar with your product or service if you intend to give a credible representation of your business. We mean *really* know the product and describe it accurately so that you can pinpoint its cash requirements and explain its impact on your financial picture. You should also be prepared to tell how it came to be, what it's made of, who designed it, what its capabilities are, what its extended possibilities are, and what its competition is. You're the expert on the subject—or should be; so plan to have all its components and idiosyncrasies at your fingertips if you're going to make a believable appeal for funds.

Sometimes the product of a business isn't what it appears to be initially. For example, one of our clients, Freund and Schiller Ltd., was to all appearances in the import-export food business. Not only was the business so described by people who had been acquainted with it for years, but at our initial meetings even the founders made no attempt to correct that impression. Not long after we began to work together, however, we realized that their financial projections were unrealistic because the sale of food products could never generate the increased sales volume they predicted. When queried about the forecasts and their viability, the clients began to elaborate on the range of products they offered and the varied markets in which they were sold.

Thus we became aware that their business was not a food business but a service business, with food just one of the products offered. The firm's prime concern was to obtain for their clients any merchandise requested at a competitive price. Since the inception of their operation, the company's merchandise had been expanded to include heavy machinery, jewelry, and cosmetics. In addition, our clients had extended the geographical area originally serviced. In light of these facts, their projections were realistic, and this important clarification became an important factor in the company's bid for a **line of credit** (an agreement that one may borrow, in increments, up to an agreed-upon maximum limit).

Having an excellent product or service doesn't guarantee sales or assure you of a loan or investment. Your chances of success in business and of raising cash also depend on your selling strategy or your marketing program.

You must know who your customer is, why that person will want to buy, and when and how to approach him or her. You doubtless have a profile of your ultimate user. But is he or she the person to whom you should be directing your marketing efforts, or should your strategy be aimed at the people controlling the purse strings, those who will buy in quantity before they turn around and sell it to the consumer?

With many routes to the marketplace, a company can easily reach a stalemate before a product catches on. How often have you heard the story of a product's creator getting nowhere until a promoter comes along with the key approach for selling it? Marketing ability is a creative and specialized talent, and brilliance in this department can mean a world of difference to the success of a business. If this is not an area in which you excel, get counsel from a specialist. Combine that with determination and persistence and you'll have an effective marketing program, one of the assets that will enhance your chances with a potential lender or investor.

SPREADING YOUR RISK

Once you have that first product off the ground, it may be time to think of adding another. To bankers or investors, not putting all your eggs in one basket is a cardinal rule of good business management. In the event that one product doesn't make it, they'd like to see what you have to back it up or what other markets you can serve if your mainstay falls through.

When a company like Freund and Schiller expands its product line and its area of distribution, it often does so merely to grab a larger piece of the action. But something else is being accomplished as well: A diversification of product or clientele gives the owner a spread of risk. This makes for a healthier business.

To illustrate this principle further, let's look at the experience of the Kensington Display Company. As its name indicates, Kensington installs displays—mainly for retail businesses. The fact that one of the company's major clients was a chain of sporting goods stores could have proven disastrous for Kensington when the drought of the middle seventies severely depressed the sporting goods industry throughout the western United States. Fortunately, someone in the company anticipated what could happen with no depth to their customer base and began to diversify before the drought hit its peak.

Compiling a list of every conceivable contact, the owners decided to approach any business for which there was even a remote possibility of using their services. Because neither owner had "grown up" in this business, they delved into their backgrounds to determine which previous experiences they might employ as a cross-reference on their newly compiled list. For example, Kensington's president, Phil Dodge, had once been production manager for a paint manufacturer. He decided to look to the painting industry, contacted some paint manufacturers, and now creates displays for a chain of retail paint outlets throughout Northern California.

For the first year that Kensington began developing its market, its business volume was small. However, the owners were fortunate in having heeded the signals when they first perceived them. That same drought had a monumentally adverse effect on countless other wholesale, retail, and manufacturing firms, including such businesses as nurseries, produce purveyors, swimming pool installation and maintenance companies, and the camping equipment industry, as well as all those involved in the boating, skiing, fishing, and hunting industries and resorts. When there was no auxiliary product and market to carry them through, many operations failed to last out dry times. Demonstrating how well you can hedge against such possibilities can net you many pluses in establishing credibility as a competent entrepreneur. And the more plus factors you can accumulate, the better your chances for raising cash.

MATCHING YOUR EXPERTISE WITH THE LENDER/INVESTOR'S

No one is going to assume you're an authority on every area of your operation, but you will be expected to have an overall understanding of your business and a firm command of certain essential procedures, particularly those affecting your company's financial position. You should be thoroughly familiar with such basic financial items as the *costs* of your product or service, *pricing* your product, your *daily cash positions* (the amount of cash your business has on hand at all times), and your *accounts payable position.*

You should also have control over **backlog,** or the number of orders on hand that haven't yet been shipped. You'll find that establishing such control is a vital factor in regulating sales continuity.

In some instances you will not only want to know the answer to all these questions but also the "age" of the key components. The age of your inventory, for example, could be a vital factor in assessing the overall financial picture of the business, particularly if you are in something like the apparel business, where styles are dated and last season's dress or suit is no asset to your stock.

KNOWING YOUR COMPANY'S QUIRKS

There are many that are vital to your particular situation, and you must have tight control over them if you are to demonstrate your ability, which translates into credibility. Take a look at Table 1.1. You may recognize some of the quirks with which you have to cope in your operation.

For a close-up of one of these quirks, let's take the case of Gotschalk Sales, importer of electronic sound equipment from Britain, a company that has to keep on top of foreign currency fluctuations.

Gotschalk contracted for twenty speakers at £2,000, deliverable within ninety days of the date the contract was signed. Whenever Gotschalk pays his bill, whether it's next week, next month, or three months from now, he will owe his British colleagues £2,000, the amount agreed upon when the contract was signed. The cost of the speakers in terms of U.S. dollars, however, will depend on the official exchange rate when Gotschalk pays the bill or purchases the pounds to make payment. The speakers may cost him more in dollars than he anticipated. If that's the case, he will have to adjust his price for the sale of the speakers (if he can) in this country so it covers the disadvantage he experienced in the exchange rate.

Being an astute business operator, he will hold out as long as possible in assigning a price to his product until he is fairly sure he has control over the cost of merchandise. Should he want to avoid keeping such close surveillance of the exchange rate (which affects his costs), Gotschalk could arrange to make the purchase with U.S. currency. This ploy, however, leaves the problem of currency conversion with the exporter, and, as you might imagine, that arrangement is not always acceptable.

Table 1.1 Business Quirks

Type of Business	Quirk
Import-export	Foreign currency fluctuations
Any service business	Productive time versus nonproductive time
Department store and other retail business	Sales dollar per square foot and theft rate
Real estate investor, developer, landlord	Cost of vacancy
Airline, bus, and other transporter	Unused space
Manufacturer	Downtime of equipment (the time machinery and other equipment is not in use), cost of manufacturing seconds
Restaurateur	Portion control
Produce and other purveyor	Cost of spoilage
Vintner	Cost of aging process
Computer software developer	Cost of developing versus cost of maintaining product

Although currency fluctuations are one of the important variables to contend with in one business, in yours it might be something else. Be aware of what the factors are and control them in order to let your potential lender/investor know that you are on top of the situation, thereby enhancing your chances for financing.

DON'T BE CAUGHT OFF GUARD

It's to your advantage to be constantly alert to as yet uncovered surprises in your business and to be candid about discussing these revelations when meeting with a potential lender/investor. (Once again, tell the bad with the good.)

One example of an unexpected lesson occurred when we were computing cost (the price of the merchandise) and **markup** (the difference between the cost and the selling price) with a client in a retail fashion operation.

It was the end of this woman's first year as owner of Weddings Inc., and she closed the twelve-month period with a modest profit—quite an achievement in light of many adverse situations she had confronted during a long and difficult initiation.

At the onset of our relationship as client and CPA firm, we had established appropriate benchmarks for the business, one of our targets being a 50 percent **gross profit** (the difference between total sales and cost of sales), which is standard in the retail business. When we examined gross profit at the end of the first year, however, we discovered it was only 44 percent. Further review of the problem revealed that we had failed to consider the adverse effect of the sale of sample merchandise on that profit.

In this business, sample merchandise was used to display the various styles in which a garment was available. Thus at the end of a season, prior to the arrival of new lines, inventory was cleared by selling samples at a fraction of their original retail prices.

From then on, in controlling costs (and conversely, in computing gross profit) we resolved to consider the costs of the samples. Hence through a moderately expensive lesson we learned one of the basic idiosyncracies of that particular business: Beware of hidden costs.

You may have the same concern, or there could be any number of other situations that could catch you off guard if you fail to keep close watch over the various aspects of your business. You should now see how every action you take affects your credibility positively or negatively. Your grasp of all the elements we've discussed helps demonstrate the believability for which you're aiming. Once that's accomplished, your chances for raising cash should be excellent.

ACTION GUIDELINES

If you're not willing to take a risk for your business, you can't expect anyone else to. Your chances of raising cash depend on the kind of credibility you can establish with a potential lender or investor. Before you try to get financing, ask yourself these questions:

- Do I have solid experience and qualifications as the chief administrator of my business?

- Do I have a good product?

- Do I have a sturdy capital base?

- Is my marketing program effective?

- Can I diversify my products and markets?

- Does my business show or have the potential to show a profit?

- Am I thoroughly familiar with the idiosyncracies of my operation?

- Am I willing to make adjustments in those areas where I am deficient?

2

Determining How Much You Need, How Much You Can Get, and Which Way to Get It

This chapter will

- Describe the relationship between goal setting and determining the amount and kind of financing you need

- Help you appreciate the necessity for planning and the effect of time on financing

- Make you aware of your investment potential

- Teach you to assess your borrowing capacity

- Show you how to decide whether you need a loan or an investment

Before you can specify how much money your business needs, ask yourself what you need the money for. Once you've given time and thought to the project, you'll find that defining your objectives will help you run a more efficient operation as well as give you a figure to aim for.

DECIDING HOW MUCH YOU NEED

Setting Your Goals

Goals or objectives usually fall into two categories—short-term and long-term. Every entrepreneur is familiar with short-term goals, which are often represented by a project as routine as meeting next week's payroll, formulating a sales pitch, or finding the perfect marketing manager. A long-term goal might require building a new plant for more efficient production, introducing an alternate line of goods to complement an existing group of products, opening another territory, or acquiring a similar business in a neighboring area. It could also be diversifying your business into an allied field or expanding a product line to give you a larger share of the market.

Beyond this, many entrepreneurs have an even longer range objective for their businesses, which could be called an ultimate goal. An example of this is to become one of the country's top producers of computer software.

Planning

Planning your business gives you, among other things, a strategy with which to reach your objectives. Goals give you something to measure against, but planning enables you to determine whether your performance is good, poor, or somewhere in between. Planning also enables you to *anticipate the need to raise cash*, allowing you to get a financing program into operation before a crisis arises. You'll do a better job when you have sufficient time in which to formulate your proposal, hence your credibility will be that much greater.

The Importance of Time

Time is crucial to determining the amount of money needed, and the kind of financing you seek often depends on the length of time required to accomplish a goal or convert a plan to action.

Initially, you will need cash to get your business started, often obtained in the form of investments. Later, if your debt-equity ratio is imbalanced, you may need additional investment. During growth peaks, you may need a loan to support inventory, or while you're waiting for the conversion of sales to money (receivables to cash), you may need financing to help sustain your business. Rarely does any operation consistently generate enough cash to provide an even flow. Many businesses have a seasonality factor to consider, that is, periods of time when they know they will have to open a line of credit or have access to a loan. The sporting goods retail industry, for example, has the busy summer and winter periods. Many other businesses have a big Christmas season to finance. And a vintner financing a red wine inventory has more of a time problem because it may take as long as two years before the red wine grape is converted to a salable product.

The list is endless with respect to mismatching of cash in and cash out. Thus the *length of time* you will need the cash helps determine the *amount* of money you'll need, the *type* of financing (loan or investment), and the *cost* of getting it. If it's a cash investment, for example, your cost will be incurred in the percentage of ownership you have to give up. And if it's a loan, you're going to have to pay **interest.**

Interest is determined by the following formula:

$$I = PRT$$

Interest equals the principal, times the rate, times the time. In other words, the cost of borrowing money is determined by multiplying the amount you want, times the lender's rate for renting it, times the length of time you'll need it.

To illustrate, let's assume you've determined that in order to meet your goals you need to borrow $50,000 for one year. You find a lender and settle on a rate of 15 percent per annum. Applying the formula, you find the cost of the loan will be $7,500. Now let's reduce the length of time you borrow the funds to half a year. The cost to you then drops to $3,750, or half as much. In either case, you'll need to add the cost of the money to the amount you need, and the length of time will have a major effect on the cost. But successful financing is more than just a favorable interest rate. The amount you can get—and the terms under which you can get it—are equally important.

DECIDING HOW MUCH YOU CAN GET

Once you've formulated your goals, done the required planning, determined the length of time you'll need the funds, and computed the cost of getting the cash, you'll have a general idea of how much to ask for. But don't cut yourself short; try to get more than you think you'll need. Asking for extra funds will give you a dual advantage. First, you'll have more bargaining leverage in the event you're forced to reduce the amount you're seeking. Second, if you receive what you request, you have some leeway. You can reevaluate your objectives without the pressures of being strapped for cash. In naming a figure, however, you will have to consider capacity.

Examining Your Investment Capacity

There are no exact rules for examining investment capacity, the amount of money your business can actually obtain. This will depend, to a large extent, on the kind of credibility you can establish. A dramatic illustration of this is the story of John Z. DeLorean, a former executive of General Motors who quit GM and went to Ireland (where unemployment was rampant) to build a plant for the manufacture of sports cars. After risking $4 million of his own money, he raised another $270 million among dealers, a limited partnership, and the United Kingdom, with the latter contributing nearly $150 million in the form of grants, loans, and equity participation. This, to be sure, is an unusual situation; but if you can demonstrate unusual ability and have a project in mind that will inspire investment, the sky is the limit. On the other hand, there are definite guidelines to observe in assessing borrowing capacity.

Assessing Your Borrowing Capacity

Capacity to borrow relates basically to the amount of burden a business can comfortably carry. One way of interpreting this is simply to gauge the extent to which a business can support the **debt servicing** required, that is, how much it can afford to pay back comfortably within a specified period of time. This means paying back not only the amount on loan but the interest.

For example, assume that your business earns $250,000 a year after taxes and expenses and you've determined that you need $500,000 for two years. The question you have to ask yourself *before* approaching a potential lender is whether the business can pay back the money within the time frame proposed. Is the time realistic? Have you given yourself some degree of maneuverability to allow for something to go wrong?

It's important that you approach a prospective lender with potential problems already resolved because he or she inevitably will challenge the feasibility of your plan and the chances of your accomplishing your goal within the specified time.

In our example, you would have virtually no room to pay back the money borrowed with any degree of comfort. So you are either going to have to alter your plans to allow for an amount you can pay back or increase the time during which you will make the payments.

Because the lender is interested only in the ultimate payback—at a profit—all you must do is convince that person of your ability to borrow and make payments within the designated time. Or in the case of an investment, you must convince the concerned party that you can provide a better than average return on his or her investment.

Borrow as much as you can but don't wait until you desperately need it.

Understanding the Ratios

Lenders follow specific guidelines to determine borrowing capacity. One of these is the debt-equity ratio which is determined from your balance sheet and indicates whether your business has a higher level of equity than debt.

To illustrate, assume that after dividing your company's total liabilities (debts) by capital, you find that you have a debt-equity ratio of 3.2 to 1. In other words, your business is carrying a debt equal to 3.2 times its capital. Is this good or bad? What will a financial analyst or your potential lender/investor think of it? The first thing he or she will do is compare it with ratios maintained by similar businesses of about the same size as your company. These statistics are available through a number of publications such as Robert Morris Associates *RMA Annual Statement Studies,* a book of ratios and statistics, or the Bank of America's Small Business Reporters series.

After comparing your company's debt-equity ratio with that of similar companies, the financial analyst will view your business from still another angle. To illustrate, assume your balance sheet shows you own 24 percent of your company's assets and your creditors own 76 percent. In some businesses this would be an overleveraged situation, and who would risk lending money to such an operation? There is, however, a way to circumvent such a disadvantage.

Before getting a loan, you might attempt to alter your capital base (and concurrently your equity) by finding an investor to inject some money in return for a share of the business. Just how large that share should be— and still allow you to retain control of your company—may be determined with the help of your attorney, CPA, and perhaps your banker. Such an investment could be the key in turning around your debt-equity ratio so it compares favorably with similar businesses and increases your borrowing capacity.

There is one other ratio in which a financial analyst will be interested: the **current ratio,** or the relationship between current **assets** (or resources) and current **liabilities** (or debts). Again, this ratio will be compared with that of businesses of comparable size. This ratio tells the inquirer whether your business has sufficient current assets to pay off your current debt. "Current" on the balance sheet is usually interpreted as convertible to cash within one year if it is an asset or due and payable within one year if it is a liability. Thus a business with a 2 to 1 current ratio has covered its current liabilities two-fold, or has twice the current assets required to pay off its obligations within one year.

Examining Your Comfort Zone

You are now familiar with some of the yardsticks a third party will apply, but don't assume that is all there is to debt capacity. What about your views on borrowing? How comfortable do you feel with the concept? Many people have been raised to believe borrowing should be avoided. Thus they have strong reservations to overcome before they take the plunge.

Even if you have such reservations, you must admit that if every entrepreneur shared your reticence, our economy would be stifled. Most commerce would come to a halt if both buyers and sellers abolished credit because good, healthy borrowing is essential. Even the government borrows—in the form of the bonds it issues. Banks borrow from you every time you put money into a savings account, and they borrow from larger banks as well. Corporations borrow by issuing debentures (loans).

Actually, borrowing is simply an expression of the rental principle. But in this case the asset is money instead of office or warehouse space. And rather than pay rent, you pay interest. Borrowing helps a business with limited capital flourish. It may also indicate that a business is healthy and is experiencing a normal growth pattern. Don't be afraid of it, but don't abuse it.

DECIDING WHETHER YOU NEED A LOAN OR AN INVESTMENT

Base your decision on whether to seek a loan, an investment, or a combination of the two on an assessment of your overall situation. Do you need cash to start a new business, or do you have a business with problems? Do you need money for a short term or for years? Will it buy new equipment or help you expand your inventory? Do you need an investment to give you a debt-equity ratio that is considered healthy in your industry? The answers to these questions lead you right back to goals or objectives. Thus the purpose for which you need to raise cash, and the length of time you need it, will help determine the kind of financing to aim for. Because your capacity also will influence the way you go, you will have to consider your capital base and your debt-equity ratio. To help you visualize the process more clearly, let's take a look at a couple of our clients as they made their financing selections.

> Grautmann-Brock Associates was a new business selling computer software. Though not unique, their situation was somewhat problematical in that the product was unproven and the owners of the company were inexperienced in running a business.

They knew they needed operating funds, but because there was virtually no capital in the company, they realized their chance of getting a loan was small. They had to get some additional "seed" money (capital) first, and they had to get it quickly. At the same time, both owners wanted to retain as much control as possible and had no intention of selling off a major interest in the business.

After determining the amount of money needed, we met with an attorney experienced in securities law. A review of the various options indicated that a **limited partnership** (see Chapter 14) would offer investment opportunities that would best meet our client's needs. Thus plans were made to restructure the company and to design an agreement that would be attractive to potential investors. Within a relatively short time, the investments came in. Our clients acquired their capital base and could then approach the banks for additional financing.

We were candid in our approach, spelling out drawbacks as well as advantages. And although the first two banks we approached didn't go for the presentation, the third one bought it. Impressed with what we had already accomplished, the loan officer with whom we met agreed to match the amount of money raised through the limited partnership agreement. We got what we needed (and a little bit more), and everyone was happy. Thus in obtaining the required financing, Grautmann-Brock settled upon a combination of loan and investment. No magic formula was utilized. With no history to refer to, we resorted to logic and common sense; and in obtaining our capital, we had to decide on a selling price (for the individual partnerships) geared to the type of investor who would find this particular arrangement attractive. Then in seeking funds from the bank, we used an amount comparable to the equity in the company as the basis for determining what the bank would lend.

To see how another problem was handled, let's look at a business with a completely different set of circumstances.

The owners of the fifteen-year-old Scientific Distributing Company (SDC) needed cash in order to acquire additional product lines so they could expand an already successful business. Although it had been profitable for a number of years, SDC had an inadequate capital base because it had not retained its profits in the business. Instead, the company had set up a profit-sharing trust so it could distribute the profits among its employees and simultaneously reduce its tax bill.

We knew that as soon as the balance sheet was reviewed, it would be obvious that the company was undercapitalized, which would be one of the first criticisms any bank or other lending agent we approached would levy.

Therefore, in his presentation to the bank, the owner emphasized that no further contributions to the profit-sharing trust would even be considered until the debt-equity ratio reached a predetermined level (until that point, it had been left open so it might be negotiated with the bank). Naturally, the bank was well aware of the company's reasons for contributing to the trust and of the fact that the contributions would resume once SDC's equity situation was rectified. Company management had to compromise its situation temporarily by deliberately increasing its tax bill for a specific period of time. Yet the loan the company was able to raise as a result far exceeded the amount of tax it had to pay.

In both these cases, a business seeking financing has its unique set of considerations. The advice that emerges from these examples is to be flexible.

> Be creative in the type of financing instruments you put together; consider your organizational structure; and be ready to compromise. In the case of a new business, be willing to restrict your goals, amend the scope of your plans, or trim your budget if necessary.

You'll get your full financing eventually and then be able to expand — as soon as you've proven your ability. If yours is an older business, regardless of how you plan to use the money, you are probably in the position of being able to choose from a number of approaches or solutions to your financing problems. Though it's wise to confer with your financial counsel, you must finally select the type of loan or investment.

ACTION GUIDELINES

In deciding how much cash you need to raise, ask yourself these questions:

- What do I need the money for?
- How long do I need the money?
- How much will it cost me in terms of interest or in benefits to investors?
- Will the amount I'm specifying give me enough bargaining room in case I have to cut back?
- Is the amount sufficient to allow me to accomplish my goals?

To assess your investment potential, review the credibility checklist at the end of Chapter 1. To assess your borrowing capacity, ask yourself the following:

- Have I allowed my company enough time to pay back the loan?
- How does my debt-equity ratio compare with other companies in the industry?
- How much of my company's assets do I and the other investors own?
- How much of the assets do my creditors own?

Assess your overall situation when deciding whether to seek a loan, an investment, or a combination of the two. Whatever you choose, be flexible. If your answers to the following questions are positive, an investment should solve your financing problems.

- Am I starting a new business?
- Do I have a low debt-equity ratio?
- Is my company undercapitalized?

A loan or investment may be the way to go if you can answer yes to the following questions:

- Do I need operating capital?
- Do I need new equipment?
- Do I need expanded facilities?
- Do I have a sluggish cash flow?

PART TWO

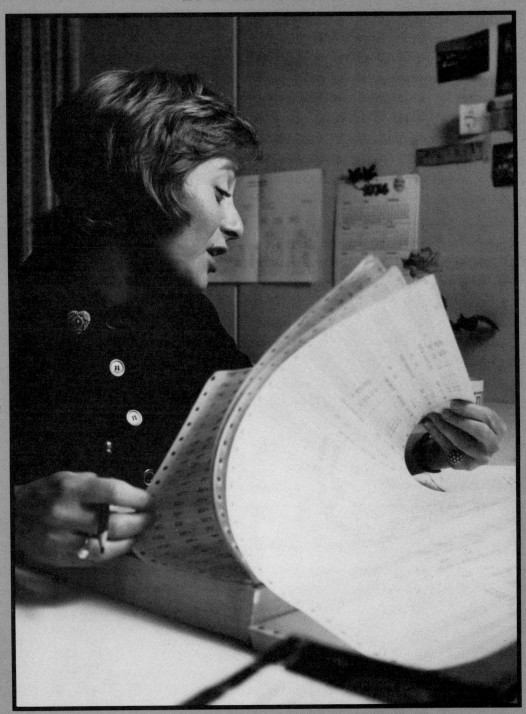

CONTROLLING YOUR BUSINESS

Because credibility with a potential lender/investor depends on your ability to control and operate a profitable business, the next three chapters deal with the tools that enable you to accomplish those objectives. It may seem we have reversed the order in which the material should logically be presented. We examine the end result of the financial controls or the accounting/bookkeeping function — the financial statements — in Chapter 3 and discuss the systems required to prepare the statements in Chapters 4 and 5. An appreciation of the end product is necessary before you can fully comprehend what makes it work.

You may wish to read Chapters 4 and 5 first and come back to Chapter 3 or reread Chapter 3 after Chapters 4 and 5.

3

Coping with Accounting/ Bookkeeping and Understanding Financial Statements

This chapter will

- Explain the importance of the accounting/bookkeeping operation

- Describe financial statements and their components

- Teach you how to choose between audited and unaudited statements

- Explain how to get the most for your accounting/bookkeeping dollar

The first step in exercising financial **control** of your business, which is a prerequisite for obtaining financing as well as for making a profit, is understanding the accounting/bookkeeping function and the financial statements. This part of the business is often relegated to the back room — in thought as well as in fact. When this happens, chaos results.

An example of such chaos occurred in the stock brokerage business during the great bull market of the late sixties and early seventies, when the number of transactions handled daily set records. Unfortunately, the flood of paperwork accompanying that volume became totally uncontrollable under the systems then in use. Stocks were not delivered; customers weren't billed; employees weren't paid; and, of course, management reports were not accurate. Confusion reigned. Tremendous **reserves** (allowances for potential losses) had to be established on the books of account, and for many firms that spelled technical bankruptcy. The upshop was merger upon merger, until some of the oldest and most stalwart names in the business were phased out of existence. All the confusion on Wall

Street can be attributed to inadequate controls in the back office and management's reluctance to understand, or become involved in, the mechanics that would have kept the wheels turning. We hope you will never be prone to such negligence. However, you cannot expect to handle all the jobs in your operation yourself. What you can do is make sure you fully comprehend the function of the accountant/bookkeeper, recognizing that your understanding is important both in hiring competent employees to provide you and your lender/investor with timely financial communications and in utilizing that data to run your business.

Essentially, the job is that of a reporter. The accountant/bookkeeper uses numbers to record permanently every transaction that takes place in your business, whether it's writing a paycheck or recording a sale.

> There is no area in which you can effectively proceed without referring to your financial data because every one of these records relates to an action already taken and affects a decision yet to be made.

When you receive an order from existing customers, for example, you'll want to check their credit history with your company. Before purchasing equipment, you'll need to determine whether you can project a reasonable return on your investment, and you'll want to know the best way to pay for it. Will you be able to pay cash, or will you need some kind of financing? If you want a loan, are you in shape to get one? Thus the data must be up to date, accurate, and comprehensible.

DETERMINING WHO DOES WHAT

By way of introduction, we have referred to the bookkeeper's and the accountant's jobs as if they are one and the same. Actually, who does what depends to a great extent on the size of your business, on what you can afford, and on the abilities of the person you hire. Bookkeepers are generally responsible for filing payroll tax returns, providing data for insurance requirements, and complying with a lender's requests for periodic updating on accounts receivable. They also accumulate and classify financial transactions — documenting the latter with every receipt, invoice, and check that enters and leaves your business — and reconcile bank statements and accounts receivable balances.

Once the data are grouped by like transactions and accounted for in your journals and ledgers, the accountant usually takes over and interprets the information. Then the accountant (or CPA, who is licensed by the state and subject to certain state and national requirements) sets up the system you use for reporting and maintaining your accounts. There are exceptions, in that the bookkeeper, not the accountant, sometimes interprets the figures because he or she recorded the transactions. Whether one uses an accountant or bookkeeper is often a matter of preference. Depending on their training, many accountants perform the same services that a CPA might perform, except to certify an audit, a procedure that always requires a CPA. But regardless of who handles the procedures, the objective is the same: to summarize all the facts on your **financial statements,** a presentation that could be viewed as your company's financial biography. Thereafter the statements are used not only as an important management tool but also to show a potential lender/investor. Thus you must understand the financial statements.

UNDERSTANDING FINANCIAL STATEMENTS

Comprised of a **balance sheet,** an **income statement,** and often a **cash statement,** the financial statements illustrate the actual results of your business via numbers, thereby enabling you to focus on where to apply pressure, where to make adjustments, and where to reevaluate your objectives. The financial statements also communicate the progress of your operation to third parties, such as creditors (including lenders) or investors.

Although your bookkeeper or accountant prepares these statements, you are responsible for the sales, commitments, or purchases summarized thereon. We'll take a closer look at a balance sheet and an income statement, but will not review the cash statement (which shows receipts and disbursements, illustrating your cash flow) here because most entrepreneurs are familiar with it. We do, however, discuss and illustrate the cash statement in Chapter 10 and we include an example of it in the business plan in Appendix A.

The Balance Sheet

The balance sheet shows three major components:

1. Assets (all items your business owns that can be measured in terms of dollars)

2. Liabilities (the amounts your business owes)

3. Equity (the amounts invested by you and your fellow investors plus the amounts of money earned and retained by the business since it began)

Also called a *statement of financial position,* a *statement of assets and liabilities,* or a *statement of assets, liabilities, and capital,* the balance sheet shows the financial health of your company as of a particular date. It thus summarizes every transaction that has taken place since your business originated.

However, contrary to popular belief, the compilation of a balance sheet is not necessarily an exact procedure. It involves considerable judgment in recording transactions, such as estimates (sometimes referred to as reserves or provisions) for losses on accounts receivable, unrealized losses on inventory (markdowns), and depreciation on fixed assets.

Accounting procedures do not allow for appreciation, even during periods of inflation. And the balance sheet does not indicate customer demand for your product (which is evidenced by your backlog of orders) or record your purchase commitments to suppliers. Therefore, to get an accurate financial picture of your company, you must consider these factors when you analyze the balance sheet. Your ability to amplify and interpret the statement (to yourself or to a third party) will be important, not only in raising cash but in helping you run a well-controlled and profitable business. With this in mind, let's examine the hypothetical balance sheet shown in fold-out Figure 3.1. In this illustration we compare two periods so you can see the changes that have taken place in the time frame shown. With your own balance sheet, comparisons may also be made to budget or to other periods, depending on your needs (a process we will demonstrate later in this chapter when we discuss the income statement).

The Income Statement

Also referred to as a **profit or loss statement** or **earnings statement,** the income statement discloses the amount of money your company earned or lost within specified periods of time. (For example, it may be compiled for a month, a quarter, or a year.) A simple equation describes the income statement:

$$\text{Income} - \text{Expenses} = \text{Net Income or Loss}$$

Although income is generated in a variety of ways, the most common being the sale of merchandise or of a service, the cost of doing business must be subtracted from that income in order to have a valid figure. Typical costs include the price paid for the merchandise you sell, rent, telephone, and sales reps' commissions. If income exceeds expenses, you have a profit. But if expenses exceed income, you have a loss.

There are several refinements of the basic income statement components. Those shown in Figure 3.2 include sales (which account for income) and cost of sales, selling and general and administrative costs, and income tax.

EVERYMAN'S MERCANTILE COMPANY
January 1, 19X3 to June 30, 19X3

	CURRENT MONTH					YEAR TO DATE				
	Actual		Budget		Favorable or (Unfavorable) Variance	Actual		Budget		Favorable or (Unfavorable) Variance
	$	%	$	%	$	$	%	$	%	$
Sales[a]	85,300	100.0	95,000	100.0	(9,700)	575,300	100.0	550,000	100.0	25,300
Cost of Sales[a]	44,779	52.5	49,400	52.0	(4,621)	317,500	55.2	286,000	52.0	31,500
Gross Profit[a]	40,521	47.5	45,600	48.0	(5,079)	257,800	44.8	264,000	48.0	(6,200)
Selling and General & Administrative Expenses[b]	34,090	39.9	29,725	31.3	(4,365)	188,764	32.8	181,500	33.0	(7,264)
Operating Profit	6,431	7.6	15,875	16.7	(9,444)	69,036	12.0	82,500	15.0	(13,474)
Income Tax	3,000	3.6	7,900	8.3	4,900	34,500	6.0	40,000	7.3	5,500
Net Income	3,431	4.0	7,975	8.4	(4,544)	34,536	6.0	42,500	7.7	(7,964)

[a]See Figure 3.3.
[b]See Figure 3.4.

Figure 3.2 Condensed comparative income statement

Although the income statement may be examined from various points of view — management's or that of an outside analyst — we will assume management's point of view. For that reason, we will compare actual figures with budget, providing what we believe is the most helpful management tool. For example, in order to appreciate the significance of the sales figures, you should know your current goal for sales volume. With such a basis of comparison, you may more easily spot a trend. However, most income statements do not compare actual figures with those budgeted or projected. If yours does not, ask the person who prepares your financial statements to follow that procedure so you will have an effective tool with which to work.

Because the condensed statement in Figure 3.2 shows merely the highlights of the operation, there are a number of questions that may be answered only by a detailed schedule. For example, there is a favorable variance in sales. How did this happen, particularly when there is an unfavorable variance in gross profit? Similarly, selling and general and administrative expenses show an unfavorable variance. Without a detailed analysis of the expense schedule, it would be impossible to understand such discrepancies. Figure 3.3 illustrates a detailed comparison of sales, cost of sales, and gross profit. As with the balance sheet, annotations keyed to line items on the detailed statement should help you understand the report.

(A) Sales   An effective evaluation of selling effort is essential to a successful operation. If you had relied on an evaluation of total sales dollars alone, you would have been severely misled. Note that even though there is a favorable variance in sales, Bumpkins show a favorable variance while the product Widget is unfavorable. Thus you must review the segmentation (mix) of your products in relation to their contribution to profits. And even this evaluation may not be enough. For example, it could be that 10 percent of your sales force is providing 75 percent of sales. Or perhaps 25 percent of your sales produces 50 percent of profits. Total sales alone, unrelated to product mix or sales performance, provide no insight whatsoever.

(B) Cost of Sales and Gross Profit   Computing gross profit requires that you determine the difference between two important elements or variables—sales and cost of sales. For example, if you had a sale of $110, with $60 representing the cost of the item sold, the gross profit would be $50, or 45 percent of sales. Simple, yes, but there is where simplicity begins and ends. In the event that your goal is a higher gross profit, you might conclude (if your marketplace will allow it) that you need only set a higher price on

EVERYMAN'S MERCANTILE COMPANY
January 1, 19X3 to June 30, 19X3

	CURRENT MONTH					YEAR TO DATE				
	Actual		Budget		Variance	Actual		Budget		Variance
	$	%	$	%	$	$	%	$	%	$
SALES (A)										
Widgets	22,700	26.6	45,000	47.4	(22,300)	253,300	44.0	287,500	52.2	(34,200)
Bumpkins	62,600	73.4	50,000	52.6	12,600	322,000	56.0	262,500	47.8	59,500
Total Sales	85,300	100.0	95,000	100.0	(9,700)	575,300	100.0	550,000	100.0	25,300
COST OF SALES (B)										
Widgets	9,080	40.0	23,000	51.1	(13,920)	116,518	46.0	146,625	51.0	(30,107)
Bumpkins	35,699	56.7	26,400	52.9	9,299	200,982	62.4	139,375	53.0	61,607
Total Cost	44,779	52.6	49,400	52.0	(4,621)	317,500	55.2	286,000	52.0	31,500
GROSS PROFIT (B)										
Widgets	13,620	60.0	22,000	48.9	(8,380)	136,782	54.0	140,875	49.0	(4,093)
Bumpkins	26,901	43.3	23,600	47.1	3,301	121,018	37.6	123,125	47.0	(2,107)
Total Gross Profit	40,521	47.4	45,600	48.0	(5,079)	257,800	44.8	264,000	48.0	(6,200)

Figure 3.3 Detailed comparative statement of sales, cost of sales, and gross profit

your product, passing the burden of increased costs of sale on to the consumer. Unfortunately, the procedure isn't that easy because, in the complex problem of pricing, you must contend with competition. So it may be fine to settle on a gross profit of 50 percent, but the actual pricing of the item may be determined by the manufacturer. The manufacturer knows that the distributor as well as the retailer must make a gross profit. The following illustration shows the chain of gross profit or markup:

	Selling Price		Cost		Gross Profit	
	$	%	$	%	$	%
Manufacturer	110	100	60	55	50	45
Distributor	165	100	110	67	55	33
Retailer	330	100	165	50	165	50

As you see, the manufacturer's selling price is the distributor's cost, and so on. Thus the manufacturer knows what the distributor and the retailer will have to pay and charge for the product. And if either of the latter is not given the opportunity to make a gross profit, there is absolutely no chance of the product being sold successfully. Without adequate incentives, who would want to handle it? Know your profit and understand the lines of succession.

The other variable in the gross profit formula is costs. One can increase gross profit even if one does not raise selling price—by reducing the cost of the product. The lower down the line of succession, the less control one has on cost. That is, the retailer must get the product from the distributor, who must earn a reasonable gross profit without giving the retailer any room to negotiate. However, there still may be an opportunity for the retailer—by taking advantage of special purchases or through better negotiations. The manufacturer, on the other hand, may be able to run a more efficient operation and thus reduce costs. If the manufacturer is successful in reducing costs, he or she may pass on the savings to the distributor and the distributor, to the retailer. However, before you can arrive at lower costs, you must know what they are, and it is important that you segment these also by product line.

In the detailed comparative statement illustrated, Everyman's Mercantile Company shows a higher gross profit on its Widget line. And even though sales are significantly off budget, the correlating gross profit is not that far off the mark. Bumpkins are producing sales beyond goal; yet gross profit is not on target. Clearly, further discussion should be held with sales reps and production people to determine what is happening. Perhaps a discussion with key customers will shed additional light on these variances and help you form better strategies for the sale and purchase of product lines.

The entrepreneur who has learned to think in terms of percentages often attempts to represent selling and general and administrative expenses (also referred to as **overhead**) as a percentage of sales. Although not totally invalid, particularly if the sales volume of an organization remains relatively constant, it is not that useful either because some expenses (administrative, for example) are not directly related to sales. However, if sales volume fluctuates, you should conduct a more comprehensive analysis of the expense section of your income statement. To focus on this portion of the income statement, we have prepared a separate schedule of the various selling and general and administrative expenses of the Everyman's Mercantile Company (see Figure 3.4).

Note that the schedule is divided into two components—fixed and variable. **Fixed expenses** are fairly constant, regardless of sales volume; **variable expenses** go up and down in direct proportion to sales volume.

It is important to understand the difference between **controllable expenses** and **noncontrollable expenses**. You can increase or decrease the former whenever you choose. Expenses you cannot change, such as payroll and property taxes or utilities, are noncontrollable. Both fixed and variable categories have controllable and noncontrollable expenses.

An expense may be variable, but not controllable (for example, a sales rep's commissions, which you might have to maintain at 6 percent of sales or risk losing your sales rep). Sometimes an uncontrollable expense may be converted to one that is controllable. Even fixed expenses, although they don't vary in direct relation to sales, fall within the categories of controllable and noncontrollable expenses. A case in point is insurance. The premium remains the same for a specified amount of coverage, but you could alter the amount of coverage, thereby controlling your expense.

The more controllable expenses you have, the better you can manage your business.

Take time now to classify the various expenses in your business. Which are controllable? Which are not? With that task completed, you can decide who in your operation will prepare the financial statements.

DECIDING WHO PREPARES THE FINANCIAL STATEMENTS

Either a bookkeeper or an accountant can assume responsibility for the job that culminates in the financial statements. Your needs, the size of your

EVERYMAN'S MERCANTILE COMPANY
January 1, 19X3 to June 30, 19X3

| | CURRENT MONTH | | | | | YEAR TO DATE | | | | |
| | Actual | | Budget | | Variance | Actual | | Budget | | Variance |
	$	%	$	%	$	$	%	$	%	$
FIXED										
Controllable Expenses:										
Officers' Salaries	2,700	3.2	2,850	3.0	150	16,200	2.8	15,050	2.7	(1,150)
Office Supplies	1,800	2.1	1,500	1.6	(300)	9,700	1.7	3,000	.6	(6,700)
Dues & Subscrip.	490	.5	200	.2	(290)	2,625	.5	1,200	.2	(1,425)
Repairs & Mainten.	3,140	3.7	375	.4	(2,765)	6,250	1.0	1,250	.2	(5,000)
	8,130	9.5	4,925	5.2	(3,205)	34,775	6.0	20,500	3.7	(14,275)
Non-Controllable Expenses:										
Rent	2,000	2.4	2,000	2.0	—	12,000	2.1	12,000	2.2	—
Union Wages	7,800	9.2	7,400	7.8	400	43,150	7.5	44,400	8.1	1,250
Utilities	980	1.1	1,200	1.3	(380)	6,800	1.2	7,200	1.3	400
Property Taxes	1,400	1.6	1,500	1.6	(100)	9,700	1.7	9,000	1.6	(700)
Payroll Taxes	1,800	2.1	1,900	2.0	100	10,500	1.8	11,400	2.1	900
	13,980	16.4	14,000	14.7	20	82,150	14.3	84,000	15.3	1,850
VARIABLE										
Controllable Expenses:										
Advertising	4,100	4.8	1,500	1.6	(2,600)	23,200	4.0	22,000	4.0	(1,200)
Travel and Entertainment	680	.8	750	.8	70	2,800	.5	5,500	1.0	2,700
	4,780	5.6	2,250	2.4	(2,530)	26,000	4.5	27,500	5.0	1,500
Non-Controllable Expenses:										
Salesmen's Commissions	4,800	5.6	5,700	6.0	900	30,100	5.3	33,000	6.0	2,900
Freight Out	2,400	2.8	2,850	3.0	450	15,739	2.7	16,500	3.0	761
	7,200	8.4	8,550	9.0	1,350	45,839	8.0	49,500	9.0	3,661
Total Expenses	34,090	39.9	29,725	31.3	(4,365)	188,764	32.8	181,500	33.0	(7,264)

Figure 3.4   Selling and general and administrative expenses

business, and the availability of talent will all help determine who prepares these reports. However, there are a few more factors to consider, such as the advantage of internally prepared financial statements over those prepared outside the company.

Internally Prepared Statements

Completed periodically throughout the year, with frequency contingent on your needs, internally prepared statements should provide you with as much accurate and timely information as possible on the current status of your business. The comprehensive information in these statements is usually significant only to management, and most companies would not want them released to the general public.

Sometimes, however, they are shown to third parties (perhaps a potential lender or investor) who are not thoroughly familiar with the company's background. When this happens, it's wise to expand on all those matters the reader might question. Such disclosure may take the form of footnotes to the balance sheet and income statement, describing such details as bank lines of credit, obligations under rental agreements, or methods used to depreciate assets. Because the internally prepared statement is usually reserved for management, an outside accountant or CPA may be called in at year's end to prepare a more formal presentation for use outside the company. That statement could be either **audited** or **unaudited.**

Audited Statements

Audited financial statements are prepared by a CPA following an intensive examination of original documents (such as sales invoices, shipping reports, bank statements, and so forth), a study of inventory (when inventories are a material part of the business), a confirmation of accounts receivable, and usually a third party's (customer, banker, or supplier) verification of an asset or an **accounts payable.**

The audited statement is always accompanied by a letter of certification. Although the audited and certified statement is required of all **publicly held corporations**, the **closely held** (or privately owned) company may also be required to obtain an audited statement if a bank or other lender/investor demands it. Sometimes there are other situations in which the certified audit becomes necessary, such as the case of the bus company that had to have an audit before it could bid on contracts with a school district. However, in view of the sizable expense involved, we hesitate to recommend an audit unless it becomes really necessary.

Unaudited Statements

Though the material summarized in unaudited financial statements is not examined in the same detail as it would be in an audited statement, it also is often prepared by an accountant or CPA. Many businesses prefer to have the outside professional perform this service, expanding on internally prepared statements so they conform to disclosure rules compiled by the CPA organizations. In these instances, the accountant or CPA must accompany the statements with a letter describing the extent of the service rendered.

This procedure, too, costs money, but you can economize by having a professional combine the project with another, such as preparing the company's tax returns. This makes the job worthwhile for the professional and keeps the fee within reasonable limits.

There are two types of unaudited financial statements an accountant or CPA may present. One is the **review;** the other is the **compilation** service. With a review, the professional analyzes those accounts that enable him or her to assure a third party that no material changes are necessary in the financial statements for them to conform with generally accepted accounting principles. In the jargon of the trade, this service is a **"half-audit."** As far as bankers are concerned, it is often a satisfactory sustitute for an audit for certain loan customers.

The least complex of the reporting services performed by an accountant or CPA is the compilation. Through this process, the professional presents financial information in standard reports solely for management's benefit, without expressing any assurance to third parties. This type of service may be provided periodically, as needs dictate, when a company does not have an internal staff to prepare its financial statements.

GETTING THE MOST FOR YOUR ACCOUNTING/ BOOKKEEPING DOLLAR

Before incurring any accounting/bookkeeping and related expenses, you should know just what you'll be getting for your dollar and how you will use the service or product you're paying for. For example, a CPA's audited statement or review is compiled only after extensive and thorough research into a company's financial affairs. But the resulting report is so condensed that it is of little use as a workable management tool. Internally prepared statements, with all their detailed summaries, can do a much better job in that department.

Recognize the advantage in having an in-house bookkeeper, accountant, or accounting staff, the size of which will depend on your company's needs.

In addition to providing more detailed financial information, an in-house person is always on hand as a resource for the origin of the data, not to mention the subject of allegiance. The in-house person will be working solely for your firm.

If you don't need a permanent, full-charge bookkeeper, hire one part-time. We frequently design simple bookkeeping systems the entrepreneur can easily handle with a part-time, assistant bookkeeper. Together, they ultimately produce a comprehensive and rather sophisticated set of financial statements. Call in a CPA, when necessary, to supplement your book-keeper's technical skills, periodically to review and evaluate your company's financial affairs, including systems and internal controls, and to provide tax-planning assistance.

Don't misuse your accounting/bookkeeping dollar by hiring a CPA for bookkeeping chores. The asute CPA will often refuse the "write-up" work (recording and posting of transactions) because it is not lucrative, thus not worth his or her time. Those who will accept write-up work should be suspect because they may be charging more than you should have to pay for this service. So stay involved, or at least keep in touch, with the back room operation, not only to avoid the kind of chaos that can result if you don't but also to take full advantage of your financial data as a management tool.

ACTION GUIDELINES

Understanding the accounting/bookkeeping operation will enable you to

- Hire competent personnel for this function
- Comprehend and utilize the financial data essential to a well-controlled business
- Give an effective presentation to a third party

If you are to get the most out of your accounting/bookkeeping dollar, you should

- First assess your company's needs in this area
- Employ your own full-time or part-time bookkeeper and/or accounting person or staff
- Utilize internally prepared statements whenever possible because they are not only less expensive but provide the most workable management tool
- Use a CPA strictly for professional services, such as evaluation or counsel on your company's financial affairs, including systems and controls; tax planning; and audit, review, or compilation services when necessary

A productive interpretation of your balance sheet should include

- Amplification of each line item under assets, liabilities, and capital
- Computation of your debt-equity ratio

When interpreting a comparative income statement, you should understand

- Variances in sales, cost of sales, and gross profit
- Techniques of manipulating gross profit
- The composition of selling and general and administrative expenses and which of these can be controlled
- Net income and be objective as to whether it is high enough to keep your company going without additional capital

4

Creating Your Accounting System

This chapter will

- Describe the purpose of an accounting system
- Explain the objectives of a financial reporting system
- List the components of a financial reporting system
- Tell you the choices available in creating your own system

Now that you have learned how important it is to keep your finger on the pulse of the back room operation, you'll want to know how the various accounting/bookkeeping functions can be most efficiently interrelated. What you need is a system, an established routine through which a combination of procedures accurately reports your company's financial health or provides you with the managerial controls with which to run your business in a timely fashion. Within your system there are subsystems, including your financial reporting system, the goal of which is the production of your financial statements. Your system also includes the tools with which your company executes these procedures. In the case of a financial reporting system, these consist of the books of account, ledgers, and any business machines or computer services utilized.

Through your system, your company's performance records are maintained and your financial statements are prepared. Thus you can take corrective action—reduce costs, contract inventory, tighten accounts receivable, raise capital, or extend your line of credit—if and when it is called for. A well-designed and tightly administered system provides controls with which to run a successful operation. It will alert you to areas that need attention and give you the opportunity to turn the situation around.

RAISING COST CONSCIOUSNESS

A good system can direct your attention to any department—accounts receivable, inventory, sales, or costs. An illustration of good control in the area of costs is the case of a client who initially engaged us to install a cost control system and then broadened our assignment to have us help expand his line of credit.

Expanding his line of credit proved to be an easy task precisely because this man had kept his eye on expenses. When it became obvious that sales would be substantially lower than originally forecast, he had contingent plans ready to make the necessary cost cuts. The upshot was that profits, which were predicated on sales, nearly matched his original predictions. Thus when we accompanied him to the bank, we didn't avoid the fact that sales missed the target. We focused on profits, stressing the attention the owner had given to his company's expense pattern. The bank was duly impressed and readily agreed to his line of credit.

KNOWING PEOPLE'S FUNCTIONS AND PROCEDURES

After you decide what your system should accomplish, you or your systems designer will decide which procedures you should incorporate. In a newly formed business, for example, a procedure has to be developed for everything—paying bills, recording sales, collecting accounts receivable, and so on. You must establish order so everyone—employees, customers, suppliers—understands the guidelines and objectives.

In an older firm, these guideline procedures exist but presumably should be periodically reevaluated, particularly in a fast-growing business, to determine if and how the system might be improved. If you've employed people who are sensitive to the details of your company's operations and maintain open communications with them, you will be alerted that much sooner to any changes that might be in order.

All too often we have heard entrepreneurs complain of an employee's failure to understand a particular situation when the employer had never taken the time to explain what needed to be accomplished. Any business starts with people.

You cannot assume your employee is going to know what you want if you don't explain your needs.

No matter how educated your employees might be in their particular fields, they must be familiar with the overall requirements of the business and how their job fits into them.

A case in point is the experience one controller had while working for a relatively large company. With a staff of thirty in the accounting department, the firm had partially converted many procedures and was on the verge of computerizing the balance of the system. As soon as the decision was made, the controller called a staff meeting, thereby preempting the inevitable rumor circulation and any subsequent buildup of anxieties. Informing everyone of what was about to happen, he assured them no jobs would be sacrificed to automation.

Then he explained why the company was automating. Management needed more information from existing records. The fastest and most economical means of delivering it was via computer. The controller stressed that the staff's help was essential to a successful transition and asked that every employee cooperate by providing incoming programmers with a thorough briefing of his or her functions in the department. Next he held individual meetings with everyone, reiterating that no job was in jeopardy as he described how each one interrelated with the department and company as a whole. Predictably, the entire staff wholeheartedly got behind the new assignment, all because management communicated its needs and everyone knew where he or she fit into the overall scheme.

COMMUNICATING YOUR REQUIREMENTS TO THE DESIGNER

In putting any system together, the designer (who may be your CPA or financial consultant) first must determine your company's needs, particularly as they pertain to the functions you want controlled and the kind of reports you want produced. In a financial reporting system, for example, these reports would make up the basic fundamental statements described in Chapter 3: the cash statement, the balance sheet, and the income, earnings, or profit or loss statement. They may also include the operating budget, cash forecast, and long-term forecast (reports we discuss in Chapters 6 and 10, with instruction for their preparation presented in Appendixes B, D, and E). Internal reports on such information as order entry, sales backlog, daily cash receipts, and inventory requirements should also be integrated into the system.

Your designer should describe all the procedures available to you and provide you with a format for all the reports you will receive before finalizing the job. Evaluate them. Have your staff review them and comment. An awareness of the kind of data that can be made available is essential if your system is to be really productive. Make sure you will be getting what you need. Sometimes the entrepreneur does not.

> For example, one client of ours was not aware that **segmentation** of product lines (a method of separating products or groups of products in order to determine their contribution to overall profits) was available through the accounting system being created. Unfortunately, we were unaware that the partners in this business disagreed over the profitability of a particular product line. The argument was ultimately settled when the questionable line was dropped, but only after a long and tedious accounting was prepared by the partner who prevailed.

An awareness of the kind of data that can be made available is essential if your system is to be really productive.

FINANCIAL REPORTING TOOLS

Although an accounting system has a number of objectives, financial reporting is of major concern in this book because the information it provides is vital to any potential lender/investor. We will examine the tools used in financial reporting in this chapter. These tools are the chart of accounts, the journal or book of original entry, the general ledger or book of secondary entry, and the subsidiary ledger.

The Chart of Accounts

Once he or she knows your reporting requirements, the systems designer creates a **chart of accounts** (a list of all the accounts or classifications the bookkeeper or accountant is to control). This chart provides uniformity in the recording of transactions by assigning a specific code to each account affected. When a rental expense is paid, for example, a code number designating that particular expenditure will be used, thereby creating classification uniformity throughout the system.

The chart of accounts must accommodate government demands because the Internal Revenue Service has numerous requirements. It must also be coordinated with your organizational structure, that is, the way your business is set up, the products you sell, and management's responsibilities.

Figure 4.1 illustrates a chart of accounts. Note that it is laid out like the balance sheet and the income statement. Current assets, property and equipment, liabilities, and capital are listed first. Income and expenses follow. Although some revision is inevitable, when the chart of accounts is created, the designer should consider the predictable growth of the business to avoid constant updating and revision.

The Journal

All financial transactions are entered chronologically in the **journal** or **book of original entry** before they are listed anywhere else. Most journals have a separate book for each group of similar transactions. For example, you may have a journal for recording cash receipts, one for cash disbursements, one for sales, and another for purchases. Depending on your needs, you might have a journal for payroll and for sales returns and allowances, or you may incorporate two of these procedures into the same journal. For miscellaneous entries posted from time to time, there is a general journal. Figure 4.2 shows a cash disbursements journal.

The General Ledger

From your journals, every transaction is summarized and posted in a **general ledger**, which lists each item on your chart of accounts. In your general ledger, or **book of secondary entry,** you'll find the debits and credits from which you may determine the balance of each account. Under "asset and expense accounts," debits record increases and credits record decreases. Conversely, under "liabilities and income accounts," credits record increases and debits record decreases.

To illustrate, suppose we were looking at your cash account in a ledger (an asset account) as in Figure 4.3. Remember that the information contained therein is compiled from several books of original entry, in this case, probably the cash receipts journal and the cash disbursements journal. Assume that you started the account with $10,000. The cash receipts journal discloses that $15,000 in receipts have been recorded; the cash disbursements journal tells you that $12,000 has been spent. You thus end up with $13,000—the amount summarized in the general ledger cash account.

We have illustrated a manually prepared ledger, but you can compile the information by machine or computer, depending on the overall system you select.

EVERYMAN'S MERCANTILE COMPANY

BALANCE SHEET

Sub No.[a]	Gen No.[b]	Account Title
CURRENT ASSETS		
01	102	Petty Cash
02	102	Cash-Checking Account
01	122	Accounts Receivable-Trade
02	122	Accounts Receivable-Other
03	122	Accounts Receivable-Employee
	130	Allowance for Bad Debts
01	150	Inventory-Finished Goods
02	150	Inventory-Work in Process
03	150	Inventory-Raw Materials
04	150	Inventory-In Transit
PROPERTY AND EQUIPMENT		
01	205	Building-New Mall Location
02	205	Building-Inner Urban Location
01	207	Manufacturing Equipment
02	207	Computer Room Machinery
01	209	Furniture & Fixtures-New Mall
02	209	Furniture & Fixtures-Inner Urb.
01	211	Executive Automobiles
02	211	Delivery Trucks
01	271	Leasehold Improvements-Sales Office
	278	Accumulated Depreciation and Amortization

INCOME STATEMENT

Sub No.[c]	Gen No.[b]	Account Title
INCOME		
01	501	Sales-Manufactured Product
02	501	Sales-Retail Products
03	501	Sales-Distributed Products
COST OF SALES		
01	651	Inventory Change-Mfd. Products
02	651	Inventory Change-Retail
03	651	Inventory Change-Distributed
01	653	Purchases-Mfd. Products
02	653	Purchases-Retail Products
03	653	Purchases-Distributed Products
01	656	Direct Labor-Mfd. Products
MANUFACTURING OVERHEAD		
01	666	Depreciation
01	668	Equipment Rental
01	669	Indirect Labor
01	670	Insurance
01	671	Maintenance & Repairs
01	675	Payroll Taxes
01	676	Rent
01	678	Utilities

BALANCE SHEET

Sub No.[a]	Gen No.[b]	Account Title
OTHER ASSETS		
01	281	Goodwill
02	281	Organization Expense
CURRENT LIABILITIES		
01	302	Note Payable-Banks
02	302	Note Payable-Other
	309	Contracts Payable
	313	Accounts Payable
	325	Accrued Expenses
	333	Payroll Taxes Payable
LONG TERM DEBT		
	385	Contracts Payable
CAPITAL		
	433	Common Stock
	436	Preferred Stock
	439	Retained Earnings

INCOME STATEMENT

Sub No.[c]	Gen. No.[b]	Account Title
SELLING EXPENSES		
	751	Advertising
	756	Business Promotion
	759	Commissions
	775	Payroll Taxes
	786	Trade Shows
	787	Travel
GENERAL & ADMINISTRATIVE EXPENSES		
	807	Automobile
	809	Bad Debts
	811	Bank Charges
	823	Depreciation
	825	Dues & Subscriptions
	831	Interest
	833	Insurance
	843	Miscellaneous
	847	Office Expense
	849	Office Salaries
	855	Professional Fees
	859	Rent
	869	Taxes
	875	Telephone
OTHER INCOME		
	940	Other Expense

[a] Describes location on balance sheet
[b] Describes general classification and determines ranking order
[c] Describes product code (where sub no. is deleted, no allocation has been determined to product)

Figure 4.1 Chart of accounts

DATE	PAID TO / RECEIVED FROM	Check #		Check Amount (Cr)	653 Purchase	676 Rent	751 Advertising	833 Insurance	543 Miscel	847 Office Expense	General Ledger ACCT.	Amount	
1/20/X3	General Telephone Co	972		176 19							825	176 19	
1/21/X3	Thompson Supply Co	973	1	88 64					88 64				1
1/21/X3	J P Patrick & Co	974	2	95 73					95 73				2
1/22/X3	Flow & Flow	975	3	435 00							855	435 00	3
1/22/X3	Montpelier Adv	976	4	896 55			896 55						4
1/25/X3	Crumble Oil Co	977	5	177 98							807	177 98	5
1/26/X3	Dina's Eatery	978	6	97 80							756	97 80	6
1/26/X3	Jane's Express Co	979	7	27 56					27 56				7
1/27/X3	Philips Rete Co	980	8	248 95							807	248 95	8
1/27/X3	The Miller Co	981	9	500 00		500 00							9
1/27/X3	Orsloup's Steel	982	10	585 00	585 00								10
1/27/X3	Screw Machine Co	983	11	49 58	49 58								11
1/27/X3	Kirschner & Co.	984	12	55 98	55 98								12
1/27/X3	Goldman Supplies	985	13	685 00						685 00			13
1/27/X3	Kelly Rental Inc.	986	14	168 50						168 50			14
1/27/X3	Franklin Auto	987	15	79 60							807	79 60	15
1/27/X3	Quist Advertising	988	16	175 00			175 00						16
1/27/X3	Shaw Insurance	989	17	600 00				600 -					17
1/27/X3	Health Plan Inc	990	18	895 00				895 00					18
1/28/X3	Extra Services Co	991	19	58 70					58 70				19
1/28/X3	Inner Urban Loc.	992	20	700 00		700 00							20
1/28/X3	New Mall	993	21	650 00		650 00							21
1/28/X3	Packing Supplies	994	22	748 70	748 70								22
1/29/X3	Larry Order Sup	995	23	129 50						129 50			23
1/29/X3	Ellis Professional	996	24	1250 00							835	1250 00	24
1/29/X3	Linda Henry	997	25	75 00			75 00						25
1/29/X3	Sand Energy	998	26	85 00	85 00								26
1/29/X3	Spitzer Casualty	999	27	785 48				785 48					27
1/29/X3	American Group	1000	28	68 25	68 25								28
1/29/X3	Simplify Systems	1001	29	350 00						350 00			29
1/29/X3	O'Mally & Co	1002	30	79 90					79 90				30
				25099 07	7633 01	1850 00	9186 55	2280 48	350 51	1333 00		2465 52	

Figure 4.2   Cash disbursements journal

Note that the columns simplify the most crucial classification of expenses. Each check is recorded chronologically and coded with the appropriate number from the chart of accounts.

GENERAL LEDGER
ACCOUNT   Cash
SHEET   NO.

ACCOUNT NO.
02-10r

DATE 19X2	DESCRIPTION	POSTING REF.			CHARGES	CREDITS	✓	DR OR CR	BALANCE
		Opening Balance			10 000 -		✓	Dr	10 000 -
Jan 10		CR 1			15000 -		✓	Dr	25 00 -
30		CD 3				12 000		Dr	13 000 -

Figure 4.3 The general ledger

The column labeled "Posting REF" describes the source of the posting to the ledger. In the January 10 entry, "CR1" refers to cash receipts journal, page 1. Thus if you want the description of the transactions or from whom the money has been received, you must open to the appropriate page of the cash receipts journal. The January 30 entry refers to cash disbursements journal, page 3, and you must look to that journal for details of cash disbursed. These cross-references to books of original entry are called **audit trails.** The better the trail, the better the control.

The Subsidiary Ledger

Because many accounts in a general ledger represent voluminous data, only a condensed summary is posted. A detailed summary is listed in a **secondary** or **subsidiary ledger.** The account in the general ledger is referred to as the **control account.** A listing of each account in the subsidiary ledger is taken at the end of every business cycle. If the sum of the schedule agrees with the control account, the ledgers are presumed to be correct. If not, the ledgers must be cross-checked.

Subsidiary ledgers are often used for accounts receivable, with a page for each customer. They are also used for accounts payable, with a separate listing for each vendor, for certain fixed assets or notes receivable, and for any other purpose that would require a separate, detailed accounting.

The format in the subsidiary ledger is usually the same as that in the general ledger. Although the data posted in the subsidiary ledger is almost the same as the data posted in the general ledger, there is one exception: The general ledger is posted with totals and the subsidiary ledger records

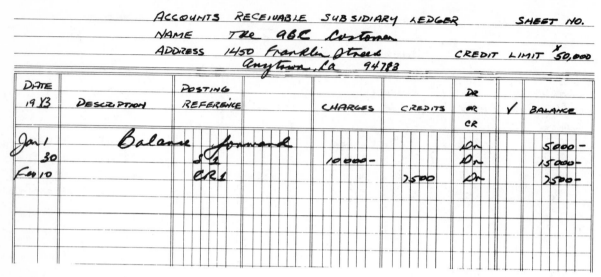

Figure 4.4   Subsidiary ledger

details. Note that in Figure 4.4 we have again used an excerpt from a manually prepared ledger, but the same information can be compiled by machine or computer, depending on your overall system.

The posting in the subsidiary ledger is restricted to the transactions with the ABC customer. The folio reference of January 30, S1, refers to the sales journal, page 1. The February 10 posting, CR1, refers to the cash receipts journal, page 1. Accounts receivables are an asset account; so debits refer to increases and credits refer to decreases. A reading of this account provides that customer's sales and payments history, thus detailing the amount owed.

Figure 4.5 reviews the order in which you use the tools in your financial reporting system.

> System components are, at the same time, both its products and its tools.

CHOOSING YOUR SYSTEM

In selecting the best system for your needs, you might choose a manual system geared to maximum flexibility. With it, you're free of the restrictions imposed by either an automatic or semiautomatic system; automation forces you to follow specific rules for machines to operate properly. However, flexibility is just one requirement. Speed, accuracy, low operating

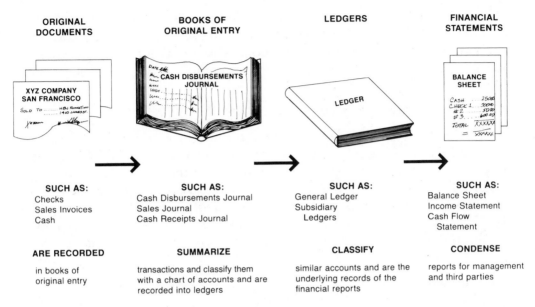

ORIGINAL DOCUMENTS	BOOKS OF ORIGINAL ENTRY	LEDGERS	FINANCIAL STATEMENTS

SUCH AS:
Checks
Sales Invoices
Cash
	SUCH AS:
	Cash Disbursements Journal
	Sales Journal
	Cash Receipts Journal
		SUCH AS:
		General Ledger
		Subsidiary
		  Ledgers
			SUCH AS:
			Balance Sheet
			Income Statement
			Cash Flow
			  Statement

ARE RECORDED in books of original entry	**SUMMARIZE** transactions and classify them with a chart of accounts and are recorded into ledgers	**CLASSIFY** similar accounts and are the underlying records of the financial reports	**CONDENSE** reports for management and third parties

Figure 4.5   Flowchart of a financial reporting system

costs, and the information the system is designed to produce are also important concerns. The semiautomatic system offers less flexibility but provides more speed. The ultimate is the computer, offering maximum speed but minimum flexibility. Even the slightest error will be maximized.

Manual Systems

The traditional manual system may conjure up images of the bookkeeper sitting on a tall stool, head bent, wearing a green eyeshade, and meticulously recording business transactions with a quill pen. Strange as it may seem, there are many companies that still find this basic system effective—with appropriate concessions, of course. The quill long ago lost out to the ball-point pen.

However, a major updating of this system evolved some years back when several manufacturers developed forms for the "one-write" system, a procedure that allows you simultaneously to write a check and make an entry in a journal as well as in a subsidiary ledger, all facilitated by the use of specially coated or carbonized paper, a ball-point pen, and the technique of placing the check on the journal so all forms are aligned.

One-write systems require maximum discipline on the part of the bookkeeper because they require that all forms and carbons be aligned properly and that the bookkeeper press very firmly when making an entry, and supply costs are higher than with the traditional manual systems. But efficiency benefits are great in that costly transcription errors are avoided and the investment is still minimal (a few hundred dollars for the forms) compared to the several thousand dollars required for a bookkeeping machine or the even greater expense of a computer.

Semiautomatic Systems

At some point in the development of your business, you're going to consider a semiautomatic system, a combination of manual effort and bookkeeping machines, with the latter operating in much the same way as the one-write system. Entries are typed and the machines have a computational capacity for addition and subtraction as data is entered. Fairly adaptable, bookkeeping machines may be integrated with either a one-write operation or a computer in order to provide a complete system geared to your needs.

Automatic Systems

The heart of the automatic system is the computer. Today the computer is available in a range of sizes, prices, and capabilities to fit almost any budget, and computer service bureaus offer prepackaged programs and services. Yet businesses of all sizes have wasted millions of dollars when their staffs were not sufficiently trained to utilize these exacting and sophisticated machines.

We discuss this subject at length in the next chapter; here we'll simply point out that your basic consideration, prior to bringing a computer into your business, should be whether the procedures you require warrant it and your available personnel will adapt to it. Let caution and research be your guides.

IMPLEMENTING YOUR SYSTEM

> With any system, you must fully understand all your objectives before you and your bookkeeper, accountant, or CPA can begin to create it.

After you have determined your company's performance goals, you will want to evaluate them periodically and detect the cause of any deviations from the original plan. Whatever your goals, once your system is designed, put it into operation as soon as possible. Don't delay between creating it and making it operative; delays and the catching-up process can be extremely costly, both because of errors resulting from incorrect information and because you'll probably have to call on professionals to square away the mess.

ACTION GUIDELINES

Before you and your systems designer create any system, be sure you can answer the following questions affirmatively:

- Do we understand my company's requirements?
- Have we decided which procedures should be incorporated into the system?
- Do I have sufficient staff to adapt to the system?
- Have I communicated openly with my staff about plans and progress of the system?
- Have we determined whether hiring additional staff is warranted?
- Will the system prepare timely and accurate reports?
- Do I have a clear picture of the initial and continuing costs of the system?
- Is my internal bookkeeping staff competent to deal with the procedures to be followed?

    The tools used in financial reporting are

- The chart of accounts
- The journal or book of original entry
- The general ledger or book of secondary entry
- The subsidiary ledger

    The three types of accounting systems, from most to least flexible and least to most expensive are

- Manual
- Semiautomatic
- Automatic

5

Should You Computerize
Your System?

This chapter will

- Show you how to weigh the advantages and disadvantages of a computerized system

- Describe the alternatives available within a computerized system

- Help you decide whether any kind of computerization is feasible for your business

- List the precautions to take if you go the computer route

- Provide alternatives to owning your own computer

There was a time when the computer was a giant machine, occupying substantial space and holding court only in the hallowed halls of huge corporations. The data-processing functions it performed were strictly a prerogative of big business. But that was years ago.

Now there are the mini- and microcomputers and computer service bureaus. As the machine got smaller, smarter, and, in most cases, less expensive, computerized information became available to very small businesses. Appropriate computer systems can now be easily developed for even the novice entrepreneur with a modest budget; and as long as the business doesn't need the flexibility offered by a manual or semiautomatic system, the advantages it might derive from a computer are enormous. A manual or semiautomatic system can be changed almost instantly simply by making the appropriate adjustments; alterations in a computerized system require considerable effort and time because they necessitate a change in program, instructions, or procedure. With proper programming, computers can handle everything from tedious postings in journals and ledgers to the cumbersome preparation of reports, sales analyses, and unit breakdowns in any format management selects (such as area, sales rep, customer, or product) as well as a simple to complex payroll.

All this is made possible because the computer can calculate (add, subtract, multiply, and divide) speedily and accurately, producing computations that are almost always correct. Sometimes, however, a worn part or some other machine malfunction can cause a miscalculation. Computers can also sort, classify, store, and remember a vast amount of information very quickly.

The computer's recall ability, a byproduct of its infallible memory or storage facility, enables it to retain a formidable supply of data. It produces the data on demand in neatly typed, easily read reports, usually referred to as printouts in the computer industry. The potential of this stored data is great. Representing one of the most valuable features of the computer, it may be utilized for anything from accounts receivable analyses to inventory processing to comparative sales reports. The list of possibilities is limited only by the needs or requests of management and the imagination of the programmer. But herein lies the computer's major flaw. In spite of its versatility, it is still a machine, capable of doing *only* what it is expressly told to do. Thus the efficiency or accuracy, success or failure, of a computer installation (or an entire system) hinges on the *people* who process the data and instruct the machine. If these functions are not performed correctly, the information produced will be invalid. Therefore if you've ever thought a machine can solve all your processing problems, you're wrong. People are what count.

In light of this consideration, you may wonder whether automation is really worth the investment. How do you decide whether electronic data processing would be an asset to your company? Specifically, how do you weigh the flexibility of a manual or semiautomatic system against the benefits in speed and volume of a computer? And if you choose the latter, how do you determine which way to go? Do you buy your own, share time, use a service bureau, or involve your business in a joint venture? There are many options available and many considerations within those options. Thus in this chapter we'll explore each alternative within a computerized system, pointing out its advantages and disadvantages.

Your initial task is to determine whether you should use a computer at all. To arrive at this decision, we suggest you seek the assistance of a professional—your CPA, financial adviser, and/or a computer consultant. If you're unschooled in this field, avoid doing the research and making all the preliminary decisions yourself. In the long run, you'll save money if you enlist the help of a consultant with solid experience in computer systems.

STEPS AND CONSIDERATIONS IN AUTOMATING
Investigation and Planning

First, your adviser will typically do a feasibility study, which should answer such questions as the following:

> Does the *volume* of transactions in your business warrant conversion to a computer?
>
> Is there enough consistency in the *type* of transactions your business handles to benefit from a computer? If not, a computer would probably not be feasible, although inconsistencies might indicate you should revise your system whether or not a computer is involved.
>
> If your responses to the first two questions are affirmative, are competent personnel available in your company or area to guarantee efficient system performance?
>
> Which of the available alternatives in using a computer would work best for your business?
>
> If you buy your own computer, is the location of your business such that you would have a variety of vendors from which to make your selection and obtain service and equipment backup?

If you're going to use a computer, try to see an installation in operation. You might inquire whether a colleague or customer has one you can look at. Your adviser should be able to show you a system. Also try to get an opportunity to speak with the user to determine his or her company's experience with it.

As you go through this introductory phase, you also should itemize what you'll use the computer for. Again, you'll benefit from the help of your professional because you may not know all the functions a computer can perform. For example, if you're a distributor and want to determine your backlog of orders by customer, product, or sales rep, you may think that such information is not worth the effort required to obtain it or that it would be obsolete by the time you receive it. You would be mistaken on both counts. Avoid underestimating the abilities of this potential addition to your staff. The procedures over which you're deliberating may well be a matter of simple routine for the computer. So if there is any information that would help you operate your business more effectively, you'd do well to investigate the possibilities of getting it.

During this period, communication with each department of your company is vitally important because you must not only consider the needs you're aware of but also those your sales and marketing managers, manufacturing chief, warehouse supervisor, and shipping departments perceive. Encourage everyone to let his or her imagination run wild, and perhaps separate the proposed functions according to those that are required and those that are desirable. (This often enables you to determine whether the incremental cost of information is worthwhile, assuming you choose a computerized system.) After culling all the requests, you'll be in a better position to identify realistically the actual needs of your business.

Then, if you've been organized about your approach thus far, it should be relatively easy to narrow your alternatives and focus on the best solution for your company. Although you will again need some guidance, remember *you* are the user, and the system you're considering is being designed for *your* convenience to enable *you* to manage and operate your business more effectively. Don't delegate the final decision to anyone else.

Design and Development

Should you decide that a computer is for you and you have selected the alternative you're going to go with, the most important person in the transition will be your systems designer, whose task is to review all your company's requirements and incorporate them into the plan.

> The systems designer may be your CPA, accountant, or a specialist referred by either of them, a colleague, a customer, or your bank.

It's good practice for you, the user, to prepare a timetable for implementation that can then be reviewed by all persons involved, including your employees, vendor(s), and CPA or other consultant.

When this process is completed, your systems designer will concentrate on such specifics as equipment delivery dates, availability of personnel, and coordination of the timing sequence of conversion procedures with the priorities of your business. Installation proceedings are complex enough without the added burden of peak season business demands. This holds true whether you are buying your own computer, sharing time on an off-premises machine, embarking on a joint venture, or using a computer service bureau.

Software or Program

If you have decided to buy or share a computer, one of your major concerns will be the software, or program, which integrates the data you want processed with instructions, enabling the machine to deliver the information you need. This can be a tricky business. Because instructions have to be precise, many hours and dollars can be wasted while a program is being perfected.

Fortunately, there have been great strides in the development of computer language, and today there are alternatives to employing your own programmer. For example, "canned" or mass produced programs are available. Should you consider this option, it's essential that you obtain references from your potential software vendor so you can determine the kind of experiences other companies have had with the program you're considering.

Assuming you find one to buy, get documentation of the program so your company will have detailed information on its composition. This will enable another software vendor or someone on your own staff to control or alter it when necessary. If you want to change the kind of information your computer provides and your vendor has gone out of business, you could really be stuck if you don't know how the program was put together. Documentation also helps management understand the system and your accountants audit it if necessary.

Personnel

If programming is vital to the success of the computerized system, then the people who run it are even more so. In fact, without capable programmers and technicians, your system wouldn't have a chance.

You may have heard the expression GIGO (garbage in, garbage out). This term sums up the situation with untrained personnel or with undocumented or untested procedures. If the computer is fed either incorrect material or inadequate instructions, the results are unintelligible, useless reports or, worse, misleading reports upon which incorrect decisions are made. When this happens, the computer is rarely at fault. More often it's the programmer, the keypunch operator, or the data-processing technician, all of whom share the responsibility of making sure the machine gives you the information you need to control your business.

It may be feasible to employ an in-house programmer when you own your own computer, if you decide not to use commercially available programs. However, it's unlikely you would also need your own technician. Often a systems manager or the controller of a company—sometimes an accounts payable or accounts receivable clerk—can serve this function.

Hardware

When you first consider purchasing a computer, your major concern is invariably the hardware, or the computer itself. Yet the consensus among professionals in the field is that hardware should be third on the list of priorities. Your first thought should be the availability of qualified personnel for all aspects of data processing and computer operation and maintenance.

Your second consideration should be the program, or software. Any number of manufacturers offer comparably excellent equipment; so hardware is the least of your problems, although prime considerations in buying a computer would be your vendor's financial stability (ask your bank to check on the company's credit if it is not a firm with a well-established reputation) and the continued service and backup you are entitled to expect. Keep in mind that if the business isn't going to be around a few years hence, servicing your installation could be a problem. Other factors to check if you buy your own computer are how expandable, flexible, reliable, and maintenance-free the equipment is in relation to the growth potential of your business.

> Because of the phenomenal evolution in computer technology, many models have become obsolete by the time they're installed. However, this will have no effect on the performance or service you can expect from the equipment.

With both hardware and software, investigate the hidden costs involved in upgrading your equipment when necessary. If at all possible, avoid making separate contracts with software and hardware vendors. Experience in such situations has proven that when something runs amok, each vendor tries to blame the other, which leaves you holding the bag as you wait for them to settle their argument. If you buy your own, attempt to find a manufacturer who can provide both hardware and software. Or at least seek a software firm that has experience with the hardware involved. The firm should also have a history of success in using the program language contemplated for the selected equipment.

Your contract with either or both vendors should incorporate many, if not all, of the specifications discussed during the screening process. To accomplish this, list your requirements in a request for proposal. In turn, the vendor will submit a proposal, spelling out everything to be covered in the contract.

USING YOUR EQUIPMENT TO CAPACITY

Make full use of your equipment. Consider the projected growth of your company when your system is designed; but remember, the computer does not "run down" and it is only doing its job when dealing with large numbers of transactions. When it is not used to capacity, you don't get your money's worth.

A classic case of a firm not getting good service from its equipment was Freund and Schiller, the import/export company we introduced in Chapter 1. When we came on the scene, the business was growing rapidly with an annual sales volume of just under $5 million. Although the company had its own computer, it used it merely as a glorified accounts payable machine.

Had management been more alert, the equipment would have been programmed for additional uses because with the growth that was taking place, there was a tremendous need for more information. For example, a sales rep was hired to conduct business in Asia, and it was difficult to compute the profitability of that area without sorting through large numbers of transactions. Yet when the computer was finally programmed to do the job, sorting was accomplished in no time and a financial report was produced on all the company's geographical areas. Thus management could discuss profitability and predict potential sales for each area.

An additional benefit was the control of accounts receivable, a procedure accomplished by reorganizing the company's credit policies to machine readable language. When a customer approached or exceeded the company's credit limits, the computer produced the necessary notice, which could then be accompanied by action from the credit and/or sales department. The ability to monitor profitablity had a number of far-reaching advantages.

ALTERNATIVES TO OWNING YOUR OWN COMPUTER

Computer Service Bureaus

There is no reason you can't have a computerized system and avoid, or at least postpone, some of the problems involved with owning your own computer. One alternative is a computer service bureau. This may serve either as a transition to another arrangement or as a permanent solution.

Along with offering a valuable product, service bureaus require no investment in either hardware or software. Because both have already been tested by the bureau's other, presumably satisfied, customers, the debugging process has been completed. Not only will you be able to choose the specific procedure you want processed (such as payroll, accounts receivable, accounts payable, inventory, or general ledger) you may even find it convenient to use two or more service centers if one is cheaper than another. One center may not have all the applications you want processed, or a certain bureau may do a better job than another on a specific application.

You'll discover too, that there are other facilities that offer the services in which you're interested. Many banks and some accounting firms offer computerized payroll applications, including processing employees' checks and preparing quarterly payroll tax returns. They also provide programs for processing financial reports (corollaries to both accounts receivable and accounts payable functions) and detailed sales and inventory reports. Another attractive feature is that the costs for this kind of processing are relatively low, and though the program used may be largely unalterable, you will have no responsibility for computer personnel or equipment maintenance.

As always, you will have to weigh your goals against the alternatives available and compare prices. However, to show you just how successful this solution can be, let's take a look at a very small business using a computer service: Weddings Inc., another firm we introduced in Chapter 1.

This business was started on a shoestring, with both partners doing almost everything themselves. Neither had had any training in bookkeeping, and neither had time to learn it. When the computer came to their rescue, the two women took advantage of one popularly used and widely available (general ledger) program that fully prepared their financial reports (the profit or loss statement, balance sheet, and a cash statement).

After only four hours of training, they were fully equipped to prepare the material for processing and, with the computer's assistance, were producing professional-caliber reports. Not only were they able to share these with their creditors, but even more importantly, they utilized them as a valuable tool to control their business. Not long after the system was in operation, they were able to train a novice bookkeeper to prepare the input data and, in so doing, demonstrate complete mastery over their accounting/ bookkeeping function. Clearly, they got their money's worth, although any advantages the computer afforded were made possible only through the efficient preparation of the data that went into it.

An important consideration in availing yourself of a computer service bureau is turnaround time—the time required to process your material and get it back to you.

If you own your own computer, you need only be concerned with which phase of your business is given priority at a particular time. However, if you're using a service bureau, remember that your company will be one of many customers, and although turnaround time with many service bureaus is very short, you may have to wait for your job to come through.

In view of this, you may want to give some thought to other options.

Time Sharing

Time sharing means exactly what its name implies: Your business shares a computer with other companies. Usually located in some remote or faraway place with access through the telephone lines, a computer in California may be shared by a company in Wisconsin and one in New Jersey.

Sharing time on someone else's computer typically allows you to have a terminal on location and avoid having your documents leave the premises. You also have almost immediate turnaround time. Data is usually accumulated, perhaps for a day, to be transmitted in bulk form, and the processing frequently occurs during off hours. Thus if you need a report on sales, someone in your company might transmit the data in the middle of the night—if that is the computer time assigned to your company—and you would have a report by morning.

Time sharing, of course, solves your hardware problem, but you still have to provide the software, or program, for your company's needs. Therefore you have to have someone on your staff develop it or purchase one, either from a software vendor or from a similar business that uses a program for comparable purposes.

A company on a computerized system often combines time sharing with the facilities of a service bureau. Inventory, for example, is an application that easily adapts to time sharing because a company constantly needs an updated inventory on its premises. This arrangement, coupled with a service bureau's processing of other requirements, might be the most feasible way to construct your system. In general, processing costs tend to be high even though data storage on a time-shared computer may be relatively inexpensive.

Joint Venture

Joint venture refers not only to a means of structuring and financing one's business; it may be the route to go when you consider computerizing your accounting system. This arrangement involves two or more businesses subsidizing the cost of both the installation and operation of the facility. A form that has become common in certain industries, particularly banking, savings and loan, hospitals, and construction, joint ventures lend themselves well to any two or more companies in the same field. However, such ventures require formal agreements, which should include commitments regarding the software to be used, formulas allocating equipment and operating costs, buyout provisions, management accord over the location and operation of the facility, methods of resolving disputes, and compatibility over use priorities. If you are interested in this alternative, you might inquire through your trade organization whether such ventures have been successful in your industry.

But regardless of the vehicle you favor in putting together a computerized system, *do* get advice from the professionals—your CPA, financial adviser, and/or computer consultant. They can offer you objectivity you may not get from your staff or the computer sales people. They also have the advantage of experience in many different computer-related problems; so they can be of invaluable assistance in conducting a feasibility study, setting up controls, determining which applications to computerize, selecting hardware and software, testing the facility, monitoring performance, and drawing up contracts with the hardware and software suppliers or with the other users and/or owners if you enter into a time share arrangement or a joint venture.

BACKUP

All systems (except one integrated with a computer service bureau) should have some kind of backup in the event of a major disaster, such as fire, theft, or earthquake. Sometimes the equipment vendor has a similar machine in his or her shop that is available to run your program, or he or she may make some arrangement with another customer so that each of you can depend on the other for support. Just as you must have a contingent plan for cash shortages, you should have an emergency plan in the event your computer breaks down. Similarly, you would do well to have a data backup, particularly for your master files, in the event material is lost or destroyed when away from your premises.

To review the procedures you should monitor in your study and transition to automation, take a look at the checklist in Figure 5.1. The flowchart in Figure 5.2 will help you visualize the sequence your data goes through as it is processed for your use.

DEVELOPING AN ACCOUNTING SYSTEM: A CASE HISTORY

Just as architects must be aware of the use to be made of the buildings they design, so should designers of an accounting system be aware of the ultimate uses of the system they develop. For a case in point, let's look at what happened when one of our clients, the Ohio Corporation, called on us to design a new accounting system with several objectives.

Vehicle	Selection to be Preceded by Feasibility Study	Professional Counsel (Throughout)	Design & Development	Competent Personnel	Software (Program)	Documentation of Program (If Predesigned Program Not Used)	Hardware	Turnaround Time Problem	*Contracts or Agreements	Using Your System to Capacity	Backup
Owning a Computer	√	√	√	√	√	√	√	—	× #	√	√
Computer Service Bureau	√	√	√	√	—	—	—	√	—	—	—
Timesharing	√	√	√	√	√	✕	—	—	× ▽	✕	√
Joint Venture	√	√	√	√	√	√	√	—	× # ▽	√	√

KEY: √ × # ▽ Indicate that the task referred to requires attention
✕ Indicates that the task referred to may or may not need attention
— Indicates that no attention is needed
*Contracts with Software Vendor ×
Contracts with Hardware Vendor #
Agreements with Other Owners and/or Users ▽

Figure 5.1   Transitional and operational checklist for computerization

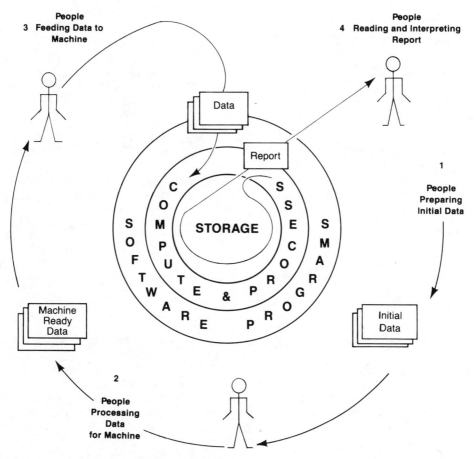

Figure 5.2   Overview of computer work flow

This family-owned business imported stereophonic equipment from Europe and Asia. Though definitely the major force in the operation, the founder and chief operating officer was assisted by a four-person management team covering marketing, sales, administration, and product procurement. He was also guided by a group of advisers retained on an annual basis to help review such operations as budget, pricing, marketing strategy, and gross profit performance. During their periodic meetings, these advisers became real participants in administering this well-controlled organization.

When we came on the scene, the company was about to increase its line of credit; and at some of the earliest meetings between client and bank, the bank outlined its reporting requirements, which included quarterly comparative financial statements and periodic information on accounts receivable. Thus the bank's requests had to be taken into consideration in system design.

Other factors that had to be considered were various managerial controls the company wanted instituted. For example, this business maintained a very small inventory with relatively high unit prices, and management wanted to maintain gross profit control for each product (this being tantamount to establishing separate profit centers, an excellent control device to determine product profit contribution—see Chapter 7).

Also important was the fact that the company's customers were somewhat unstable, moving shakily in and out of their respective retail businesses. Thus tight control of accounts receivable was a top priority.

We had the usual concern with costs, not only original but also continuing costs, because the system would presumably be in service for a long time. And because people operate a system, a major continuing expenditure is personnel costs. Thus we focused on the firm's accounting/bookkeeping staff, which consisted of

1. A full-time bookkeeper who doubled as office manager

2. An assistant bookkeeper, primarily responsible for invoicing and accounts receivable

3. A part-time clerk who maintained **perpetual inventory control** (a method of determining quantities and type of inventory on hand without counting each item)

Prior to our involvement, this staff had manually prepared financial statements showing total sales, gross profits as a whole (but not by product category), and a detailed breakdown of general and administrative expenses (referred to as fixed costs on the following report). To illustrate, take a look at Figure 5.3, the profit or loss statement prior to conversion of the accounting system. Note that comparisons are impossible because budget data is not an integral part of the report. (Compare this manually prepared report with the comparative statement of earnings in Figure 5.9.)

Accounts receivable reports were another area that suffered because they had to be prepared manually by an already overburdened bookkeeping staff. Because of insufficient time, it was not a report of **aged accounts receivable** (a listing of accounts showing the length of time each invoice has been outstanding) and it was not prepared on a regular basis. To see the advantage of an aged accounts receivable report over a current listing of accounts receivable, compare the manually prepared list in Figure 5.4 with an aged accounts receivable report (Figure 5.8).

Equipped with this background and an evaluation of the existing accounting system, we were ready to begin creating a new one.

Because we were restricted in making additions to the staff, we decided to utilize computer service bureaus and commercial data-processing programs. Not only would these produce versatile reports with considerably less

Period 7–30–X3	Company Ohio Corporation	
Acc. no.	Item	Actual
	GROSS SALES	704,695
	LESS DISCOUNT	54,565
P 1	Net sales	650,130
P 2	Landed cost of prod. sold	370,843
P 4	Gross profit	279,287
P 5	Gross margin	
P 6	Other revenues	
P 7	Other costs	
P 8	Internal service	
P 9	Costs internal service	
P 10	Internal gross profit	
P 11	Internal gross margin	279,287
	INDIRECT COSTS	
P 14	Fixed costs, appendix	258,458
P 15	Administrative costs	
P 16	Result before depreciation	20,829
P 21	Depreciation, appendix	
P 22	Operating result	
P 24	Interest gains	
P 26	Interest expenses—group	
P 27	Interest expenses—non-group	
P 28	Other financial revenues/costs	
P 29	Sum of exchange rate fluctuations	
P 31	Financial reserves	
P 32	Income tax	
P 36	Net result this period	20,829

Figure 5.3　Statement of earnings prior to system conversion

Period 7-30-X3	Company Ohio Corporation	
Acc. no.	**Item**	**Actual**
	FIXED COSTS	
F 1	Personnel wages	64,951
F 2	Personnel salaries	
F 3	Personnel travelling, repr.	39,944
F 4	Personnel misc.	
F 5	Buildings, premises, etc.	11,237
F 6	Cars & vehicles, etc.	
F 7	Machinery & equipment	
F 8	Fees	4,799
F 9	Telephones, telex, postage	8,903
F 10	Stationery	758
F 11	Delivery costs	27,311
F 12	Misc. other services	40,723
F 13	Advertising, PR, etc.	41,105
F 14	Insurance costs	4,279
F 15	Delivery delay, cancellation	
F 16	D & B	1,200
F 17	Guarantee costs	13,248
F 18	BAD DEBT	
P 11	Total fixed costs	258,458
	DEPRECIATION	
D 1	Buildings	
D 2	Cars & vehicles	
D 3	Machinery & equipment	
D 4	Depr. rechargeable	
P 14	Total depreciation	

Fig. 5.3   (Continued)

Ohio Corporation
List of Accounts Receivables
April 30, 19X3

Abrams Company	$ 638.58
Amfarco Dealers	2,797.22
Alana Corp.	< 12.73 >
Beehre Inc.	197.50
Beta Group	58.75
Boston Sound Company	4,989.50
Brown Stores	598.90
Charlie Cooper	289.75
Darwin & Company	< 59.90 >
Essex Sales	852.50
Georgia Hi-Fi	75.00
Hallinan House	119.50
Jack & Jills	75.00
Kennedy & Shapiro	485.00
Zincola Corp.	< 875.00 >
Morrison & Cooper	12.50
Max Pona	110.00
Maxton Group	75.00
Melody Company	989.17
Noonan & Jones	17.50
Nixon Dispensing	98.22
	11,531.96
	Carry fwd.

Figure 5.4 Manually prepared current listing of accounts receivable

effort, but they would provide management with each product's contribution to gross profit. Our project was simplified by the fact that most of the data required for commercial data processing was available through one source: the sales invoice (see Figure 5.5, which highlights the criteria utilized).

We knew that by providing the computer with standard costs of products and cash collections, we could meet many of our financial reporting requirements. Thus began our search for a computer service bureau, and we selected one that met many of our needs by producing the following reports: sales by sales rep, sales by product and profit margins, and aged accounts receivable trial balance. We would go elsewhere for the balance of our requirements. The sales by sales rep report in Figure 5.6 analyzes sales for each sales person and serves as the basis for preparation of sales commissions.

A report showing profit contribution by product line indicates to management when to "push" or support a product that is earning its way and perhaps delete one that doesn't hold its own. Figure 5.7 shows such a report.

A detailed aged accounts receivable report (see Figure 5.8) tells management where customers stand on their credit obligations and in which cases collection efforts have to be intensified. It also demonstrates whether it is worthwhile to continue selling to certain customers.

Now we had a series of reports that provided invaluable information, and the cost of producing them represented only one-sixth of the monthly cost for an additional assistant bookkeeper. Moreover, the input information that would generate the reports was already prepared, in a different format, perhaps, but not so different as to burden the staff.

However, there was another important requirement to meet—the comparative financial statements. The bank had stipulated quarterly statements, but management wanted them monthly so they would always have a current working tool illustrating the relationship between actual performance and budget. We again used as much existing data as possible to avoid any additional burden on the staff. The result (see Figure 5.9) was all the company had hoped for. Not only did the system produce a comparative report in an easy to read format, but it pointed out all the variances to budget.

After providing for the comparative financial statements, we were left with the final task of verifying the managerial reports prepared by the first computer service bureau with the financial reports prepared by the second. This was accomplished manually (Figure 5.10). By reconciling these two reports, we had excellent guidelines in providing reliable data for the entire reporting system, a reality made possible when we compared the **standard cost of goods sold** (the cost you allow for in setting the selling price for merchandise) with the actual cost of goods sold.

The company was thereby able to realize all its objectives through the use of a computer service bureau and commercial programs readily available to companies of any size at a reasonable cost.

INVOICE

ohio corporation

605 Market Street, San Francisco, CA 94105

INVOICE NO.

2312

SOLD TO:

DALY SOUND COMPANY

370 Franklin Street

Anytown, U.S.A.

SHIPPED TO:

''SAME''

DATE 2/14/X3	DATE SHIPPED 1/27/X3	SHIPPED VIA UPS	YOUR ORDER NO. XX31269	F.O.B.	TERMS Plan B	CUST. NO. 670123	SALESMAN'S NO. 36
QUANTITY	PRODUCT CODE	DESCRIPTION			PRICE		AMOUNT
1	AB22	Speakers			60.00 ea.		60.00
			Freight				3.48
							63.48

Figure 5.5   Sales invoice

OHIO CORPORATION
SALES BY SALES REP

SALESMAN — JOE BROWN — INDIANA AND ILLINOIS

CO. NO. ___   REPORT ___   DATE 4/30/X2   PAGE NO. ___

PROD. CLASS PRODUCT NO.	PROD. CLASS DESCRIPTION / ITEM NO. AND DESCRIPTION	CURRENT PERIOD VOLUME	CURRENT PERIOD VALUE	CURRENT VOLUME	YEAR-TO-DATE VALUE	YTD LAST-YEAR VOLUME	YTD LAST-YEAR VALUE
P/C 02 LS1	SPECIAL SPEAKERS						
5043		39	550.44	80	1,080.80	75	945.00
TOTAL PROD. CLASS 02		39	550.44	80	1,080.80	75	945.00
P/C 04	SWITCHING COMPONENTS						
5043	DAMP			2			
5046	CENTRAL CONTROL			1	1,050.60		
5046	CENTRAL CONTROL			1			
5043	AMP 1			1			
5051	PHONO			1	210.00		
5052	SPEAKER			1	420.00		
5054	SPOTLIGHT			2	2,120.00		
TOTAL PROD. CLASS 04				8	3,800.00		
P/C 05	PHONODISCS						
CR01	RECORD			10	94.40		
RD03	RECORD	26	271.95	26	271.99	20	200.00
RD04	RECORD	2	18.90	2	18.90		
7742	RECORD			12	113.28		
7761	RECORD	20	184.10	30	278.50		
7762	RECORD	5	42.50	15	138.90	15	147.50
7763	RECORD	4	34.00	14	128.40		
7770	RECORD	4	34.00	14	128.40		
7782	RECORD	5	42.50	27	254.38		
7784	RECORD	4	34.00	15	130.90		
7785	RECORD			14	128.40		
7788	RECORD			12	113.28		
7792	RECORD	10	94.40	37	349.28		
TOTAL PROD. CLASS 05		80	756.35	228	2,149.01	35	347.50
P/C 06	PREMIUM CABLE						
PH015	CABLES	27	783.92	27	703.92		
PH075	CABLES	47	602.60	47	602.60		
PH090	CABLES			33	207.48		
TOTAL PROD. CLASS 06		74	1,386.52	107	1,514.00	—	0
P/C 07	ACCESSORIES						
ACC77	CARTRIDGE			4	375.40	20	1,877.00
ACCRK	RACK					60	83.40
ACC40	CABLES	40	55.60	40	55.60		
ACC50	CABLES	40	77.60	40	77.60	75	145.50
ACC70	CABLES	40	66.80	40	66.80	80	137.50
TOTAL PROD. CLASS 07			200.00		575.40		2,243.40
TOTAL SALES—JOE BROWN			2,893.31		9,119.21		3,535.90

Figure 5.6 Sales by sales rep report

OO.NO   REPORT

OHIO CORPORATION
SALES BY PRODUCT AND STANDARD GROSS PROFIT
SPECIAL SPEAKERS

DATE 4/30/X2   PAGE NO. 1

PRODUCT NO.	ITEM NO. AND DESCRIPTION	VOLUME	CURRENT PERIOD			CURRENT YEAR TO DATE		
			NET-VALUE	TOTAL COST	MARGIN	NET-VALUE	TOTAL COST	MARGIN
ALL00	SPECIAL SPEAKER	1,666	18,694.00	11,029.46	7,664.54	53,689.17	26,762.07	26,927.10
BASS3	PARTS MA					75.46	48.00	27.46
BASS4	PARTS MA					48.32	30.73	17.59
BASS5	PARTS MA					31.18	19.84	11.34
BASS7	PARTS					28.92	15.20	13.72
BASS8	PARTS					200.00	159.70	40.30
81500	TURNTABLE							
LS1	SPEAKERS	2	120.00	44.34	75.66	4,245.00	1,795.77	2,419.23
LS4	STANDS					585.00	345.80	239.20
LS5	STANDS	4	144.00	54.60	89.40	1,108.80	464.10	644.70
MA1R	SPEAKER ROSEWOOD	4	1,224.00	714.40	509.60	7,680.60	5,000.80	2,679.80
MA1W	SPEAKER WALNUT	8	2,288.00	1,403.76	884.24	15,041.00	10,177.26	4,863.74
MA3W	SPEAKER ROSEWOOD					11,811.60	7,908.06	3,903.54
MA3W	SPEAKER WALNUT					11,851.00	9,178.40	2,672.60
MA4R	SPEAKER ROSEWOOD	8	220.00	96.80	123.20	2,380.00	2,063.20	316.80
MA4W	SPEAKER WALNUT					4,445.00	4,048.00	397.00
MA5R	SPEAKER ROSEWOOD	12	830.00	354.00	476.00	4,498.60	3,064.16	1,433.84
MA5W	SPEAKER WALNUT	12	1,824.00	1,057.44	766.56	5,092.00	3,172.32	1,919.68
MA7R	SPEAKER ROSEWOOD	4	440.00	252.56	187.44	385.00	252.56	132.44
MA7W	SPEAKER WALNUT					2,700.00	1,970.24	729.76
MA8R	SPEAKER ROSEWOOD	8	1,056.00	630.00	426.00	1,782.00	1,102.50	679.50
MA8W	SPEAKER WALNUT	16	1,920.00	1,231.52	688.48	5,028.00	4,002.44	1,025.56
M103	PARTS MA					60.40	57.63	2.77
TWEE1	PARTS MA					52.32	33.28	19.04
TWEE3	PARTS MA					120.80	76.84	43.96
TWEE4	PARTS MA					52.32	33.28	19.04
TWEE5	PARTS MA					52.32	33.14	19.18
	TOTAL PROD. CLASS 02		28,760.00	16,868.88	11,89112	133,044.81	81,815.92	51,228.89

Figure 5.7 Sales by product and profit margin report

OHIO CORPORATION
DETAILED AGED ACCOUNTS RECEIVABLE REPORT

DATE 4/30/X2   COMPANY NO.   DIV. NO. 00   PAGE NO. 1

INVOICE NO.	TC	TRANS. DATE	ORDER NO. CM. NO.	COMMENT	C TERMS C DAYS	TOTAL BALANCE	CURRENT	1 MONTHS	2 MONTHS	3 MONTHS	4 MONTHS AND OVER	OVER-CR. LMT
186011-0-00			DALY SOUND COMPANY			ATLANTA, MAINE		30340 TELE. NO. 781-9858			CREDIT LIMIT 2000	
000311	10	1/31/X2	INV.			66.96				66.96		
002312	10	2/10/X2	INV.			60.00			60.00			
000419	10	3/06/X2	INV.			233.88		233.88				
	30	3/27/X2	ADJUST.			114.24-		114.24-				
			INVOICE TOTAL			119.64		119.64				
000441	10	3/06/X2	INV.			1,656.41		1,656.41				
			CUSTOMER TOTAL			2,022.65		1,895.69	60.00	66.96		
			AGING PERCENT					93.72%	2.97%	3.31%		
						*******						
200003-0-00			DEFINITIVE			SEATTLE, INDIANA		98105 TELE. NO. 333-0948			CREDIT LIMIT 1500	
000454	10	3/06/X2	INV.			259.25		259.25				
	30	4/10/X2	PYMT.			233.76-		233.76-				
	30	4/10/X2	DISCOUNT			25.49-		25.49-				
			INVOICE TOTAL			.00						
			CUSTOMER TOTAL			.00						
			AGING PERCENT									
						*******						
2000011-0-00			DELL CORP.			PALO ALTO, GEORGIA		94301 TELE. NO. 777-8756			CREDIT LIMIT 4000	
000584	10	4/04/X2	INV.			172.63	172.63					
	30	4/12/X2	PYMT.			172.63-	172.63-					
			INVOICE TOTAL			.00						
			CUSTOMER TOTAL			.00						
			AGING PERCENT									
						*******						
300017-0-00			DIGIT			VIRGINIA CITY, NEVADA		23462 TELE.NO. 415-3259			CREDIT LIMIT 4500	
000692	10	11/08/X2	INV.			277.75					277.75	
			CUSTOMER TOTAL			277.75					277.75	
			INVOICE AGING PERCENT								100.00%	
						*******						

Figure 5.8   Detailed aged accounts receivable report

OHIO CORPORATION
COMPARATIVE STATEMENT OF EARNINGS
FROM JANUARY 1, 19X2 TO MAY 31, 19X2
UNAUDITED

DOLLAR ROUNDING. BRACKETED VARIANCES ARE VARIABLE.

| | FROM MAY 1, 19X2 TO MAY 31, 19X2 | | | | | YEAR TO DATE | | | | |
| | ACTUAL | | BUDGET | | VARIANCE | ACTUAL | | BUDGET | | VARIANCE |
	AMOUNT	PCNT.	AMOUNT	PCNT.	AMOUNT	AMOUNT	PCNT.	AMOUNT	PCNT.	AMOUNT
INCOME										
SALES										
SALES—SPECIAL SPEAKERS	$28,760	100.0	$29,980	100.0	$(1,220)	$133,045	100.0	$150,000	100.0	$(16,955)
TOTAL SALES	28,760	100.0	29,980	100.0	(1,220)	133,045	100.0	150,000	100.0	(16,955)
ALLOW & CASH DISCOUNTS	(1,944)	(6.8)	—	—	(1,944)	(2,447)	1.8	—	—	(2,447)
TOTAL RET ALLOW DISC	(1,944)	(6.8)	—	—	(1,944)	(2,447)	1.8	—	—	(2,447)
NET SALES	26,816	93.2	29,980	100.0	(3,164)	130,598	98.2	150,000	100.0	(19,402)
COST OF SALES										
BEGINNING INVENTORY	16,000					26,792				
MATERIALS CONSUMED PURCHASES—SPEAKERS	37,076		17,398			54,747		91,150		
FREIGHT—AIR	1,501		200			38,254		1,100		
TOTAL AVAILABLE INVENTORY	54,577	—	17,598			119,793	—	92,250		
LESS ENDING INVENTORY	35,975					35,975				
COST OF SALES	18,602	64.7	17,598	58.7	(1,004)	83,813	63.0	92,250	61.5	(8,432)
GROSS PROFIT	8,214	28.6	12,382	41.3	(4,168)	46,780	35.2	57,750	38.5	(10,970)
GENERAL & ADMIN. EXPENSES:										
SALARIES	2,400	8.3	3,000	10.0	600	12,797	9.6	15,000	10.0	2,203
RENT	750	2.6	1,000	3.3	250	3,750	2.8	5,000	3.3	1,250
TELEPHONE	413	1.4	375	1.3	(38)	2,881	2.2	2,000	1.3	(881)
OFFICE EXPENSE	283	1.0	250	.8	(33)	2,211	1.7	1,250	.8	(961)
DELIVERY COST	176	.6	500	1.7	324	1,773	1.3	2,500	1.7	727
INSURANCE	312	1.1	500	1.7	188	2,522	1.9	2,500	1.7	(22)
TOTAL GEN. & ADM.	4334	15.1	5,625	18.8	1,291	25,934	19.5	28,250	18.8	2,316
EARNINGS BEFORE TAXES	3,880	13.5	6,757	24.9	(2,877)	20,846	15.7	29,500	19.7	(8,654)

Figure 5.9 Comparative statement of earnings, also called profit or loss or income statement

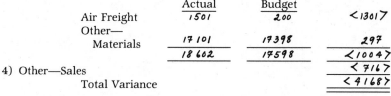

OHIO CORPORATION
Analysis of Gross Profit Variances
Product ___*Speakers*___
Period ___*May, 19 X 3*___

Per Comparative Financial Statements:

	$	%
Actual	8214	28.6
Budget	12382	41.3
Variance	<4168>	<12.77>

Components of Variance

		Variance
1) Allowances & Discounts from Standard Prices:		
Actual	<1944>	
Budget	—	<1944>

2) Sales Volume Variance

$$\frac{41.3}{\text{Budgeted Gross Profit}} \times \frac{1220}{\text{Sales Variance}} \qquad <504>$$

3) Materials Consumed Variance

	Actual	Budget	
Air Freight	1501	200	<1301>
Other— Materials	17101	17398	297
	18602	17598	<1004>
4) Other—Sales			<716>
Total Variance			<4168>

Figure 5.10   Manually prepared analysis of gross profit variances

ACTION GUIDELINES

Before you decide whether you can and should use a computer in your business, consult a professional—a CPA, financial adviser, or computer consultant. You and your adviser(s) should be able to answer the following questions affirmatively if you opt for automation.

- Have we investigated the potential applications of a computer to my business and planned exactly how it will be employed?

- Have I seen an installation in operation?

- Have we sought input from personnel who will use and generate the reports?

- Have I considered whether to employ a programmer or buy the software?

- Are qualified personnel available to accomplish the tasks of data processing and computer operation and maintenance?

- Is the hardware vendor established and reliable?

- Have we planned for system change as my company grows in order to continue to use the equipment to capacity?

There are alternatives to buying your own computer. You may employ the following as a transition to owning your own system or as a permanent way to have the advantages of automation:

- Computer service bureau

- Time sharing

- Joint venture

PART THREE

PLANNING YOUR BUSINESS

6

Financial Planning

This chapter will

- Explain breakeven and how to manipulate it

- Discuss the principle of long-term forecasting

- List the benefits of a cash forecast

- Describe the function of operating and capital budgets

- Discuss the value of a projected balance sheet

- Explain how all of the above relate to financial planning

Getting your accounting system into operation is a major accomplishment, but hardly an end in itself. The smooth implementation of procedures—whether manual, semiautomatic, or computerized—facilitates your control over your business and helps you plan your company's future. *Effective planning* of your operation also reinforces your credibility with potential lenders/investors, customers, and associates.

We're going to examine the *tools* of financial planning, such as breakeven and long- and short-term forecasting (specifically, cash forecasting) and the *results* of planning, which include the operating and capital budgets and the projected balance sheet. Later, these components will reappear in the financial section of your business plan, thereafter to be presented to your potential lender/investor.

FINANCIAL PLANNING TOOLS
Breakeven

One of the fundamental ingredients of financial planning is your **breakeven** point on sales. When you think of sales, any profit goal you might set for yourself is meaningless until you have reached your breakeven point.

A survival figure for every operation, breakeven serves as a barometer to keep you and your lenders/investors informed of your progress toward your sales goals.

If you proceed too slowly toward breakeven, you may have to apply more pressure on your sales force, revamp your marketing or promotional program, make personnel changes, or reduce overhead (including such essentials as rent, utilities, most administrative expenses and selling costs, or expenses incurred to offer your product for sale, such as advertising, promotion, and sales reps' commissions).

Expenses are both fixed and variable, and within each category, they may be controllable or uncontrollable. You may want to review some of the examples cited in Chapter 3, but the point is that you can do a lot of juggling to control expenses—something you must accomplish in order to break even. If you can understand breakeven and control overhead, you can readily monitor the progress of your business.

Now let's translate breakeven into numbers. We'll assume you've already determined that you'll earn a gross profit of 40 percent (a conclusion you may have arrived at through previous experience, knowledge of the product, and industry averages). Let's also establish that fixed costs are $30,000 and variable costs are to be kept at 10 percent of sales. The short-form income statement with a varying level of sales in Figure 6.1 illustrates the breakeven concept. Suppose

$$BE = \text{Breakeven}$$
$$S = \text{Sales}$$
$$FC = \text{Fixed costs}$$
$$VC = \text{Variable costs}$$
$$CS = \text{Costs of sales}$$

MAKE OR BREAK COMPANY

	Less than Breakeven	Breakeven	Over Breakeven
Sales ($1 per unit)	$80,000	$100,000	$120,000
Cost of sales (.60 per unit)	48,000	60,000	72,000
Gross profit	32,000	40,000	48,000
Variable costs ($.10 per unit)	8,000	10,000	12,000
Marginal contribution	24,000	30,000	36,000
Fixed costs (same at all levels of sales)	30,000	30,000	30,000
Net	$(6,000)	$ –0–	$ 6,000
	Loss	Breakeven	Profit

Figure 6.1   Short-form income statement

Using the equation

$$S - [CS + VC + FC] = BE,$$

we can substitute the figures from the income statement:

$$100,000 - [60,000 + 10,000 + 30,000] = BE$$
$$\text{Therefore } \$100,000 - \$100,000 = BE$$

Consequently, you know that by maintaining cost of sales at 60 percent, fixed costs at $30,000, and variable costs at 10 percent of sales, you will have to sell $100,000 worth of goods simply to break even. Thus your breakeven figure represents a decision-making and planning tool with which you can calculate the sales required before you make a profit and determine what kind of profit or loss you've attained at any sales level.

Using the factors from the previous example but changing your goal from breakeven to a $12,000 profit, you can determine what level of sales will provide you with your goal:

$$S = CS + VC + FC + \text{Profit}$$
$$S = [.60S + .10S] + [30,000 + 12,000]$$
$$S = .70S + 42,000$$
$$.30S = 42,000$$
$$S = 140,000$$

Any change in *any* factor will affect breakeven. If you reduce fixed or variable costs, you can lower your breakeven. If you increase your gross profit, you can lower your breakeven. But if you go that route, be sure to consider all the ramifications of increasing gross profit discussed in Chapter

3. You must have a firm grasp of all your breakeven factors if you are going to keep your business in control. Another reason for having these components firmly in hand is that breakeven is a preliminary step in preparing your operating budget, a vital procedure in financial planning. You *must* be able to determine breakeven before you can forecast any other sales goals, investments, or expenditures.

Short-Term and Long-Term Forecasting

Unlike breakeven, forecasting is not a figure but a *technique* used in financial planning and in determining results of various actions. It predicts whether you are going to achieve your goals. If based on sound assumptions, your forecasts will tell you whether your goals are realistic. (See Chapter 10.)

> You can use a forecast in many areas of financial planning, particularly to project costs, sales, gross profit, cash (reviewed later in this chapter), accounts receivable, or inventory.

Use **short-term forecasts**, which pertain to factors relevant to a period of less than one year, to prepare an operating budget. **Long-term forecasts** deal with the same factors as they affect your business for a period beyond one year. For example, if you plan to enter a new market five years hence, use a long-term forecast to project sales, costs, and cash to determine whether the objective is feasible.

A forecast represents projections based on past performance and available information on costs and market and industry factors. Rather than an exact computation, it is more of an educated guess, but it gives you a general idea of where you're heading—a glimpse into the future that should help you decide what you must do now to prepare for what's ahead. Thus equipped, you will be able to put together your operating budget (discussed later in this chapter).

Cash Forecasting

A fundamental technique used in financial planning, **cash forecasting** is the projection to which most entrepreneurs can best relate. It's the process through which you determine how much cash is available and how much you will need to implement the goals in your operating and capital budgets.

It should motivate you to act in time if you learn that you will have a cash shortage and need to seek financing.

Cash forecasting requires that you analyze the components of *both* your operating and capital budgets in order to determine the timing of receipts and expenditures. If you hope to compile a reasonably accurate cash forecast, you must also consider certain company policies, such as

- Paying all bills promptly in order to maximize cash discounts
- Maintaining an even production flow in your factory (if applicable)
- Establishing goals for inventory and/or accounts receivable levels

All these functions are really an extension of your convictions, so you can't delegate this aspect of your job to an accountant or bookkeeper. The decisions to continue or abandon the policies are up to you.

Sales: The Key   Your disbursements will affect the cash forecast, but the common denominator for all aspects of cash forecasting is your projected sales figure.

> If you're going to anticipate your receipts realistically, then you need an idea of how much you're going to sell.

One procedure always affects another when it comes to running your business, and there is no better example of this than in the process of cash forecasting. For example, if you are to avoid an inventory shortage, which would in turn prevent you from shipping on schedule, you must order raw materials at the right time to be able to go into production. Yet the amount of raw materials you order must be contingent on your sales projection. Ordering an insufficient supply will affect your inventory, therefore your sales, and subsequently your cash forecast. Ordering too much, or over-production of inventory, can ultimately force you to close out goods at markdown prices (see Chapter 7), which again affects your cash forecast. Figure 6.2 illustrates this cycle.

Frequency   Because so many decisions hinge on your company's cash flow, you may wonder how frequently you should prepare a cash forecast. This depends entirely on your company's needs. Some companies prepare one daily, others weekly or monthly. The longer the time between cash forecasts, the less exact each one is because so many changes are occurring

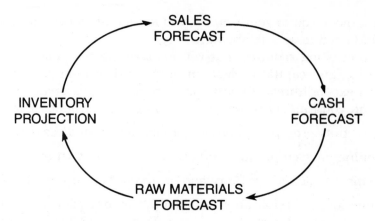

Figure 6.2   One procedure affects another

constantly. And the more accurate the cash forecast, the less chance you'll be caught unprepared in your financial planning. Thus we recommend you prepare cash forecasts continually throughout the year, if only to enable you to monitor your needs. Then a formal presentation prepared annually for your lender/investor should be sufficient. Some companies even attempt to prepare a five-year forecast, but this is merely to get a feel for where the company is going in the long run.

With a cash forecast, you will know what your projected cash flow may be. But what about the position of your other assets or liabilities? What other resources do you have in the event that you need to rely on them? What is your projected level of accounts receivable or inventory? What borrowing position will you be in at the bank or with your other creditors? To answer these questions, you must project a balance sheet. This will give you the full perspective with which to do an adequate job of financial planning.

RESULTS OF PLANNING

Operating Budget

Unfortunately, many entrepreneurs balk at the mere suggestion of constructing a budget. They complain that such a device is too restrictive, saying, perhaps, "Budgets are for really big business—not for me," "I've got my budget in my head. I don't need to put it on paper," or "In this economy it's difficult to guess which way things will go. I'm not going to lock myself into a budget." Considering that the typical entrepreneur is a doer, an active person, this reluctance to commit him or herself to certain guidelines might be understandable. But it points up a lack of appreciation for what a budget can actually do for you.

At the very least, an **operating budget** (also called a projected profit or loss statement or income plan) will point out the risks in the route you're pursuing. That awareness enables you to cope with swings in the economy, changes in market conditions, competition, and seasonal factors. It allows you to plan ahead and thus enhances your credibility with a potential lender or investor by informing him or her that you have anticipated many problems you might face and are equipped to handle them. In addition, a budget gives you a point of reference when actual results are tallied, allowing you to compare accomplishments with a forecast and then analyze any deviations so you know where to make adjustments in the future.

No successful entrepreneur can run a business one day at a time. The present builds on the past, just as the future builds on the present. Moreover, you're never really "locked into" a budget that you see is not working.

> To be truly effective, an operating budget should be reviewed regularly and updated when necessary.

And by working with your budget periodically, you avoid reinvesting the amount of time you put into the original plan.

One effective technique for evaluating your budget is to note just how it integrates the past, the present, and the future. Figure 6.3 shows how this is done. By completing the columns for any line item on the income statement (sales, cost of sales, or expenses), you can see how the success or failure (column 4) of the plan (column 3) ties the past (column 1) with the present (column 5).

For example, let's assume that last year's sales totaled $500,000. After deliberating with your sales reps and analyzing the market, you plan to sell an additional $125,000 of merchandise, for a total operating plan (or current year's budget) of $625,000. However, when you made your plans, you neglected to consider the possibility of a recession. Because your sales fell short of target by $25,000, you are left with current sales of $600,000. Therefore from this analysis you know you have to do something to boost your sales program.

But you may choose not to undertake such a lengthy evaluation of your budget. In that event, it would be simpler to compare your budget with actual accomplishment. To illustrate, look at the statement in Figure 6.4.

	Column 1	+ or (−)	Column 2	=	Column 3	+ or (−)	Column 4	=	Column 5
	PRIOR YEAR ACTUAL		PROJECTED CHANGES		CURRENT YEAR BUDGET		SUCCESS OR FAILURE		CURRENT YEAR ACTUAL
	Your Track Record		Planning		Operating Plan		Variance		Results
Sales	$500,000		$125,000		$625,000		$(25,000)		$600,000
Cost of Sales	275,000		50,000		325,000		(7,000)		318,000
Gross Profit	225,000		75,000		300,000		(18,000)		282,000
Selling Expenses:									
Advertising	25,000		12,500		37,500		(4,500)		42,000
Commissions	30,000		8,500		38,500		2,500		36,000
Rent—Sales Offices	10,000		1,500		11,500		(6,500)		18,000
Travel	10,500		2,000		12,500		500		12,000
Miscellaneous	9,500		9,250		18,750		(5,250)		24,000
Total Selling Expenses	85,000		33,750		118,750		(13,250)		132,000
Expenses									
Salaries	15,000		2,750		17,750		(7,250)		25,000
Rent—Administrative	10,000		3,500		13,500		1,500		12,000
Office Expense	5,000		1,250		6,250		(550)		6,800
Telephone	4,500		3,250		7,750		2,350		5,400
Insurance	5,500		3,000		8,500		1,200		7,300
Professional Services	6,000		1,775		7,775		1,200		5,750
Miscellaneous	9,500		4,500		14,000		1,600		12,400
Total General & Administrative Expenses	55,500		20,025		75,525		875		74,650
Total Expenses	140,500		53,775		194,275		(12,375)		206,650
Pretax Profit	$ 84,500		$ 21,225		$105,725		$(30,375)		$ 75,350

Figure 6.3.   Comparative budget report

ATLAS SALES COMPANY
January 1, 19X3 - January 31, 19X3

	Actual		Budget		Variance	
					( ) = unfavorable variance	
	$	%	$	%	$	
Sales	575,300	100	550,000	100	25,300	(A)
Cost of Sales	317,500	55	286,000	52	31,500	
Gross Profit	257,800	45	264,000	48	(6,200)	(B)
Selling Expenses						
Advertising	40,739	7	46,500	8	5,761	
Commissions	35,100	6	33,000	6	(2,100)	
Rent-Sales Office	13,200	2	12,000	2	(1,200)	
Travel	12,800	2	15,500	3	2,700	
Total Selling Expenses	101,839	17	107,000	19	5,161	(C)
General & Administrative Expenses						
Salaries	19,205	3	18,000	3	(1,205)	
Rent-Admin.	12,000	2	12,000	2	-	
Miscellaneous	32,500	6	31,400	6	(1,100)	
Total Gen. & Admin. Expenses	63,705	11	61,400	11	(2,305)	(D)
Total Expenses	165,544	28	168,400	30	2,856	
PRETAX PROFIT	92,256	17	95,600	18	(3,344)	

KEY:
(A) As far as *sales volume* is concerned, the statement shows that sales targets are being exceeded. We could respond to this trend by increasing inventory.
(B) In respect to *gross profit variance*, even though sales are in excess of budget, we aren't making as much money as projected. Costs are exceeding original estimates by 3 percent. (Note budgeted cost of sales is 52 percent and actual is 55 percent.) Gross profit would have been even lower had sales not exceeded goals. Thus, if we order more merchandise now, we might be able to get a better purchase price.
(C) Our *selling expense variance* indicates that we have developed a favorable drend. Because sales are up, the advertising program that was budgeted seems more than accurate, but let's watch this. Commissions, rent, and travel are in proportion to sales. These bear close watching, too, to see if this favorable trend continues.
(D) A variance in *general and administrative expenses* shows that salaries are over budget by $1,200. However, we know that the sales department had to hire some temporary staff to handle additional volume. Thus if sales continue on the upswing, we should consider adding a permanent member to staff, which would be less expensive than hiring temporary help.

Figure 6.4   Comparative income statement

As you see, your budget serves as a guide, confirming that you should continue on course if results are positive or indicating that you should change course if they are not.

Such a tool also serves as an integral part of the financial section of your business plan (see Chapter 10), and you'll prepare a better budget when that need arises if you have been using one as an ongoing part of your operation.

Components   Like breakeven, your operating budget is comprised of fixed and variable costs, sales, and gross profit. And just as breakeven components may be adjusted and manipulated, so may those in your budget. There will be times when you will need to increase certain expenses. Other times you will want to reduce them. The only requirement is that all your expenditures relate realistically to sales volume, as indicated on the comparative income statement (in the financial section of your business plan—see Chapter 10). If not, you're going to be low on cash and the various segments of your business will be disjointed rather than merge into a cohesive, smooth-running operation.

Preparation   Because it is a rather technical procedure, many of you will need guidance in the actual preparation of an operating budget. Detailed instructions are included in Appendix B. It is important, though, that you understand the chain of responsibility in compiling your budget.

The person ultimately responsible, of course, is you; but if your business is large enough, the head of every department should accept the task of preparing the budget for that department.

By having the individuals who will be administering the budget become involved with planning it, you will have the additional advantage of your staff's personal commitment when the concepts are employed.

After each department prepares its portion of the budget, it is usually passed on to the accounting office for tabulation and consolidation. There it is your responsibility either to approve or disapprove the various segments. Should you feel that part of it is out of line, you will have to return it to the department head, following which he or she must either convince you of its validity or revise it. If you're going to hold department heads responsible for their budgets, they had best prepare, amend, and justify them if necessary.

Capital Budget

In contrast with the operating budget, which concerns itself with the day-to-day management of your business, the **capital budget** is used to allocate company funds and establish boundaries (financial limits) for expenditures that generate benefits extending over one year and sometimes far into the future. These expenditures usually pertain to such assets as land, buildings, machinery, equipment, furniture, fixtures, or automobiles.

There may be any number of reasons for a capital expenditure. They range from routine operating requirements (which may necessitate a machinery replacement), to expanded production (which calls for additional plant facilities), to the desire to improve employee working conditions. Whatever the reason, the allocation of funds for any long-term asset is called a **capital investment,** sometimes requiring the postponement of immediate benefit for some future benefit. And because the very reason you are seeking financing may be for a capital budget expenditure, it is essential that the budget be compiled with care.

Because the commitment to a capital investment is somewhat irreversible, it has a long-term effect on your company's resources. Once you've planned to construct a new building, for example, your business is going to be locked into the decision for a long time. Thus capital expenditures should be scrutinized carefully to make certain you are getting the best deal possible for the amount of money invested over the time span involved. To do so, you must evaluate the contemplated expenditure in comparison with other potential investments.

To illustrate why you should compare two possible expenditures, suppose you need to expand your facilities and you also need a computer. You don't have enough funds for either and you know you can't get financing for both. Which will make the better investment? Also, which expenditure can you either get along without or provide for in another way (perhaps by leasing)? Evaluation requires that you discount the value of two cash flows—that is estimate the **present value** (see Appendix C) of the amount going out and the present value of the amount the investment brings in. Determine both cash flows on an after-tax basis (that is, consider the tax ramifications of the investment).

Capital budgeting is *not* just a matter of deciding that you need, say, a piece of heavy equipment and then planning how to pay for it. It is a many-faceted process that includes the following:

- Determining the most profitable investment or expenditure

- Assessing how much the investment would add to overall profits or whether the funds would be put to better use elsewhere

- Projecting how much the investment will cost, how much of the cash you'll have, and whether you need financing

- Evaluating tax benefits and after-tax costs on a *discounted* basis (see the explanation of discounted cash flow methods in Appendix C)

- Providing for the needed equipment, machinery, or facility in the event you decide not to invest in it (in this respect you must consider not only the cost of owning versus leasing the equipment but the cost of maintaining it, the kind of wear and tear it is likely to sustain, and its predicted life span, allowing for early obsolescence)

Now you must be aware that:

1. Your capital budget is a planning function that affects your resources for a long time

2. There are numerous considerations involved in each capital investment

3. Your cash forecast is going to be one of the factors involved in your investment-making decision

Projected Balance Sheet

The **projected balance sheet** summarizes the results of your operating budget and your cash forecast. It shows your company's projected financial health regarding assets as they relate to liabilities or obligations and equity as it relates to liabilities or obligations. The projected balance sheet is identical to the balance sheet referred to in Chapters 2 and 3 except it shows the condition of your business at some *future fixed time*. (See the projection columns in Figure 10.3.)

Because the task of assembling the projected balance is so technical, we suggest that if you don't have someone on your staff to complete this job, you call in your CPA or financial adviser to help you with it.

Don't try to save a few dollars in professional fees and prepare something that is apt to be unreliable.

The professional can also help you interpret the key ratios to be deduced from the projected balance sheet, which will be of utmost interest to a potential lender/investor. Such ratios include the debt-equity ratio, discussed in Chapters 1 and 2. It describes whether there is a sufficient amount of capital in the business to cover current and long-term obligations.

$$\frac{\text{Liabilities (debt)}}{\text{Net worth (equity)}} = \frac{30,000}{40,000} = .75 \text{ to } 1$$

If there is more debt than equity in a company, a lender could be reluctant to add to the entrepreneur's burden and thus refuse a loan. An investor, however, might take a different view of the situation because even an overleveraged company might represent an attractive opportunity to acquire a large equity interest in the company. You should thus be aware of your future position so you can knowledgeably deal with whatever situation you will have to confront in a negotiating session.

Another ratio to be determined from the projected balance sheet is the current ratio, which indicates whether you can pay off present obligations with current assets. You compute the current ratio by dividing all present assets by current liabilities:

$$\frac{\text{Current assets}}{\text{Current liabilities}} = \frac{100,000}{50,000} = 2 \text{ to } 1$$

Most analysts will react favorably to a 2 to 1 ratio. If it is less than that, be prepared to do some explaining.

The third ratio to be deduced from your projected balance sheet is the **quick asset ratio** (also called an **acid test ratio**), which is the sum of cash and accounts receivable (cash equivalents or close to it) measured against your current obligations. A 1 to 1 ratio is considered good in most industries, indicating you have just enough cash to cover your current debt. Anything more would appear even better to a potential lender/investor. Compute your quick asset ratio as follows:

$$\frac{\text{Quick assets}}{\text{Current liabilities}} = \frac{7,000}{6,000} = 1.16 \text{ to } 1$$

The projected balance sheet indicates what you *hope* to accomplish; a balance sheet is a measure of your past operating ability, showing the lender/investor what *has been* accomplished. Seldom does a balance sheet dictate operations, although a poor balance sheet can limit one's aspirations. Thus we suggest you keep a conscientious watch on this scoresheet.

The frequency with which you prepare a projected balance sheet depends largely on your company's needs. In most cases, putting together an annual projected balance sheet should be enough, although certain key assets, such as cash, accounts receivable, and inventory, need to be forecasted regularly along the way.

Your capital budget, prepared annually, will probably provide you with sufficient data to give you a handle on the level of capital investment; so you need not be concerned with a continual forecast of fixed asets throughout the year.

In addition to forecasting asset positions, keeping a close watch on your liabilities will allow you to determine how much financing you need in order to maintain the assets your business requires. If you're aware of the total level of financing your business needs, you can begin to seek sources of cash to service it. For example, if you know you need total financing in the amount of $500,000 and you can depend on your suppliers to provide financing up to $200,000, you know you will have to raise $300,000. Thus you can avail yourself of the various sources available to arrive at your total financing package.

Keep in mind, too, though, that there are alternatives to increasing your debt. By evaluating the assets on your balance sheet, you can determine what they are. Can you get rid of some equipment or property? Do you really need all that inventory? Are your customers taking advantage by not paying their bills?

ACTION GUIDELINES

Determining your breakeven point requires that you calculate the sales you must achieve before you can make a profit. You can change your breakeven point by

- Reducing fixed costs
- Lowering variable expenses
- Increasing gross profit

Use forecasting to

- Prepare an operating budget
- Compile a capital budget
- Assemble your projected balance sheet

Your cash forecast should enable you to answer the following questions:

- How much cash will I have?
- How much financing will I need to implement my goals?

- Must I alter my operating budget?

    An operating budget is the result of short-term forecasting. It should answer the following questions:

- Can I increase sales?

- Can I reduce the costs of sales?

- Can I adjust gross profit?

- Can I alter selling or general and administrative expenses?

    Your capital budget, which is the result of long-term forecasting, should answer the following questions:

- What permanent assets should my company invest in?

- How much will they cost?

- Are these investments feasible compared to other potential investments?

- Am I going to need financing?

    Your projected balance sheet should answer the following questions:

- Is there enough capital in my business to cover my long-term debts?

- Are my assets sufficiently valuable to pay off my debts?

- Does my business have enough cash and accounts receivable to cover my debts?

- Am I eligible for financing?

7

Keeping Cash Flowing and Profits Growing

This chapter will

- Discuss two major obstacles to cash flow—accounts receivable and inventory—and how to control them

- Describe how inventory affects gross profit and how to mark down your inventory without destroying profits

- Explain the importance of segmenting your business by product or service so you can assess each according to its profit contribution

Though effective financial planning depends on many factors, the common denominator is cash. It determines your forecasting and affects your budgets and goals. Some of your goals call for expenditures. You hope you will have the cash to pay for them so you can avoid expensive financing, keep it to a minimum, or at least anticipate the amount of cash you'll have to raise.

But cash can be elusive. Your business is growing, sales are at a peak, orders are pouring in, and profits are up; but you don't have the cash to prove it. You wonder where it is.

Chances are it's in your accounts receivable or in your inventory—the most common obstacles to a smooth cash flow. In this chapter we examine accounts receivable and inventory, both critical areas of your business you must control if you are to plan effectively and not only make a profit but have the cash as well. Without close surveillance of your accounts receivable and inventory, all efforts at financial planning are futile.

ACCOUNTS RECEIVABLE

Representing the amount of money your customers owe you, accounts receivable are an integral part of any operation that conducts business on credit. However, an excessive accumulation of accounts receivable becomes a problem. Overaccumulation can occur when a company experiences extremely rapid growth. It may also evolve through lack of planning or as a result of inadequate control. Thus you, as well as your credit manager, bookkeeper, and/or accounts receivable clerk, must be alert to the slow collection syndrome, using any and all tools available to keep your accounts under control.

Control Techniques

One of these tools is a **schedule** or listing that shows the total each customer or client owes. Another tool is an accounts receivable **aged trial balance,** an expansion of the schedule. This record, maintained by almost every business, discloses not only the amount owed to the business but how long each segment of the balance has been outstanding. This tool is so valuable that when a business seeks financing, many financial analysts will request a copy of it in order to determine the probability of collecting the accounts receivable. From the aged trial balance the analyst can evaluate each customer's accounts and decide which need close watching. Figure 7.1 shows a section from a typical accounts receivable aged trial balance.

According to Figure 7.1, CDE and XYZ companies are considerably past due. Thus a review of the terms of sale with these customers should be the next order of business. If the terms were thirty days, you should take action on collection. But if you had agreed on payment, say, six months following a sale, you would have established a **dating program** and must be alert to the collection problems that can ensue when so much time has elapsed after delivery.

RALOS PRODUCTS

CUSTOMER	TOTAL AMOUNT DUE	CURRENT UNDER 30 DAYS	30 DAYS PAST DUE	60 DAYS PAST DUE	90 DAYS PAST DUE	OVER 90 DAYS PAST DUE
ABC Company	$2,000	$2,000				
CDE Company	2,000			$1,000	$1,000	
XYZ Company	1,300		$1,000			$300
TOTAL	$5,300	$2,000	$1,000	$1,000	$1,000	$300

Figure 7.1 Section of an accounts receivable aged trial balance

Effect of Dating Programs

You might establish a dating program with suppliers as a means of financing goods or services you need for your business. However, you may use this concept in reverse as well, encouraging the sale in June, perhaps, of merchandise for which you will receive payment in December.

Dating programs are often used to secure the preseason sale of a product and to enable it to compete more effectively in the marketplace. They might be an adjunct to a sales program. An excellent example of this is the deferred payment plan many department stores use during Christmas.

Strict credit policies and tight collection procedures are imperative with dating programs. Careful cash forecasting at the onset of the agreement is also essential if your business is going to survive.

Red Flags to Watch For

You should also be alert to the unplanned dating program (occurring when there are deviations from your sale agreement) and such other forms of slow payment as invoice skipping, attempts to return merchandise long after payment is due, payments on account rather than on specified invoices, and payments made by postdated checks. Any of these ploys can create a buildup of accounts receivable, even by one customer, if that customer is large enough.

Evaluating Your Credit Policies

Any pains you take to review accounts receivable or to reevaluate terms of sale are meaningless unless you act to reverse the trend causing the problem. This is where you rely on your credit policy, frequently one of the weaker links in the chain of operating controls because most entrepreneurs are more concerned with making a sale than with credit policies. In fact, some entrepreneurs focus so intently on their sales figures they even refuse to heed signals that are an integral part of their financial controls. A case in point was the Flair Wheel Company, an auto supply business that had gone to considerable effort and expense to have its accounts receivable effectively monitored.

This company's computerized system prepared regular aged accounts receivable trial balances and established firm credit limits for every customer. The computer then cranked out warning letters to customers that were over-extended. Theoretically it was an efficient, fool-proof arrangement, yet it had a serious flaw. There was one person in the company who could override the computer. That person was Bill Wheel, owner of the business, and, unfortunately for the company, Wheel frequently chose to exercise his prerogative.

Before founding Flair Wheel, this entrepreneur had long been a top notch salesman. Though he *said* he realized the importance of collections, as far as he was concerned, sales was still the only name of the game. When Wheel was alerted to the fact that many customers had exceeded their credit limits, his response was that the country overall was experiencing a slight recession and that Flair Wheel would have to carry these customers if it wanted to stay in business. At the same time, the company's controller warned Wheel that this philosophy could only cause the business trouble. He also expressed concern that many customers being sold were reputed to be uncredit worthy even before Wheel gave them a chance to accumulate substantial receivables. The controller projected a severe cash flow problem for the company because cash simply was not coming in, and, if Wheel persisted in this suicide course, he predicted, the company would go bankrupt. But, in spite of the warning, Wheel persisted in indulging his customers. Fortunately, an astute banker and the company's CPA realized what was happening and by the time the company was on the very brink of bankruptcy they were finally able to convince Wheel that his company's survival actually depended on his observance of the warning signs being flashed by the computer and the advice dispensed by the company controller.

Obviously, you can't exist without sales, but you can't exist without cash, either. Nor can you plan to seek financing evey time you have a cash flow problem. When you seek financing—for whatever purpose—you must demonstrate control over your accounts receivable. Therefore just as the creation of a sales program requires imagination, persistence, and planning, the cash collection process also demands planning, creativity, and follow-through. In the successful business, the two go hand in hand. It is not unusual to use sales to enforce collections, as in the case of utility companies, which simply disconnect a service when the bill isn't paid within the specified period. If you happen to have a monopoly on a service or sell a product that is in great demand, you have an advantage.

Analyzing your accounts will enable you to determine whether you are allowing customers to carry balances that facilitate their financing problems while jeopardizing your cash flow. If so, you will have to decide how important it is to you to retain slow-paying customers or clients, and during the process, you will have to assess your customers' credibility in light of their promises to pay in the future.

Setting credit limits and charging interest are policies to consider. Before taking any action in that direction, however, we suggest that you discuss the matter with your attorney so you comply with all legal requirements in charging interest.

> A sound credit policy, reinforced by effective follow-up procedures, is essential if you are going to control your accounts receivable, thereby facilitating your cash flow.

It is possible, though, that your accounts receivable are *not* where the cash is hiding. It could be in your inventory.

INVENTORY

When excessive cash is invested in inventory, most businesses are going to be in trouble because inventory must be converted to a receivable before it goes full cycle and reverts to cash. Moreover, when inventory is old or there is too much of it, at least some of it will have to be marked down (that is, sold at a lower price than was originally planned). So unless yours is a service business, in which case inventory isn't an issue, being sensitive and responsive to **inventory turn** (the number of times your inventory is sold within a specified period of time) is vitally important if you want to keep cash flowing *and* achieve the highest possible gross profit.

Computing inventory turn requires that you divide your annual cost of goods sold by your average inventory level.

$$CGS \div AI = T$$

$$CGS = \text{cost of goods sold}$$

$$AI = \text{average level of inventory}$$

$$T = \text{inventory turn}$$

Select the appropriate figures for the equation from Figure 7.2.

If you add your beginning inventory of $100,000 to your ending inventory of $250,000 and divide the sum by two, you will determine that you have an average level of inventory worth $175,000. If you substitute the figures for cost of goods sold and average level of inventory in the aforementioned equation, you will find

$$\$525,000 \div \$175,000 = T$$

$$T = 3$$

Sales		$900,000
Cost of Sales:		
Beginning Inventory	100,000	
(Inventory for the period		
beginning Jan. 1 of that		
calendar year)		
Purchases	675,000	
Available for Sale	775,000	
Ending Inventory	250,000	
Cost of Goods Sold		525,000
Gross Profit		$375,000

Figure 7.2   Partial profit or loss or income statement for the 12 months ended Dec. 31, 19X3

Now you know you have three inventory turns per year, or an average of one inventory turn every four months. You may compare this with industry standards (use Robert Morris Associates' *RMA Annual Statement Studies*). If your turn has been lower than the average and you want to increase it, you will have to lower your inventory investment or increase sales if you want to maintain the same level of inventory. Increasing your turn requires not only controlling inventory but understanding your basic goals and sometimes making a capital investment, enabling you to improve facilities or provide additional equipment as well.

To show you just how important the relationship between goals and inventory can be, let's take a look at what happened when two partners in a bookstore sought our advice in financing their growing business. These young women had limited funds with which to meet expansion plans, and in our initial discussion, we learned that their business was marked by a large stock of unusual and rare titles concentrating on handcrafts. This, they felt, was what made theirs a viable business, distinguishing it from larger, more commercial bookstores with smaller departments devoted to the subject.

An analysis of their problems revealed a fallacy in their reasoning because 10 percent of the books they carried accounted for more than 80 percent of their sales. When the partners approached us, their bookstore had an annual (sales) volume of $330,000; cost of sales was $200,000; and inventory was $80,000. Simple division revealed 2.5 turns annually, compared with industry statistics showing an average rate of 4 turns a year for an inventory mix of hardbound and paperback volumes. We knew that if they could begin to control expenditures and stock books that yielded maximum sales, they could reduce (inventory) investments, thereby freeing a sizable portion of funds needed to finance their plans.

Granted, our clients had to be willing to compromise on certain ideals, but they were aiming at a goal that was within their grasp. Reaching it did not depend on some elaborate financing program, and when we convinced them of this fact, they were willing to trade off a small adjustment in their store's image.

Their starting point was the construction of an **aged inventory,** a relatively simple task requiring paper and pencils and a few hours to research dates of purchase. Next, inventory had to be related to sales with a detailed analysis of the latter. This proved to be a bit more cumbersome to produce and could continue to be a burden as time went on. To simplify that chore in the future, the business leased a computerized sales register that coded all sales and summarized the number of copies of each title sold. This procedure was so effective that after several months of comparing inventory titles to sales volume by title, our clients no longer questioned the necessity of reducing inventory in certain areas. Consequently, they closed out several slow-moving titles, and though they continued to carry some of their more unique books, they no longer did so in the quantities previously stocked. They kept a current count of fast-moving books and purchased them only when they reached the reorder point. Thus they reduced inventory by approximately 40 percent and freed funds previously tied up in inventory for other uses. Had the partners not increased their turn to 5, they would not have had this saving and would have had to seek outside financing.

> Monitoring inventory turn in effect helps you budget or control your inventory requirements and investments.

In the retail business, an inventory budget is called an **open to buy,** but whatever you choose to call it, it is essential and should be an integral part of your operating budget. Without one, you will tie up funds that can be better used elsewhere.

RELATING INVENTORY TO GROSS PROFIT

Because there's hardly any kind of inventory that appreciates with time, chances are you're going to have to resort to a **markdown** policy when your product does not move quickly at its original price.

Markdowns

Markdowns are inevitable with almost every business because, regardless of how well you control your inventory, rarely does an entire stock turn over. Aging inventory must be disposed of in order to free up funds and space for new, fast-moving merchandise. Thus it helps to remember that markdowns are actually a **hidden expense.** They must be built into the "cost" of inventory along with such factors as raw materials and labor, if applicable to your business. Early recognition of surplus merchandise allows you to dispose of goods at a figure as close to your original selling price as possible. Therefore a predetermined markdown policy establishes perimeters within which you may sell off inventory quickly and efficiently.

The disposition of off-price merchandise requires special techniques that usually involve established markets outside your normal distribution channels. This precaution protects your regular customers from an influx of discounted goods, though at times you may want to offer them marked-down merchandise that they in turn may feature as specials to their customers. When pursuing either procedure, however, establish guidelines to help you determine the effect on the overall disposal of markdowns. These might include decisions on how long a period should elapse before inventory is marked down, to what price it should be marked down, or to what percentage of the original price it should be marked. Such techniques enable you to determine the toll that markdowns take so you can build this real figure into your overall costs, allowing you to calculate gross profit without distortion.

Computing the Cost of Markdowns

There is a delicate balance here. In order to maintain a firm grasp on gross profit, make sure you thoroughly understand the effect of markdowns on your computation of costs. Suppose that after monitoring inventory and markdown patterns for a year or more, you determine the following:

1. You have had to dispose of 5 percent of your merchandise via markdowns, and you feel these dispositions represent a pattern likely to be sustained over the next few years.

2. You earn a 40 percent gross profit which indicates that your cost of sales is 60 percent. Therefore if you are to build markdowns into your costs, 5 percent of your costs, or $.05 \times .60$, should be the factor applied to selling price as an additional cost of goods.

SP = selling price
CS = cost of sales
CM = cost of markdowns
therefore .05 × .60 × SP = CM

If you determine that the original selling price of a product is $100, then .05 × .60 × $100 = $3, which is the cost of markdowns that the product will have to sustain. This is *not* to imply that the product is marked down by $3 but that *all* your inventory will have to bear the cost of your products that have been marked down. Thus if you want to maintain a gross profit of 40 percent, you will have to mark your selling price up by another $5 to accommodate the additional cost of $3.

Avoiding Distortion of Gross Profit

As you see, markdowns represent a real expense. However, if you keep in mind that timing is critical, you will avoid having markdowns seriously affect your gross profit by registering that expense on your financial statement as soon as you recognize the need for the markdown. To put it another way, suppose that after a major selling season you know part of your inventory will have to be marked down. You also know it will take about six months to sell off all this merchandise. In order that the recording of profits not be distorted over the next six months, you should note the loss when you make the decision to mark down the product. If you are going to maintain an even keel on gross profit, you have to balance the relationship between selling price and cost of sales—both before and after markdowns. In other words, if you average 50 percent of your selling price on your markdown merchandise, then you will have to mark your merchandise to 50 percent of the cost.

To illustrate, assume that your product is light switches and that you sell two models, Model A, with an original selling price of $2 and cost of $1.20, and Model B, which sells for $3 and costs $1.80. Both provide you with a 40 percent gross profit.

Let's further assume that Model A must be marked down to a selling price of $1 in order to dispose of a ten-item inventory and that you will continue to sell Model B switches at the original price. About five months after your recognition of markdowns on Model A, you dispose of your inventory of ten Model A switches at a reduced price of $1. You sell five Model B switches at the original price of $3. If we also assume that you did not record your markdowns at the time of recognition, five months later your profit and loss statement will look something like Figure 7.3.

If this is a valid record of what actually occurred, the psychological impact of believing that you had worked for five months and made no

Six-Month Period Ending June 30, 19X2

		$	%
Total sales:			
10 Model As @ $1.00		10.00	
1 Model B @ $3.00		3.00	
		13.00	100.00
Cost of sales:			
Inventory at beginning of period			
10 Model As @ $1.20 =	11.20		
5 Model Bs @ $1.80 =	9.00	$20.20	
Purchases - 3 Model Bs @ $1.80		5.40	
Cost of inventory available for sale		25.60	
Inventory at end of period			
0 Model As		0	
7 Model Bs @ $1.80		12.60	
Cost of sales		13.00	100.00
Gross profit		Ø	Ø

Figure 7.3   Profit or loss statement (income)

gross profit could be devastating. But in fact that was not the case. Let's see what would have happened had you marked down your beginning inventory earlier.

In keeping with a 50 percent markdown policy, if the original cost of your Model A switches is $1.20, you may compute the marked-down selling price of the product as .50 × $1.20 = $.60. Therefore the beginning inventory of ten Model A switches is 10 × .60 = $6.

Now let's revise that income statement, substituting the marked-down inventory in place of the inventory at the original cost (see Figure 7.4). This gives us quite a different picture, and an accurate one, of what your gross profit for that period really is. In reality, the $6.00 markdown is attributable to a prior period and actually should have been recorded on an earlier statement.

Verifying Gross Profit

As an essential element in controlling your business, let's make certain the markup you thought was there actually exists. If it doesn't, your figure for gross profit is inaccurate as well.

Six-Month Period Ending June 30, 19X2

	$	%
Total sales (no change)	13.00	100.00
Cost of sales:		
Inventory at beginning of period		
10 Model As @ .60 = 6.00		
5 Model Bs @ 1.80 = 9.00	15.00	
Purchases (no change)	5.40	
Available for sale	20.40	
Inventory at end of period		
(no change)	12.60	
Cost of sales	7.80	60.00
Gross profit	5.20	40.00

Figure 7.4   Revised profit or loss statement (income)

You can verify your calculation for gross profit by using two methods to compute markup and then reconciling the answers (accounting for the difference so you become aware of any variance).

The conventional method is to take an inventory count at the beginning and end of the period under scrutiny (including any additional purchases in between). Another approach is called **specific identification** (identifying the cost of every sale). However, if sales are numerous, it may be cumbersome to utilize this method without a computer, which can "cost" a sale out at very high speed by multiplying every item sold by a standard price.

When the results of the two methods you use are not in agreement, you should investigate further. (And this might be the time to call in the professional to square away your procedures.) It may seem burdensome to follow this process of verifying your gross profit, but you will find it well worth your effort. Only through gross profit control will you know whether your business is making money, whether your markup is appropriate, and whether it compares with industry averages.

SEGMENTATION

Equally important as gross profit control is an awareness of which part of your company is profitable and which is not. Such information must be an integral part of your financial reporting system if you are to make intelligent decisions regarding the direction your company should take. It is therefore essential that the profits of your business be segmented by components (by products or services or by groups of products or services). You could also segment an entire line of products, forming a division or a branch of your main operation. Segmentation is a natural succession of the diversification of product or clientele discussed in Chapters 1 and 4.

We'll refer to our segmentation classification as a division. Just as with accounting for gross profit, we are concerned with two aspects of accumulating data for this divisional reporting. These are *sales* and *costs of sales*.

Where sales are concerned, you may want to consider a grouping of products carried by each of your sales reps. Or the geography of sales may be a more logical way to create a division. Other possibilities include a classification of products or of customers. Before firming it up, discuss the matter with your accounting people. Find out what makes sense to them, but make sure they can provide you with the data you need and segment costs in such a way that they are *directly* related to the divisional grouping of your sales.

Direct costing refers to the accumulation of expenses (or costs) attributable *only* to the division under evaluation. It's a procedure requiring some very specific rules. For example, even though the president of a company may be involved in the creation of a new product or in the sales efforts of that product, his or her salary will have to be paid regardless of whether there is one product or fifty. Therefore an allocation of his or her salary to a specific product line or division is of no relative importance, nor are other administrative expenses or the cost, say, of a bookkeeper. Such non-direct costs should not be allocated to a division unless the expense is the result of having formed that division.

But if new sales invoices with a specific logo are purchased for a particular product line, the cost should be segregated. Or if there is a staff increase to accommodate a new product line, that incremental cost might be assigned to that line.

Whenever possible we suggest avoiding the allocation of costs because the procedure carries an accompanying problem of maintaining control over a natural classification of costs.

Apportioning half a salary to one department and the other half to another, for example, tends to create a situation in which neither is responsible for administering that person's job. Of course, there are times when allocations are unavoidable. When this happens, we recommend that one department be responsible for the duties of the employee in question. If not, the person working for both divisions will be accountable to neither. The underlying concern with which we are dealing here, however, is control—your control over this aspect of your company as well as over all other areas of your operation. Control enables you to plan effectively and to run a profitable business, which in turn will enhance your credibility with potential lenders/ investors when you seek financing.

ACTION GUIDELINES

If you're to determine whether accounts receivable are tying up your cash, you should have immediate access to the following:

- Accounts receivable schedule
- Aged trial balance
- Credit policies established for or with each customer

Control over accounts receivable requires that you define and implement the following:

- Credit policies
- Cash collection processes
- Follow-up procedures on delinquent accounts

You won't have a smooth cash flow unless you can answer yes to these questions:

- Are my goals flexible?
- Do I have control over my inventory?
- Have I maintained an aged inventory?
- Have I explored the possibility of reducing my inventory by increasing its turn?
- Do I have an inventory budget?
- Am I aware of the effect of markdowns on gross profit?

Maximizing gross profit requires that you

- Recognize what part of your inventory will have to be marked down
- Acknowledge when it *must* be marked down

- Record the markdown as soon as possible after recognition occurs
- Know how to compute the markdown
- Confirm or verify your gross profit

Effective profit planning requires that you be able to answer the following questions affirmatively:

- Have I determined which part of my business is profitable and which is not?
- Have I segmented my business by products or services or by groups of products or services?
- Have I focused on two areas in this segmentation—sales and costs of sale?

In regard to sales, you may segment or group your product or service according to

- Sales reps
- Geography of sales
- Classification of products
- Classification of customers

As far as costs are concerned,

- Do you know *when* costs have to be allocated to a particular division?
- Have you avoided the allocation of costs when possible?

8

Getting Help from Professionals and Peers

This chapter will

- Show you the advantages of outside advisers

- Tell you what to look for in selecting and retaining your advisers

- Describe the benefits of a board of directors

- Tell you what to expect from your board

You have come a long way toward "getting your house in order." You accepted our premise of establishing and maintaining credibility with potential lenders/investors. Having developed an appreciation of the importance of accurate financial reporting, you learned to understand your company's accounting/bookkeeping operation, instituted a smooth-running accounting system, and planned astutely as you initiated most of the procedures required for a well-controlled business.

You may have been working seven-day weeks for months on end—and very long days at that. Even so, you probably haven't accomplished all this without help from professional counsel: attorney, CPA, insurance agent, banker, maybe even a marketing specialist or management consultant. Regardless of how well you run your company, you can't be an expert in every area. Fortunately, you're smart enough to realize it. In this chapter, we'll show you how to avail yourself of outside assistance on a continuing basis, not only from the best professional counsel available but from your peers, business people like you with similar problems and varied experience. We'll give you guidelines for selecting some of the professionals who counsel you or for determining whether those already working for you are giving you the service you should be getting. We'll also give you some suggestions for assembling a full advisory group.

SELECTING YOUR ADVISERS

You may already have the beginning, or the full complement, of your outside professional help if you have a CPA and an attorney. Then you may need only to evaluate their services periodically. But if you're going it alone, you may need some help in selecting at least your first adviser. Once you get the first, acquiring the rest should be easy because an attorney, for example, can lead you to a CPA, a banker, and an insurance agent. Chances are any of the professionals you choose will have worked with the others in many capacities, and most of them know enough people in each field to be able to refer you to the advisers you need.

But if it's the first one you've yet to find, talk with the person whose business judgment you respect most. Ask this person whom he or she would recommend. Get the best. Don't scrimp on these services by hiring the man next door or the woman downstairs simply because they seem nice and it's easier to do business with someone close to home. Don't hesitate to meet with a few attorneys or CPAs before deciding which one is right for you.

> The relationship you *should* have with your professionals is one of complete confidence and trust.

If your relationships are going to be really productive, your advisers may learn more about you than your spouse knows. Therefore you must respect both their integrity and their ability and be comfortable enough to level with them.

How to Use Your CPA

When you're shopping around for a CPA firm, find out what their experience is and who their other clients are. If you're their biggest or smallest, perhaps you should keep on looking. Will this CPA have time for you? Will she have the best interests of your business at heart? Does she share your vision of where your business is going? What is her attitude toward an advisory group or board of directors? If she deems it unimportant, you should question her security and ability to interract with other professionals.

The CPA you select has to do more than supervise the keeping of your books, file your tax returns, or run interference for you with the IRS. He or she must be able to scrutinize your financial reporting procedures, evaluate your accounting system and financial controls, direct your financing program, oversee your audit if you need one, and counsel you on the general direction your business is taking. Your CPA should advise you on all aspects of your business related to financial matters as well as supervise the integration of your personal financial affairs with those of your business. At times your CPA may need to call on someone with more expertise in a particular area (such as taxes), but he or she should be competent in overall managerial accounting, recognizing when a specialist must be brought in.

How to Use Your Attorney

With your attorney, too, you should be absolutely candid about long-range plans and goals for your business as well as for your personal affairs. Determine whether she can identify with your aspirations, but *don't* use her merely to bail you, or your business, out of hot water. If you've established a working relationship with her, she may help you stay out of trouble. In the event problems do arise, she'll be better able to serve you if she knows you and your business well. Depending on the nature and size of your operation, there are numerous areas in which her counsel may be invaluable. You may call on her for labor or acquisitions negotiations, to scrutinize a lease, to establish credit policies, to secure patents, to set up pension trusts and profit-sharing plans, or elsewhere in the area of estate planning. An attorney's service to you, like that of your other professionals, depends on your needs and those of your business. But astute entrepreneurs use their attorney just as they use their CPA—for the prevention of problems as well as for their cure.

You'll often find that the matter on which you're seeking counsel requires advice from an attorney, a CPA, and an insurance agent, with you providing the overview or business perspective.

How to Use Your Insurance Agent

It's possible, though improbable, that you can continue for some time without calling on either an attorney or a CPA; but when it comes to insurance, it's impossible to do it yourself. You simply cannot acquire the protection you need without an agent. Moreover, most insureds aren't that certain about the coverage they've bought. The whole field is so involved and technical that you must do business with an agent you respect and can trust and you must have the utmost confidence in his or her evaluation, judgment, and competency to oversee the insurance needs of you and your business.

Because his services often iterrelate with law, taxation, finance, or banking, any one of your other counselors should be able to refer an insurance agent. In general, however, if the agent who oversees your personal coverage is a C.L.U. (Chartered Life Underwriter) and you have a C.P.C.U. (Chartered Property and Casualty Underwriter) supervising your casualty requirements, you're in good hands.

The insurance requirements of any person and business are unique. To serve you well, your insurance agent(s) must be thoroughly familiar with your operation. Your C.L.U. will have to relate your business insurance requirements with your personal objectives. In supervising your personal life insurance program, he may integrate life insurance protection with pension trusts, incorpoating many elements (such as profit sharing or stock options and transfers) into your estate planning. (This is an area in which your CPA, your attorney, and perhaps your banker will also have to become involved.) Among the C.L.U.'s concerns are also the health and disability protection of your employees, your family, and you.

The domain of your C.P.C.U. is everything from workmen's compensation to inventory insurance, bonding coverage for employees and for contract fulfullment, and product, accident, liability, and risk insurance of all kinds. Numerous kinds of coverage are available; and although your business could be subject to ruin without certain essential protection, you could be throwing money away with too much or a poor choice of coverage. Thus it is imperative you do business with an agent who is thoroughly competent.

How to Use Your Banker

We outline important criteria for selecting an appropriate bank and banker in Chapter 12. Financing has always been one of the most important reasons an entrepreneur seeks banker assistance. But keep in mind some of the auxiliary services a bank offers, such as computerized services for general ledger, accounts receivable, and accounts payable procedures. Beyond that, banks have a wealth of resources at their disposal and can supply you with statistics on many subjects, provide credit information on potential customers, and even put research facilities at your disposal.

Through their vast network of contacts, bankers often assist in mergers and acquisitions and introduce clients to suppliers or potential customers.

It's important to have a comfortable ongoing relationship with your banker. His or her experience could mean the difference in your success, just as a word from your banker at the right time could save you from disaster. If you form an advisory group or board of directors, a banker on the board can be a tremendous asset.

ADVANTAGES OF AN ADVISER GROUP OR BOARD OF DIRECTORS

No matter how much you like running the show, it should be reassuring to know you needn't bear the burdens of your business all by yourself.

> Though no one knows your operation quite the way you do, one person cannot know, or be, everything a company needs to keep it healthy. Common sense tells you that every business can benefit from objective input from others with whom to discuss current problems or who will reinforce decisions that will keep your business successful.

Large corporations seek assistance from professionals outside the organization and have backup from a board of directors. But a board of directors need not be limited to big business.

Even a small company like Roggi Wines, which we discussed in Chapter 1, has a board of directors, and Roggi is a five-person operation with gross sales of $500,000. Yet, if it wasn't for its board, Roggi would probably never have stayed in business. A company of almost any size would do well to utilize such a team, a sounding board for management's ideas as well as an objective auxiliary interpreting the performance of the operation. Call it what you will—board of directors, advisory group, or whatever. The name is unimportant; its function and effectiveness are what must concern you.

How to Form It

Although such a group can best serve your needs if it represents a diversity of backgrounds and thereby provides a broad spectrum of ideas, the nucleus of your team should be the professionals we have been discussing: your attorney, CPA, banker, and insurance agents. The advice of one often affects that of another, and that can entail a lot of discussing. It would be much simpler if everyone involved in your affairs was to meet and review the interrelated problems at one time rather than determine at separate sessions what each one is, or should be, doing. And because all your professionals have a common interest—the welfare of your organization—it's to your advantage to bring them together on a regular basis. The frequency of your meetings—once, twice, four times a year—is determined by your company's requirements.

Ideally, your advisory group or board of directors should also include representatives from the business community, as well as members of your staff, if your business is large enough to warrant it.

Inviting other members of the community offers you a perfect opportunity to benefit from others' mistakes or learn from their experiences. Take the problem of collecting receivables, for example. Should your banker not have an answer, a business member of the group might very well come up with a solution. Or perhaps you're discussing a business site. Your business representatives may already have gone the route you're pursuing and be able to warn you of pitfalls in a contemplated expansion. Or they may be familiar with the advantages and disadvantages of the location you're considering. The purpose of the advisory meeting is to provide a forum to discuss the progress of the business. Certainly the member(s) of the community you invite to join your group will be those whose judgment you value and who have already had some success in their own businesses.

As important as the business executives' presence, however, are the contributions of key staff people. Their input can give other board members a full understanding of the company's operations. And they can give your staff the feedback they need to help run your business effectively.

Meeting Agenda and Frequency

A definite format (an agenda) is essential if meetings are to be productive. Don't plan an informal meeting, assuming a natural exchange of ideas will occur. It won't and it shouldn't. Like anything else that's going to work, it has to be organized. Because you've gone to the effort of assembling the group to discuss your business problems, the meeting should focus on areas of concern.

Typically, an agenda might start with a financial report for the past quarter or month, depending on the frequency of your meetings. Your controller, bookkeeper, or CPA relates this information with comments on any departure from objectives. This should provide an excellent pivot for the balance of the meeting because it is from observations of what *has* occurred that corrective action may be determined.

The next order of business could be a report from your sales manager, covering such themes as customer acceptance of your product, problems between customers and sales personnel, new marketing techniques, sales for the past quarter, and an outline of projected sales for the subsequent period. Such a report might prompt a discussion of similar situations your representatives from the business community are having with their markets. Sales patterns may be symptomatic of the economic environment, a possibility your banker or CPA, who may have other clients in similar circumstances, can easily verify.

If you're involved in diversification, your staff member in charge of product development or product control might report on his or her progress in developing or finding a new product. At this point your sales manager may comment on customer requirements, pointing out problems with current merchandise or with the potential sale of a new product. Here your business representatives may again offer suggestions concerning the development of an item in their business that could lead to new ideas.

The possibilities are endless. The specifics of your agenda must be adjusted to your particular situation, just as you must determine how frequently your board or advisory group should meet.

> As a rule, the smaller the business, the less complex the problems, the less frequent the meetings; yet there is no fixed formula.

In most organizations, a semiannual or quarterly meeting is sufficient, with enough time elapsing between agendas so that a trend can be noted in assessing the company's performance.

Trending Your Business

Trending your business, one of the basic functions of your board or advisory group, must be accomplished on two levels—in terms of your own objectives and in relation to what may be happening in the world outside. "Trending" means determining the direction of sales, profits, costs, or expenses in relation to both inside and outside conditions. Your staff managers, having set their own targets, can provide valuable insight into any deviations when comparing the company's performance with its budgets and goals. Evaluation of your company's performance in relation to the industry at large or the overall economy should be the priority of the (outside) advisers who are not associated with your company on a daily basis. Their familiarity with the general business community, as well as their separation from the politics of your inner organzation, gives them a broader perspective.

In evaluating any business, and particularly in determining trends, the seasonality of your business cycle should be considered. Your banker may be the best qualified to report on this factor, but all your outside advisers should be able to judge your company's performance relative to the general economy. Based on both the internal and external factors against which your business must perform, trending should give you some perspective on where your company has been and where it's going.

Working with Your Advisers

You alone are ultimately reponsible for your company's success or failure. Don't be disenchanted with those who disagree with you and don't use your group merely to rubber stamp decisions you've already made. A dissenting voice may focus on a point that has merit. Be happy to hear it.

> Your responsibility at meetings is to listen to what your advisers have to say without fearing that they want to run your business.

Actually, they probably have problems of their own, and sitting on your board gives them perspective, too. If your board is to be effective, you must share your company's problems openly and keep your members well informed. This creates a close association in which members feel more responsible to your company. On the other hand, don't attempt to abdicate your decision-making responsibility. You're in charge.

Paying for Advisers

To be effective, your advisers must be able to interact productively with each other. Your relationship with your group should be a professional one, entailing mutual trust, respect, responsibility, and objectivity. It also requires that the members of your board be remunerated. The service they render is valuable, and you can't expect them to sit on your board out of goodwill or friendship. Occasionally, members do serve on boards with compensation in kind rather than dollars, but this is the exception rather than the rule. It's best not to take advantage of such situations.

However, the amount you pay your advisers can vary, depending on the size and age of a company, its assets, the frequency of meetings, prestige factors, and so on. Board members are usually compensated with either an annual or per-meeting fee. Your professionals and your representatives from the business community should all be paid the same amount; staff people need not receive compensation because this function should be considered part of their jobs.

The appropriate compensating arrangements for your board can best be decided upon at the first organizational meeting, perhaps following a one-to-one discussion between you and your CPA to decide on the guidelines with which you feel most comfortable. Your members should then feel free to discuss openly and decide upon a plan that is acceptable to all.

Whatever it is, it should be an equitable expression of your appreciation and serve to reinforce a constructive relationship between you and your board. In order to be productive, the relationship between an entrepreneur and his or her board must also be flexible. At times the board may be responsible for some surprising turns in the direction the company takes.

To illustrate, let's take a look at an entrepreneur we've known for a long time. Seeing how he interracts with his board will demonstrate the vital role a board can play in the life of your business and underline some of the other concepts advanced in this chapter.

Louis Baum was a prosperous apparel manufacturer, but in the formative years of his business, he was successful only in spite of himself. Baum's ability was confined to one area: He was a terrific salesman. Louis had started his company just after World War II in a small building on the wrong side of the tracks. To get his business moving, he had invited a small group of friends and business acquaintances to invest in the company and had forged them into an advisory group. As time passed, he acquired a CPA, an attorney, and an insurance agent; and in due course, they joined the board as well.

For some years, Louis's advisers were aware that the company's principal asset—Louis Baum, salesman—was also one of its biggest liabilities. Though he may have been able to sell ice to an Eskimo, Louis couldn't run a company. There were times when even he admitted to his lack of business acumen, but he refused to give up the helm.

So the advisory group finally confronted the problem. It all came to a head when the company was in dire financial straits and Louis could not deal effectively with his principal lenders. At one fateful meeting, the board made a point of praising Baum for his contributions to the company yet emphasized the need for a manager who could cope with the financial pressures of running a business.

Fortunately, Louis had an underlying respect for his advisory group. He trusted the motives behind their recommendation. This time he acquiesced to their demand. And once he faced the situation, he was not only able to accept it but to do so with considerable relief.

Even when the company outgrew its original warehouse, it made do with that facility. Then at one significant board meeting, the directors approved a concept taking the business into a new direction, even though it would further antiquate its warehousing and distributing facility. Recognizing that adjustments would have to be made, board members formed a committee to study the problems the business would face once its new plans were implemented.

Comprised of the company's attorney, CPA, and a realtor who specialized in tax shelters, the group put together projections of the financial obligations involved in constructing a new warehouse. In reviewing the figures, the advisers realized the business would be overleveraged if it undertook the project and it did not need the amount of depreciation that would be generated. Given these conditions, the committee put together a plan, which they presented at the next board meeting.

Their suggestion was to have a small group of investors form a syndicate and build the warehouse to the company's specifications. This would serve a dual prpose. First, the property could be leased to the company on a long-term basis, providing it with a much needed facility as well as with built-in financing. Second, it would provide syndicate members with a sound investment and a tax shelter.

The plan was not complex, yet it would never have been conceived, or executed, without a board of directors. As a device for meeting expansion needs, it was perfect. And, knowing each other so well, the committee assumed correctly that board members would be happy for the investment opportunity. The program was evaluated and unanimously approved.

Over subsequent months, several board members helped implement the plan. The real estate agent disposed of the old property and found a new location according to company specifications. The company's attorney drew up the partnership (for the syndicate) and lease agreements; the CPA made sure all documents met IRS requirements. In this fashion, the members of the board made the new facility a reality. Baum realized he could not have accomplished all this in such a short time without his team. In fact, without it, his business couldn't have flourished at all. With them, he was free to do what he did well—sell. And the members of his board received various compensations for doing their job—making sure the business survived.

ACTION GUIDELINES

Have you examined the various areas in which your business can benefit from an ongoing relationship with the following professionals?

- CPA
- Attorney

- Insurance agents
- Banker

Have you considered assembling an advisory group of the following people?

- Your professionals
- Two or three well respected peers from the business community
- Top staff members

An effective advisory group can do much for your company through

- A position of objectivity
- Reinforcement of policy and programs
- Input of ideas
- Noting the trends in your business
- Assistance in the decision-making process

Prior to each advisory group meeting do you do the following?

- Meet with key members of your staff for an update on each department?
- Plan an agenda for the meeting that comprehensively communicates company progress?
- Assign responsibility for reports to key staff personnel?

A successful advisory group meeting depends on the following:

- Adherence to agenda
- Encouragement of input from all sectors
- Listening to (and perhaps acting on) the dissenting voice
- Accepting the ultimate responsibility

PART FOUR

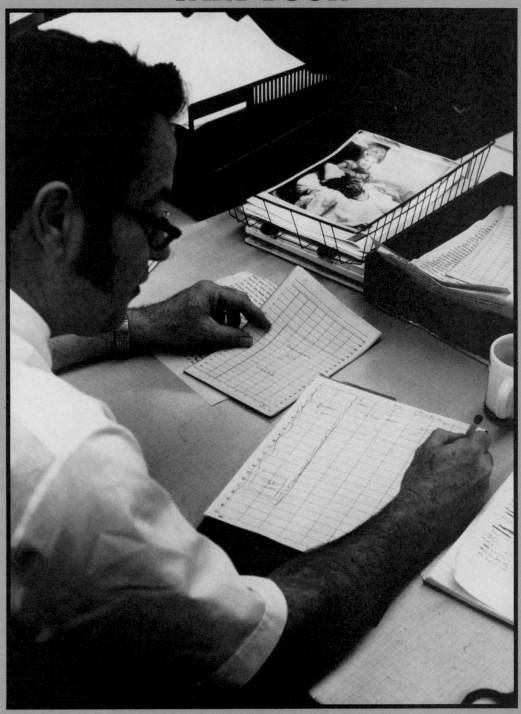

DESIGNING YOUR BUSINESS PLAN

9

How to Write Your Plan—
Prose Section

This chapter will

- Describe the advantages of a written over an oral presentation of a business plan
- List the components of the prose section of a typical business plan
- Tell you how to compile each of these components

Occasionally in this chapter, we describe in more than one section the information to be included in your business plan. This is not to suggest that you repeat this material. Rather, it can be used in any one of a number of places. We are providing an outline you should tailor to meet the needs of *your* business when putting together your own plan. A sample business plan is included in Appendix A.

WHY A BUSINESS PLAN

The objective of your business plan, which tells your story to potential lenders/investors, is to compile tangible proof of your financing readiness. Anyone willing to put up cash for your company will want a comprehensive picture of what your business is all about.

> An added dividend in putting together a business plan is that you are forced to crystallize your goals. In writing them down, you are really committing yourself to them, thereby becoming that much more effective as an administrator.

Granted, veteran entrepreneurs with long histories of successes sometimes approach a potential lender/investor equipped simply with their latest financial statements. But that is the exception. More often, even the veteran business person (as well as the new entrepreneur or the owner of a business experiencing problems) gets better results with an all-inclusive "biography" of the business. In your case, such a presentation would include a thorough description of both you and your operation, with an indication of how much money you need. You should also explain how you intend to pay it back if your financing takes the form of a loan or what kind of return you anticipate if it's an investment.

The more documentation you can supply with your presentation, the better, particularly during times of tight money, when lending institutions are more than usually selective. A case in point may be seen during the inflation/recession period of the late seventies and beginning eighties, when the Federal Reserve Bank tightened the money supply and all member banks reacted accordingly. Although money was still available, it was harder to come by and a lot more expensive, with the trend started by the banks creating a ripple effect that touched every financial institution. Thus those businesses whose houses were in order were still able to get financing.

SPOKEN OR WRITTEN PRESENTATION

Considerable information is assembled in a comprehensive business plan and then transmitted to all concerned parties. It's surprising, therefore, that some entrepreneurs would choose to give an oral rather than a written presentation of their material. There are a number of good reasons for a written presentation.

First, oral communication of massive information tends to create the appearance of "flying by the seat of your pants," an impression you hardly want to convey while attempting to establish your credibility. Second, much is lost or forgotten when ideas and data are communicated orally. Third, because many people will need access to your story, it's wise to commit it to paper and avoid risking omission or misinterpretation of data as the story is passed from one to another.

At a typical presentation with a bank, your first meeting may be with the branch manager, who will discuss your request with his regional manager. He may then appeal to the loan committee. If your presentation is written, you will remain in control of the story throughout and will have emphasized the information you want stressed.

If you dislike expressing yourself in writing, consider dictating the material onto a tape recorder or dictaphone, having it transcribed, and asking your CPA or attorney to review it.

A MULTIPLE-PURPOSE DOCUMENT

> Preparation of a written business plan represents considerable effort, but you will have a document that should serve you well on several levels.

In addition to acquainting potential lenders/investors with your business, the plan may be presented to key suppliers, who in effect grant you credit when they ship you merchandise or to select customers, who need continuity of supply and therefore are as dependent on you as you are on them. You may also show it to managerial level employees who are interested in their futures with your company. Naturally, a change of emphasis on certain parts of your operation may be necessary for some of these presentations, but such modifications are easily accomplished once you have your basic plan.

For most companies, plan contents are basically the same, although any plan should accommodate those factors important to your business. (In our sample business plan, sections one and two—on the contents covered in this chapter— have been combined.) It may be appropriate to include a detailed description of operations, for example, if your business is an unusual one, or a segment on your data-processing program if it has had a major effect on operations. Following a title page and a table of contents, the prose section of the business plan includes the following:

1. Business purpose or objectives
2. History
3. Management
4. Products or services offered
5. Selling and marketing strategy
6. Plant and facilities
7. Labor force
8. Competition
9. Administration

The length of each segment depends on how much space you need to describe the subject adequately; so there is no specific number of pages required for the overall presentation. We have seen some plans as short as ten pages; others are as long as forty. Your only concern should be to tell your story well, but without extraneous material.

PLAN CONTENTS

Business Purpose or Objectives

Whatever your reason for seeking financing—to start a new business, expand a growing business, or solve some problems with cash—your business purpose or objectives sets the tone for your entire presentation. It is here that you introduce your company and your product, explaining the purpose of your operation, your objectives, and the customer being served. Because you and your ambitions are essential to the ultimate success of your business, making sure that your potential lender/investor understands your motives may make the difference in the decision on a loan or investment.

Whenever possible, spell out your goals. For example, what kind of growth rate are you shooting for this year, and why are you confident you'll achieve it? What are acceptable profit margins for your company? Compare those of your own business with the traditional profit margins for the industry you're in (see Robert Morris Associates, RMA Annual Statements Studies), and if there's a variance, explain why.

Designate the geographical area you see as your market and discuss whether it's realistic in terms of product distribution or whether you need to expand into other locations.

If you have a new business, it's particularly important that your lender/investor understands the concept upon which your business operates, that is, how it developed and why you believe it will succeed. And while you're explaining, consider citing an authority for the development of your philosophy. You can name a spokesperson for your industry, product, or service who has substantial experience in the field. It may even be yourself, referring to past experiences and whatever factors led you to establish your own company. This information might be reinforced with documentation from articles in newspapers, trade publications, or other periodicals. Still other sources of statistics and background material are trade associations, the Chamber of Commerce, the United States Department of Commerce, the Small Business Administration, and many banks. Many of the materials are available at most libraries.

The Better Business Bureau is another organization you might utilize in order to determine whether you have competition in your area and what kind of service your competition is providing. Supplying this information will also lend authority to your presentation and do much to enhance your credibility.

Should yours be an established business, your authority would be the business itself. Having aquired a track record, you can no doubt demonstrate your ability to pay back a loan. But one cannot always rely on a company's history. Business objectives change with the times, and if you're seeking financing because your business is moving in a new direction, you may need another authority in addition to the fact that your company has been around for twenty years or so.

If you're looking for a loan because your business has problems, you not only must offer an authority for the direction your company is taking, but you have to be candid about the problem and the solutions you're attempting to institute. *Never* attempt to camouflage a situation. If you have a receivables problem, define it and describe how you plan to solve it. The same holds true for inventory or gross profit problems. Indicating your awareness of a difficulty gives you an opportunity to demonstrate that you can control it. You may also find it expedient to integrate your plans for correcting that problem with your overall objectives. In fact, this may be a good technique for coordinating all the elements in this segment of your business plan.

History

In business plans for either the expanding business or the business with problems, a brief history of your company should follow, or be combined with, your purpose or objectives.

The segment should indicate to the lender/investor that you *are* capable of running your own show, tell how long you have been in business, and indicate whether you have a partnership, sole proprietorship, or corporation. You should also list all subsidiary companies (if applicable), describing their product or service lines and the dates each was formed. Again, be specific. Tell the reader what you have accomplished over the years in terms of sales and profitability. If possible, stress the points most vital to your request for financing. To illustrate, let's look at an experience we had helping a client revise his business plan.

While working up the objectives of this company, we learned that additional equipment was needed in order to bid on an important contract. If negotiations were successful, the business was assured of an additional $800,000 a year in sales volume; yet in order even to participate in bidding, the company required financing for equipment in the amount of $500,000. To complicate matters, management had already encountered a hurdle when a lending institution refused to believe they could dispose of the equipment should they need to cut back.

Keeping this problem in mind as we recorded company history, we highlighted results of a similar situation the company had experienced some years before, when the business had faced the possible unionization of its labor force. Preferring not to comply with union demands, it tightened its belt, sold off equipment, and cut back in almost every area of operation. Rather than cover up this part of the company's history, we used it to illustrate that the business was able to dispose of its fixed assets. Not only did we show that there was a ready market for such equipment, we demonstrated that management could control the company and survive—in the face of potential disaster. Because we proved the company would not be saddled indefinitely with fixed payments, the lending institution decided to consider the resale value of the equipment. This turn of events was the deciding point in getting the loan.

Management

The typical approach in the management section is to introduce the group in general and follow with a brief description of each member. It should include that person's title and area of expertise and conclude with a summary of his or her educational background and experience. These biographies should be comprehensive but concise—not more than a short paragraph for each person.

You must also demonstrate here how members of management interrelate with one another, a task you may want to accomplish with an organizational chart. The chart indicates that you have taken the time and effort to delegate reporting responsibilities. You could also illustrate interrelationships between staff members in a description of staff meetings, citing how often they take place and the topics discussed. Such information demonstrates how one area of the operation communicates with another so that the entire company becomes a working team.

The next item to be mentioned in this section is your advisory group or board of directors, noting frequency of meetings and subjects discussed and describing how it interracts with your company.

Finally, other factors to consider including are contractual relationships between executive-level employees and the company (depending on the significance of those terms) and the share of ownership key employees have in the business, if that share is 10 percent or more.

Products or Services Offered

The next subject your business plan should cover is the product or services you offer, focusing on new products, particularly if new-product development is the reason you're seeking financing. Your product is the area in which you must excell; so if you're the manufacturer, expain how it is constructed or assembled. If your products are patented, explain the importance of the patent rights and provide the expiration dates. You may also want to enclose a letter from your patent attorney detailing your rights under the patent, a document that can add substance to a presentation.

Should your company's function be simply to market the product or products, explain the contractual rights, describing only the principal products or those products accounting for more than 10 to 15 percent of your overall sales efforts.

It may be that your principal product is actually a service formalized by a contract, in which case you should include the contract as an exhibit and in the body of your report highlight the important points of the contractual relationship and their significance to your business.

If your business is in an area of high technology, you might outine your research and development process, describing how your key products evolved and any marketing surveys you may have researched.

If you have a competitive edge on the market as the result of some proprietory technology you developed, so much the better. Explain it; yet be careful of self-aggrandizement. Factual but low key is the appropriate point of view for your presentation.

It is in this section that you should discuss diversification of your product line. Most lender/investors are not sympathetic to the one-product company. Should your company be in that position, confront the situation head on. Clarify what you are doing to expand into other product areas if that kind of action is possible. If it isn't, offer a viable reason why your product or service fills a long-standing need with the community you are serving and tell why you believe the demand will continue. Whatever you do, don't ignore the fact that you are not on solid ground if you have a one-product company.

Should yours be a distribution business, another situation you must give special mention is your relationship with your suppliers. If any one supplier provides more than 50 percent of the products you distributed, the interaction between your two companies is vitally important. Such a relationship would make you one of the principal sales arms of your supplier's company—with your stability and strength dependent on it; so you might include financial data on your supplier, with a brief rundown on that organization. Or if you are very dependent on a few suppliers, describe in detail the options available to you in the event that one of them cannot deliver a critical part of an order. This would provide yet another opportunity to make your audience aware of how you plan your business and that you can keep afloat in a crisis.

Selling and Marketing Strategy

Describing how your product is sold is one of the most important parts of your business plan because it indicates how you will get the revenue to repay the loan or provide your investor with a return on his or her capital. (In the case of a new business, you will have to make assumptions based on your research and/or on previous experience.)

If you have a sales force, describe its function. Does it provide you with detailed itineraries or call reports? What other feedback do your sales people give you? How do you provide incentives, not only dollar incentives but the necessary enthusiasm that is the key to a successful sales or distribution team? Do you have a marketing or sales manager? How often does he or she meet with your sales rep? How much time elapses between the sale and delivery of the product or between the delivery of the product and the collection of the receivable? If you use a dating program, mention it because the arrangement will affect collections. All these matters become very significant later, when your potential lender/investor views your financial statements. This section must show the timing *relationships* between sales and cash collections.

You could compare your company with the rest of the industry in terms of delivery and the percentage of the market your business claims.

If yours is other than mass market merchandise, the (potential) total market for your product is important, too. It is available in materials published by the federal government and through many state agencies. This material, also, should be available at most public libraries. You may want to indicate what percentage of the total market you're seeking if you haven't already covered this subject in your business purpose or objectives section.

When appropriate, describe how your market has grown over the past two years and the past five years. How do you foresee your future growth in the market? Have you hired consultants to advise you along these lines? If so, mention them and include in your plan pertinent parts of their reports. This segment of your presentation should coincide with the preparation of the financial section of your business plan (see Chapter 10), in which you will have to quantify sales growth over the next three to five years. Thus you will be laying the groundwork now for that projection, which will appear in the statement of profit or loss.

Finally, don't forget to mention any limiting factors on your market, such as your present facilities (are they adequate for market expansion?), a "hot" item destined for a short life, and adverse geographical factors or labor supply.

Competition

It's important to learn everything you can about your competition and benefit from it. How does your product or service differ from others from a technical or packaging point of view, in marketing, in distribution, or in sales? Because most companies seeking credit must go through a credit evaluation, you can usually obtain data that tells you how your competition operates in these respects. Dun and Bradstreet is a good source for such data. In the event that your product or service was favorably evaluated by a technical or consumer publication or by a critic, be sure to include such a report.

If you have no competition, don't assume that situation is necessarily an advantage. Many lenders/investors interpret lack of competition for a product as an absence of demand. If that's the case, you'll have to outline your plans for developing a market or at least getting a head start in a potential one. But, as always, be candid and be thorough.

> Don't try to ignore or gloss over a problem. An astute lender/investor will surely pick up on it.

Plant and Facilities

One excellent way to demonstrate that you have nothing to hide is to let your potential lenders/investors see your business in operation. Inviting them on a plant tour—a "live performance" of your company (in addition to providing a written or oral presentation)—makes it easier for them to relate to your operation. Without being obvious, lay out the red carpet, making sure that everything is in tip-top shape. But be realistic. Having a place appear spruced up to the point of being inoperative may be less complimentary than an honest approach to a well-run, well-controlled company.

The discussion of your facilities, whether part of a written plan or a guided tour, should indicate the reason you chose your present site (perhaps it put you in closer touch with the labor supply). You should also cover such key factors as capacity and what quantity of your product your present facilities can produce or service. You might consider stating capacity as it relates to sales volume, that is, your present facilities might produce enough to result in $100,000 or $200,000 in sales. Explain whether a second or third shift is feasible to increase productivity and indicate whether the costs of additional shifts would be offset by enough of an increase in productivity to warrant such a measure. In any case, indicate that you have considered it.

Should you be contemplating any major repairs or alterations to facilitate greater efficiency, say so. It's possible that your reason for raising money relates to this very factor. It that's the situation, disclose what additional profits you expect from such an expenditure and have your financial expert review your figures or assist you in preparing them.

Labor Force

A related subject in which any potential lender/investor will be keenly interested is whether the labor supply in your area is adequate and competent to guarantee continued manufacture or distribution of your product or service. Here is where you mention the size and quality of your labor force, the potential for increases in its size, and the supervisory force required. You might prepare a ratio of employee cost to dollar volume and compare this statistic with those of your peers in the same or similar businesses. Don't overlook competition for labor in your area and keep in mind that it may not come from the same industry as yours. For example, another company may employ semiskilled machinists just as you do, in which case ask yourself how your company stacks up on the pay scale or benefits being offered down the street or across town.

In today's market, most businesses provide fringe benefits for their employees. List your company's benefits, with an indication of employee acceptance of them. How does your package compare with others in your area? How does it compete with a union package? If your business is not unionized, have your employees been approached about organizing? How have you reacted? Responses to all these questions should be readily available in your presentation. It is almost inevitable that someone will ask, and your replies will reveal a great deal about your administration.

Administration/Operating Controls

Though you may think that you have covered the subject of administration in your segment on management, this section should actually deal with the nitty gritty of running your company, that is, the frequency of board meetings as well as all the detailed information on operating controls, such as order procedures, frequency of staff meetings, your monthly schedules of sales and cash forecasts, and monthly profit and loss reports. (The schedules are sometimes included in the exhibits accompanying your business plan.)

This is where you may also explain the frequency with which you receive reports on accounts receivable, accounts payable, and cash positions and how you utilize them. Indicate the system you use to keep track of trends and describe any other pertinent factors that might be typical of your business (see "Knowing Your Company's Quirks" in Chapter 1). How do you control inventory and purchase requirements? Are perpetual inventory reports maintained, and if so, who uses them? How do you track cash flow—weekly, monthly, quarterly, or annually? Many entrepreneurs work with an informal cash forecast but never commit it to paper. If you cannot do so, ask your financial adviser to give you a hand with it. Meanwhile, consider enclosing sample daily or weekly reports on cash forecast, accounts receivable and accounts payable, purchase control, and sales analyses. These exhibits can lend substance to your presentation.

This is the area, too, where you should mention insurance, focusing on such aspects as liability coverage, life insurance on company officers, and employee benefit programs. Such information demonstrates how responsible you have been in providng for the unexpected.

Profit-sharing and pension plans or bonus programs for either management or administrative employees should also be described in this section. That information indicates the extent of your financial involvements and shows how competitive your business is in these respects. If you have funds in such plans, your bank may very well have a department to help with their investment (and that association might give you the leverage you need for the bank's loan approval).

The final subject to be discussed in this segment is litigation. If none exists, say so. But if there is any pending, be up front about it. It is sure to come out if anyone does a credit analysis on your company. Being candid about the problem reinforces the credibility you have worked so hard to establish. This particular spot is a most opportune place to do just that because you are about to complete the prose section of your business plan and go on to the financial section, the preparation of which we discuss in Chapter 10.

ACTION GUIDELINES

The advantages of the written over the oral presentation of a business plan are the following:

- You could omit vital information in an oral presentation.
- Your facts might be misinterpreted when you present them orally.
- Verbal communication is subject to distortion as it is relayed down the line.

- With a written plan, the writer retains control regardless of how many persons review the material.

     A well-prepared business plan should include the following:

- Title page
- Table of contents for both the prose and financial sections
- A discourse of appropriate length on each of the following subjects:

1. Business purpose or objectives
2. History of the company
3. Biographical sketches of management
4. Products or services offered
5. Selling and marketing strategy
6. Plant and facilities
7. Labor force
8. Competition
9. Administration

10

How to Write Your Plan—
Financial Section

This chapter will

- Tell you what constitutes the financial section of the business plan

- Explain where the information for the financial section comes from

- Describe how to compile the components of the financial section

This chapter, too, is geared particularly to entrepreneurs who intend to prepare a written presentation of their business plan. Those delivering an oral presentation typically accompany it with CPA- or staff-prepared financial statements, although not in the comparative format we suggest. Financing usually takes a lot longer to finalize because the lending institution, or the investor, must prepare its own analyses and, in so doing, goes back and forth requesting supplemental material of the would-be borrower. The statements we recommend in this chapter have value not only as essential enclosures in the business plan but as important tools with which to run your business.

The prose section of your business plan is intended to acquaint the potential lender/investor verbally with your company's past, present, and future performance, and the financial part of your plan should substantiate the information you have supplied in the prose section. Because most plan reviewers are accustomed to interpreting numbers, your figures will provide them with a graphic description of how your business has functioned in the past and how well it will be performing in the future.

The heart of this plan is the following reports:

Profit or loss or income statement

Cash statement

Balance sheet

Capital budget

The first three of these reports illustrate the relationship between past accomplishments and future projections. The capital budget is an expansion of one line item on the cash statement and is not presented as a comparative statement. The information supplied in these statements culminates in your request for the amount of financing you need, along with your description of how you plan to pay it back. The first (prose) part of the plan sets a mood and establishes credibility; the second (financial) section maintains that credibility. As a rule, the financial section of a business plan includes the following:

1. Introduction
2. Assumptions used in preparing the projections
3. Profit or loss statement, actual and projected
4. Cash statement, actual and projected
5. Balance sheet
6. Ratios derived from the balance sheet
7. Capital budget
8. Accountant's statement
9. Your financial requirements
10. Exhibits

INTRODUCTION

Unlike the business purpose and objectives, which serve as the introduction to your company, the introduction to the financial section is very brief. Its purpose is solely to provide parameters with which to review the reports or statements that follow.

Because three of these reports cover not only past and present performance but forecast the future, they represent the company's long-range financial plan. Accordingly, they may be prepared for three or five years into the future. Whichever way you go, your introduction should indicate how far ahead the projections extend. In addition, it should state that the long-range plan is an essential part of your company's management and control system and explain the purpose it serves both externally and internally. It might also describe the plan's effect on management.

Your introduction should summarize the projected growth rate for the following year, along with expected profits after taxes. Consider giving a comparison with an earlier year in order to illustrate the company's recent growth rate.

The introduction puts your readers in the appropriate framework for examining the statements. However, in order to relate to them realistically, they need certain explanations, or the *assumptions* upon which the financial data is compiled. These explanations make a review of the statements more comprehensible and illuminate business trends.

MAJOR ASSUMPTIONS

Because it is impossible to include all assumptions made in compiling your plan, limit yourself to those crucial to the preparation of financial projections. For example, the profit or loss statement is usually supplemented by the following assumptions: sales, gross profit, selling expenses, general and administrative expenses, and pretax and after-tax profits.

The assumptions for cash projections cover cash receipts and cash disbursements. The balance sheet doesn't require any assumptions. The background with which you review the balance sheet is actually a summary of the assumptions used for the other two forecasts. In lieu of assumptions for the balance sheet, it's wise to include the ratio analyses that may be determined from it (see Chapter 6). However, the capital budget, which is actually an expansion of one line item in the cash disbursements section of the forecasts on the cash statement, requires its own set of assumptions because the projections contained therein may extend beyond the projections shown on the cash statement.

If you hope to provide meaningful assumptions, remember that your readers know far less about your company than you do. Moreover, they have not been involved in the strategies, preparation of analyses, or acceptance and rejection of ideas, as you have. Thus your assumptions must make the numbers on the statements intelligible and meaningful to your readers.

The assumptions may either immediately follow the introduction to the financial section, as a separate section, or the appropriate assumptions may accompany the particular statement to which they pertain. We have chosen the latter approach because each statement requires explanation for the benefit of *our* readers.

Before examining the four statements in the financial section of the business plan, you may find it helpful to review the background material on each of these documents in Chapters 3 and 6. You may also want to refer to the instructions for preparing operating and capital budgets, a cash forecast, and a long-term forecast in Appendixes B, C, D, and E.

PROFIT OR LOSS STATEMENT

The profit or loss, income or **earnings statement,** or operating budget is usually presented as the first of the four statements in your business plan because it is from the income recorded here that the lender or investor will be repaid. In addition to providing the reader with essential data on such items as sales, costs, and income, the statement also shows key percentage variations and the annual growth rate of sales and pretax income from one year to the next.

Because we are using the comparative format for the financial statements, you have an overview of the company's performance over the previous three years against projections for the succeeding three years.

> In using this format for your own financial statements—and we recommend that you do—you may choose to record performance and projections for a five-year period rather than for three years.

Not only does it enable you to visualize the company's past, present, and future performance, but you will have readily available figures to compare with industry averages. Please see Figure 10.1.

Sales Assumption

Because it is from the projected sales figure that you measure the profit (or loss) of the business, the collection and disbursement of cash, and the subsequent effects on the balance sheet, the sales assumption sets the tone for the interpretation of all the statements that follow. Thus it is essential that it be as specific as possible in order to establish the viability of the

| | PAST THREE YEARS ACTUAL | | | | | | NEXT THREE YEARS PROJECTED | | | | | |
| | 19X1 | | 19X2 | | 19X3 | | 19X4[a] | | 19X5 | | 19X6 | |
	$	%	$	%	$	%	$	%	$	%	$	%
Sales	6,429,330	100	4,058,510	100	7,010,970	100	8,500,000	100	9,900,000	100	11,500,000	100
Cost of Sales	4,181,160	65	2,923,040	72	4,427,140	63	5,440,000	64	6,340,000	64	7,360,000	64
Gross Profit	2,248,170	35	1,135,470	28	2,583,830	37	3,060,000	36	3,560,000	36	4,140,000	36
Selling Expense	514,340	8	556,680	13	570,880	8	935,000	11	850,000	8	920,000	8
Gen. & Adm. Expense	576,550	9	682,670	17	717,390	10	805,000	9	975,000	10	1,100,000	10
Total Expenses	1,090,890	17	1,239,350	30	1,288,270	18	1,740,000	20	1,825,000	18	2,020,000	18
Pretax Profit	1,157,280	18	(103,880)	(2)	1,295,560	19	1,320,000	16	1,735,000	18	2,120,000	18
Federal & State Taxes	445,200	7			619,000	9	630,000	8	840,000	9	930,000	8
Net Income	712,080	11	(103,880)	(2)	676,560	10	690,000	8	895,000	9	1,190,000	10
% Annual Growth Rate												
Sales	16.9%		(36.9%)		72.7%		21.2%		16.4%		16.2%	
Pretax Profit	16.8%		(166.0%)		1347.2%		1.9%		31.4%		22.2%	

[a]The projections for 19X4 represent the operating budget.

Figure 10.1   Statement of profit or loss or income statement

sales forecast. For example, if your forecasted sales grow significantly, note the reasons for such a projection and explain any deviance from an established trend.

To illustrate, we have prepared the following comment on sales to accompany the profit or loss statement in Figure 10.1:

> The trend in sales has not always been upward. In 19X2, the entire industry was affected by the nationwide recession, and the company has always followed industry trends, despite the fact that accomplishments in sales growth have consistently been better than industry averages (Source: Apparel Manufacturers Trade Assoc.). Recovery from the recession in 19X3 brought the company back to a more typical growth pattern. Forecasted annual growth rate correlates with projections of the Apparel Manufacturers Trade Association. The company is planning a major sales promotion in 19X4, which is projected to accomplish a better than average sales growth rate for that year. The company has employed similar campaigns in prior years, most notably in 19X6 when a sales growth rate over 19X5 in excess of 35 percent was experienced.

This assumption highlights those areas that support the financial statement the comment accompanies. The explanation should be given as much depth as possible because it provides substance that enhances your credibility.

We cited a trade association as our authority, but you should use whatever is appropriate: housing starts, perhaps, or per-capita consumption of goods. State your position as well as your authority. Maybe your forecast is more "bullish" than that of comparable industries, or perhaps your company will be conducting a major promotional campaign. If so, state your case. If seasonality is a factor in your business, mention that fact because it may be the reason for larger cash requirements during a particular period in your forecast. Also mention the condition of the economy, particularly as it relates to your industry. Perhaps the country as a whole is projecting a recession, but your locality is not because of some unusual circumstance. Highlight the situation. Be as concise as possible.

Gross Profit Assumption

The size of the gross profit you aim for affects many aspects of your business and how you run it. It influences the quality of product you handle, the volume of business you do, and the type of customer you attract. Thus the more knowledge you can communicate to the lender/investor about this aspect of your business, the easier it will be for him or her to relate to your operation.

In preparing your gross profit assumption you must again compare your projection with that of the industry. If you are doing better than average, mention your achievement. But if your position falls below the industry standard, explain why you are not doing as well as your competitors. It may be that your method of merchandising requires a lower gross profit. If so, briefly describe your approach to merchandising and distribution. Or perhaps you need a vigorous cost reduction program in your manufacturing facility. If competitive pressures prevent a price increase, mention the program you plan to inaugurate and its probable effect on your gross profit. If markdowns are excessive, explain why and elaborate on how you plan to prevent that situation from recurring.

To illustrate, the following assumption explains the gross profit situation for the profit or loss statement in Figure 10.1:

Typically, merchants in our industry earn 38 percent to 40 percent in gross profit; we have earned and project to earn in the 35–37 percent range. This situation results from an early policy decision to opt for the lower-priced markets. However, to offset the disadvantage of earning a lower gross profit, we attract a wider than average range of customers who continuously seek lower-priced goods. This in turn provides our company with stability in the marketplace and thus reduces our business risk considerably. In 19X2, the company had some abnormal markdowns on merchandise that was purchased with an anticipated sales volume that failed to materialize in light of the recession previously mentioned. To reduce our risk in the future, we have invested in a computer to help in allocating and forecasting inventory. This should reduce markdowns considerably in 19X3, enabling the company to experience an additional 1 percent gross profit margin.

Selling and General and Administrative Expense Assumptions

Generally, selling and general and administrative expense assumptions are rather brief. An overview noting relationships of expenditures to industry averages and past accomplishments is usually sufficient. However, you should note any extraordinary expenses, such as an exceptionally large amount of money you plan to spend on, say, an advertising campaign. Or if you plan to expand your staff in order to provide your company with the operating personnel with which to accomplish your sales goal, provide an in-depth explanation of that expenditure.

In our example of a selling expense assumption to accompany Figure 10.1, we indicate that there are two major points to be covered in explaining selling expenses: the historical consistency of variable expenses and a major selling campaign that accounts for increased selling expenses during 19X4.

This category has consistently varied in direct proportion to sales volume. However, in 19X4, as stated in our sales assumption, we are planning a promotional campaign budgeted at $25,000. This additional cost is expected to yield a higher sales volume in future years, thereby justifying the extra expenditure.

On our statement, general and administrative expenses are substantially below industry averages. Thus our explanation covers this unusual situation.

The basic overhead costs for the kind of business that we operate is nominal, primarily because of the low gross profit generated. Although we provide basic services to our customers, they do not in turn expect too many frills with the low prices they are paying for our goods. There are no major increases budgeted in salaries, which account for over 90 percent of total general and administrative costs. However, with the added sales volume, we expect to increase staff to cover the additional burden of handling increased volume.

Pretax and After-Tax Assumption

This assumption should compare your pretax and after-tax earnings with industry standards. The following example spells out what needs be said about these two line items on the profit or loss statement in Figure 10.1:

Income generated by our company is in excess of industry standards by an average of 2 percent of sales. We attribute this result to maintaining tight control over overhead, which is necessitated by the lower than average gross profit our business generates. In 19X6, we plan a major warehouse project and therefore have forecast expenditures of over $3,000,000 in capital equipment and improvements, of which $150,000 is eligible for a 10 percent investment credit. We have therefore reduced the provision for federal income taxes accordingly.

CASH STATEMENT

> The **cash statement,** or **cash flow,** indicates how much money you need and enables the lender/investor to determine when you will be able to pay it back.

We again suggest the comparative statement format because it best illustrates your company's record of loans and repayments. If you demonstrate your past accomplishments, lenders/investors are more likely to accept your potential capabilities.

Two assumptions pertain to forecasts and accompany the cash statement. These are the cash collections assumption and the cash disbursements assumption. Cash collections is a line item under cash receipts, which include collections on accounts receivable and projected borrowings from long-term debt and bank loans. You need not provide any detail regarding long-term debt or bank loans because these are the channels through which any cash shortage would be covered. Although you will discuss this subject in detail in the section on financial requirements, you may want to include a statement such as the following with the cash statement:

The company has projected additional debt, both short and long term, to cover any cash shortages. (See the financial requirements section.)

For the overhead expenses and income tax assumptions on the cash statement, see the selling and general and administrative expense and pretax and after-tax assumptions accompanying the profit or loss statement. Fixed asset expenditures are expanded on in the capital budget, which is accompanied by its own set of assumptions.

Cash Collections Assumption

To demonstrate the viability of future collections, we are going to rely heavily on the company's past performance (a procedure that does not follow with the other projections). But if you expect to improve upon past accomplishments, mention how you plan to do so. For example, if you propose to computerize your accounts receivable function, which in turn may streamline the administration of collections, change your credit policy, or increase staff in your credit department, cite the impact of these changes in your assumption. Any unusual industry practices, such as extended dating programs or larger than usual trade discounts, should also be disclosed.

In the cash forecast illustrated in Figure 10.2, the average number of days outstanding on accounts receivable was extraordinarily high in 19X3. This may be attributed in great part to the recession that occurred in 19X2 and slowed down everyone's collection cycle considerably. A computer was purchased in 19X3 for the primary purpose of increasing gross profit, but an additional benefit proved to be more efficient control over the collection of accounts receivable. Thus we felt that a reduction in the number of projected days outstanding for accounts receivable was realistic.

With this criteria in mind, we wrote the following comments to accompany the cash statement in Figure 10.2:

> Although average days outstanding of accounts receivable were extraordinarily high in 19X3 (due in large part to the recession), we are projecting a more bullish experience for the years 19X4 through 19X6 (that is, decreasing the average number of days outstanding to approximately forty-three from an average forty-four days). This compares favorably with an industry average of forty-five days outstanding. During the latter half of 19X3, we overcame many of the problems associated with the 19X2 recession. Moreover, to increase the collection cycle further, the company has implemented a control system facilitated by the new computer purchased in 19X3.

Cash Disbursements Assumption

The second assumption supplementing cash pertains to cash disbursements. The items that would bear comment in this area are purchases of raw materials and labor, overhead, fixed asset expenditures (or capital budget), debt repayment, and taxes. You need not be redundant, however, if any of these items are covered elsewhere in the presentation. For example, in the set of papers we are using, overhead and taxes have been covered

	PAST THREE YEARS ACTUAL			NEXT THREE YEARS PROJECTED (FORECAST)		
	19X1	19X2	19X3	19X4	19X5	19X6
CASH RECEIPTS						
Collections-Accts. Rec.	$6,403,370	$4,235,070	$6,582,550	$8,337,080	$9,799,780	$11,229,100
Depreciation	177,150	185,000	225,000	275,000	300,000	400,000
Long-Term Debt	-	-	1,000,000	-	-	1,500,000
Notes Payable-Banks	-	150,000	-	100,000	-	300,000
Other	-	-	10,050	-	-	-
Total Cash Receipts	6,580,520	4,570,070	7,817,600	8,712,080	10,099,780	13,429,100
CASH DISBURSEMENTS						
Raw Materials & Labor	4,364,860	2,631,550	4,581,920	5,695,290	6,239,370	7,168,660
Overhead Expenses	938,890	1,179,350	1,382,420	1,688,800	1,906,000	1,940,000
Fixed Asset Expenditures	452,150	600,000	1,000,000	400,000	650,000	3,000,000
Repayment of Note Payable to Bank	200,000	-	200,000	-	200,000	-
Repayment of Long-Term Note	116,000	116,000	116,000	216,000	216,000	216,000
Other Income-Other Charges - Net	17,500	2,250	-	-	100,850	91,400
Income Taxes	445,200	-	619,000	630,000	840,000	930,000
Total Cash Disbursements	6,534,600	4,529,150	7,899,340	8,630,090	10,152,220	13,346,060
Net Cash Overage or (Shortage)	45,920	40,920	(81,740)	81,990	(52,440)	83,040
Cash-Beginning of Period	255,500	301,420	342,340	260,600	342,590	290,150
Cash-End of Period	$ 301,420	$ 342,340	$ 260,600	$ 342,590	$ 290,150	$ 373,190
Average # of Days of Accounts Receivable (Industry Average - 45 Days)	38	45	50	46	42	42

Figure 10.2   The cash statement

in the profit or loss statement; fixed asset expenditures will be covered in the capital budget; and debt repayment will be discussed in the section on financial requirements. You may therefore refer the reader to the appropriate section and restrict your comments in the cash disbursements assumption to those topics not covered elsewhere in the plan.

Even the line item regarding the purchase of raw materials (under cash disbursements) interrelates directly with the inventory turn ratio that will be mentioned in connection with the balance sheet, as well as with the gross profit assumption made in regard to the profit or loss statement. However, because this item represents the single largest dollar outlay on the cash forecast, special attention should be directed to it. Thus we suggest the following:

> The company has experienced excellent relationships with its suppliers and has negotiated favorable terms on future purchases of raw materials. These terms include not only time extensions on payments but also special warehousing on select items. The latter will enhance the company's inventory turnover because it will not have to stock certain key raw materials for more than thirty days.
>
> In the past the company has experienced a turn of approximately 2.5 and is projecting an increase to an average turn of about 3.25 over a three-year period. This will be accomplished not only as a result of the aforementioned relationship with suppliers, but also through the coordination of that arrangement with decreasing inventory levels programmed and controlled by the computer purchased in 19X3.

BALANCE SHEET

The third statement in the financial section of your plan is the balance sheet, which is a summary of the results of the profit or loss statement and the cash statement. For consistency of preparation and to allow the reader to analyze the effects of the other two statements, we recommend that you continue with the comparative statement format, which also allows the reader to note company trends.

A trend analysis is usually accomplished by a computation of the key ratios (see Chapter 6). Thus we strongly advocate including those key ratios in your presentation, along with an explanation of any serious deviation from industry standards and from past accomplishments.

The balance sheet is one of your most important statements. Here your potential lender/investor learns what your capital base is, and this indicates your capacity to borrow or attract investors.

Current Ratio

The current ratio shows your company's ability to pay its current obligations. If a company can handle twice its present obligations with its current assets, its current ratio is 2 to 1.

In the balance sheet in Figure 10.3, the industry ratio is 1.80 to 1, and the company's past accomplishment and future projection improves upon the industry average in every year except 19X2 and 19X6. The explanation that would accompany the illustrated situation might read as follows:

The company has consistently maintained a current ratio of almost 2 to 1 in all years other than 19X2, when the country was in a mild recession. As a result of the recession, our accounts receivable were at an all-time high, and to meet our obligations to suppliers, we had heavier than usual bank loans, thus temporarily increasing our current debt load. We project a lower than industry average in 19X6, when we anticipate additional loans on a short- and long-term basis in order to finance the new warehouse facility. Our projections allow for the expectation that this condition will extend only through the end of 19X6, when additional profits from the new facility will further enhance the company's profitability and hence its cash position.

Quick Asset Ratio

The quick asset ratio serves much the same function as the current ratio, although it does not include inventory or prepaid expenses as part of the computation. If you maintain excellent control over accounts receivable but not over inventory, your quick asset ratio would be better than your current ratio. If that is the case, you should mention the fact and explain how you plan to correct it.

In Figure 10.3, the same factors affect the quick asset ratio as the current ratio. Thus we refer the reader to the current ratio analysis in order to explain the deviation in the quick asset ratio:

	PAST THREE YEARS ACTUAL				NEXT THREE YEARS PROJECTED		
	19X1	19X2	19X3		19X4	19X5	19X6
ASSETS							
Cash	$ 301,420	$ 342,340	$ 260,600		$ 342,590	$ 290,150	$ 373,190
Accounts Receivable	912,760	736,200	1,164,620		1,327,540	1,427,760	1,698,660
Inventory	1,519,600	1,353,110	1,555,540		1,813,330	2,012,700	2,102,860
Prepaid Expenses	55,000	47,500	60,250		60,250	100,750	151,500
Total Current Assets	2,788,780	2,479,150	3,041,010		3,543,710	3,831,360	4,326,210
Fixed Assets	2,577,900	3,177,900	4,177,900		4,577,900	5,227,900	8,227,900
Depreciation	648,900	833,900	1,058,900		1,333,900	1,633,900	2,033,900
Fixed Assets - Net	1,929,000	2,344,000	3,119,000		3,244,000	3,594,000	6,194,000
Other Assets	70,500	80,250	57,450		57,450	117,800	158,450
Total Assets	$4,788,280	$4,903,400	$6,217,460		$6,845,160	$7,543,160	$10,678,660
LIABILITIES & CAPITAL							
Notes Payable - Banks	$ 150,000	$ 300,000	$ 100,000		$ 200,000	$ -	$ 300,000
Accounts Payable	857,800	982,800	1,030,450		1,132,950	1,432,950	1,714,450
Accrued Expenses	243,850	303,850	209,700		260,900	179,900	259,900
Current Maturities of Long-Term Debt	116,000	116,000	116,000		216,000	216,000	250,000
Total Current Liabilities	1,367,650	1,702,650	1,456,150		1,809,850	1,828,850	2,524,350
Long-Term Debt	464,000	348,000	1,232,000		816,000	600,000	1,850,000
Total Debt	1,831,650	2,050,650	2,688,150		2,625,850	2,428,850	4,374,350
Common Stock	500,000	500,000	500,000		500,000	500,000	500,000
Retained Earnings	2,456,630	2,352,750	3,029,310		3,719,310	4,614,310	5,804,310
Total Capital	2,956,630	2,852,750	3,529,310		4,219,310	5,114,310	6,304,310
Total Liabilities & Capital	$4,788,280	$4,903,400	$6,217,460		$6,845,160	$7,543,160	$10,678,660
				INDUSTRY AVERAGES			
Current Ratio	2.03:1	1.46:1	2.09:1	1.80:1	1.96:1	2.09:1	1.71:1
Quick Asset Ratio	.88:1	.63:1	.98:1	.95:1	.92:1	.94:1	.82:1
Debt Equity Ratio	63%	72%	76%	80%	62%	47%	69%
Inventory Turn	2.75	2.15	2.85	2.50	3.00	3.15	3.50

Figure 10.3   Balance sheet

The same factors that affected the current ratio apply to the quick asset ratio. (See current ratio for explanation.)

Debt-Equity Ratio

In the balance sheet in Figure 10.3, the company has continually improved upon the industry average because of its consistent performance. Even in the loss year of 19X2, the company maintained a better than industry average in this all-important ratio, which shows how much of the company the entrepreneur actually owns. The following comment is appropriate here:

> The company takes pride in maintaining its debt level within the benchmarks cited by the industry. It plans to continue this policy in order to sustain its excellent relationship with its banks and other creditors.

Inventory Turn Ratio

The inventory turn ratio relates to the average number of times inventory is sold throughout the course of a year. For example, if we have an average inventory of $25,000 and cost of sales on a yearly basis is $75,000, we can say that we turned the inventory 75,000 ÷ 25,000 or three times, using the formula

$$\frac{\text{Cost of Sales}}{\text{Average Inventory}}$$

On the balance sheet illustrated in Figure 10.3, the company projects a turn that is better than industry average as a result of terms negotiated with suppliers and of having tighter control over certain key raw materials. Although we mentioned this fact in our cash disbursements assumption, we refer to it again so the reader may better understand this ratio. However, other reasons that would account for improving on a company's inventory turn might be convenient distance from suppliers (thus using the supplier's warehouse as a storage facility), a heavy demand for the product, or just good management. Whatever the reasons, if inventory is an important component of your operation, you should disclose the ratio and comment upon it.

The company maintains an inventory turnover that has surpassed industry averages (2.5) in all prior years with the exception of 19X2, when its average inventory level was approximately $200,000 in excess of projections. This higher inventory level was caused by the recession, which reduced projected sales far below expectations.

The positive trend continued, however, in 19X3, as noted on the accompanying balance sheet, when the company achieved an inventory turn of 2.85.

With the advent of a computerized purchasing system and improved warehouse facilities, the company expects further improvement in its turnover to a rate of 3.5 by 19X6, which, when measured with industry averages, represents a reduced investment in inventory of approximately $1,000,000 over the next three years.

CAPITAL BUDGET

Because the capital budget elaborates on one line item in the cash statement (fixed asset expenditures), you need not include it in your business plan unless you intend to invest in fixed assets. However, if you are trying to raise cash to finance that investment (in machinery, equipment, a building, or whatever), then the capital budget becomes a vital part of the plan.

> Your potential lender/investor will want to know not only the total number of dollars to be expended in fixed assets, but what those assets are and over how long a period you expect to pay for them.

He or she will also want to see a computation on the **internal rate of return** in order to justify the expenditure. Also called the discounted rate of return or time-adjusted return, the internal rate of return is the yield of an investment and thus the maximum rate that a company or an individual should pay for funds in order to break even on the investment.

Because the warehouse project is the largest expenditure on our capital budget, we have selected that item on which to present an internal rate of return calculation. Such a calculation is predicated on a forecast, and the forecast should consider the potential earning power of the investment if it is a new venture or the saving in labor and overhead if the investment is intended to provide a more efficient way of performing an old procedure. When you complete the calculation, you should not only consider the projected return on the investment but also the effect of the investment on your business structure and whether the funds might be invested more profitably elsewhere. (See Chapter 6, "Capital Budget," and Appendix C.)

Although you should analyze previous capital expenditures in terms of their profitability, each capital asset is unique and is not comparable with a prior period. Therefore a trend analysis is irrelevant and thus the capital budget is the only one of your four statements not submitted in comparative format.

However, because your readers may wish to analyze each capital outlay separately, you should summarize each item from the detailed bids and quotations you have received for each projected expenditure. For example, on the capital budget shown in Figure 10.4, the amount budgeted for the computer is listed as one item but is actually a compilation of hardware, software, servicing, and so forth.

The capital budget in Figure 10.4 and the net present value calculation in Figure 10.5 illustrate the points we have been discussing. Table 10.1 lists the sources of the numbers in Figures 10.1, 10.2, 10.3, and 10.4. The following annotations are keyed to items in Figure 10.5.

(A) Projected Reduction of Warehouse Expenses It is estimated that the company will save approximately $.45 per garment over the projected useful life of the warehouse. This will include storage, handling, payroll and inventory taxes, easier access to product, increased shipping ability and hence increased inventory turnover.

(B) Depreciation 15 year straight line.

(C) Effective incremental tax rate is estimated to be 48%.

(D) Assumes present cost of money at 16% for short-term funds.

(E) Property is expected to increase in value at the rate of 10% per annum. At the end of the 15th year, it is expected that it may require $500,000 of renovations. The residual value has been discounted at 16%.

(F) Assumes cost of money at 14% for long-term funds. Total purchase price $3,000,000; 20% down payment; 15 year amortization schedule.

(G) Conclusions Purchasing the facility generates a Net Present Value (NPV) of more than twice the NPV of leasing the facility. *The rate of return or interest that is equal to the operating income that the investment will yield plus the increased value of the property at the end of 15 years plus returning the original cost of the investment is slightly more than 20%.* Thus if funds presently cost 16% the investment is worthy of consideration.

Project Description	Total Amount Authorized	Additions/ (Deletions) to Project	Project as Adjusted	$ Expended from Inception of Project	Estimated Amount Required Next Three Years		
					19X4	19X5	19X6
Computer Installation	$1,700,000	($300,000)[a]	$1,400,000	$1,000,000[b]	$400,000[b]		
Warehouse Improvements[c]	3,000,000		3,000,000			550,000	2,450,000
Office Furniture	100,000		100,000			100,000	
Salesmen's Vans & Showrooms[d]	450,000	100,000	550,000				550,000
					$400,000	$650,000	$3,000,000

a. Price drop in minicomputers.
b. Phase I & II of project completed in 19X3, final phase complete in 19X4.
c. Total project expected to be completed in two years.
d. Preliminary bid was $1,450,000. Price increase anticipates additional cost of $100,000.

Figure 10.4   Capital budget

Table 10.1   Sources for the Statement Numbers

Statement	Past Three Years, Actual			Next Three Years Projected		
	19X1	19X2	19X3	19X4	19X5	19X6
Statements of actual results						
Statement of profit or loss (Figure 10.1)				See Appendix B	See Appendix E	
Cash statement (Figure 10.2)				See Appendix D		
Balance sheet (Figure 10.3)						
Capital budget (Figure 10.4)				See Appendix C		
Source: Internally prepared statements or statements prepared by your CPA				Requires technical assistance; consult with your CPA or other professional personnel		
				Source: Bids and quotations from suppliers		

	PROJECTED STREAM OF CASH FLOW					DISCOUNTED CASH FLOW
	(1)	(2)	(3) = (1) − (2)	(4) = (3) × 48%	(5) = (1) − (4)	(6)
Year	Projected Reduction of Warehouse Expenses (A)	Depreciation (B)	Taxable Income (C)	Income Tax (C)	Net Cash Flow After Taxes	Present Value of Net Cash at 16% (D)
1	$178,900	200,000	(21,100)	(10,100)	189,000	162,918
2	446,200	200,000	246,200	118,200	328,000	243,704
3	504,900	200,000	304,900	146,400	358,500	229,798
4	474,600	200,000	274,600	131,800	342,800	189,225
5	442,900	200,000	242,900	116,600	326,300	155,318
6	420,750	200,000	220,750	106,000	314,750	129,047
7	420,750	200,000	220,750	106,000	314,750	111,421
8	420,750	200,000	220,750	106,000	314,750	95,998
9	420,750	200,000	220,750	106,000	314,750	82,779
10	420,750	200,000	220,750	106,000	314,750	71,448
11	420,750	200,000	220,750	106,000	314,750	61,376
12	420,750	200,000	220,750	106,000	314,750	52,878
13	420,750	200,000	220,750	106,000	314,750	45,639
14	420,750	200,000	220,750	106,000	314,750	39,343
15	420,750	200,000	220,750	106,000	314,750	33,993

Net present value of operational results $1,704,885   (E)

Residual value of warehouse   1,300,000

Total cash inflow   3,004,885

Less discounted value of stream of cash outflow on purchase and financing of warehouse project   2,033,837   (F)

Net present value of warehouse project $ 971,048   (G)

Figure 10.5   Net present value of proposed purchase of warehouse and warehouse improvements

SOL POSTYN

CERTIFIED PUBLIC ACCOUNTANT

December 30, 19XX

Mr. Robert Frost
President
Designs First Limited
1002 Frontera Street
San Francisco, California

Dear Robert:

I have prepared the accompanying financial projections concerning your Company for the year ending August 31, 19XX.

I believe the projections reflect assumptions about future events based on present circumstances and available information, but I am not expressing an opinion on whether those assumptions are either reasonable or comprehensive.

Projections are inherently subject to varying degrees of uncertainty and their achievability depends on the timing and probability of a complex series of future events, both internal and external. Accordingly, I am not expressing an opinion on the realization of the projections or on the probability that the actual results for any period may or may not approximate the projections.

Cordially yours,

Sol Postyn

SP:bcs

Figure 10.6   Accountant's statement

ACCOUNTANT'S STATEMENT

If you have had a CPA or accountant review the forecasts in the statements, he or she should provide you with an opinion report. The accountant's statement usually looks something like the one in Figure 10.6.

YOUR FINANCIAL REQUIREMENTS

We now come to the most crucial part of your business plan—stating your financial requirements. Though you've been gearing your reviewer for this point since the beginning of your plan, the segment should be brief, not more than one or two pages. It will be in prose, may be illustrated with financial charts if you wish, and should capsulize your financial needs, telling why you need the money, what you will use it for, and what amount and kinds of loans your company has outstanding.

Be specific about what you are requesting. If you need $500,000, $1 million, $2 million, or more, say so. Then state what kind of financing vehicle you are seeking. If it's a line of credit, then indicate it. If you need a loan for equipment financing, for a new building or inventory, or for accounts receivable financing, be definite. Perhaps you need the money for more than one purpose. If so, explain. Then follow this information with a description or plan of how and when you intend to repay the loan, if it's a loan, or when you plan to give a return on an investment, if it's an investment.

ACTION GUIDELINES

The financial section of your business plan should consist of the following components:

- Introduction
- Assumptions
- Profit or loss statement or operating budget
- Cash statement
- Balance sheet (with ratios derived from it)
- Capital budget
- A CPA's statement (when applicable)
- Your financial requirements
- Exhibits supplementing both the prose and the financial sections

PART FIVE

11

Negotiations

This chapter will

- Explain the process of negotiation
- Introduce the language to be used in negotiations with a lender/investor
- Prepare you for negotiations with a lender/investor

Armed with your completed business plan and a thorough knowledge of the controls of your business and aware of what you are after in the way of financing, you've come to the point where you'll put it all together to strike the best deal. In a good negotiation, however, *everyone* should come out ahead—you and your business, the lender and his or her organization, and the investor and his or her portfolio. Because this is probably not the only time your business will need financing, seek a continuing relationship. If either party feels cheated, the basis for an ongoing association will be weak.

MEETING BOTH PARTIES' NEEDS

The object of any negotiations should be an agreement in which both participants meet their respective needs. In this case, your need or goal is cash—either invested capital or a loan—and you want to accomplish your goal at the lowest possible expense to your business and to yourself. The other participant's goal is to make either a profitable investment or a secure loan that will bring a fair return. To guarantee attaining that goal, the lender/investor will want some assurance that you are running, or will run, a profitable business. The lender will also want some additional security in the event that there are not enough profits in the business to repay the loan plus interest. These are the basics of your negotiation.

DETERMINING NEED

There are also different degrees of need, a factor that plays a significant role in negotiations. If the entrepreneur is on the brink of bankruptcy, for example, and the only obstacle to the company's survival is an injection of cash, then his need is desperate. But if the entrepreneur is interested in refurbishing the facade of her building in order to enhance her company's image, she has a less urgent need.

Inevitably, the greater the urgency, the higher the price one must pay for cash. This is to be expected because when the need is desperate, the business is usually on shaky ground. When the entrepreneur approaches a negotiation in this vulnerable position, he or she is already at a disadvantage. Thus it's good business to have an entree to cash when you least need it.

LAYING THE GROUNDWORK

There are many sources of financing, and we discuss several in Chapters 12, 13, and 14. You should cultivate as many as possible and maintain those relationships that represent viable sources of funds. You never know when you might have to call on them. The benefits of this advice were demonstrated to us by a successful real estate investor.

One day when a really big deal came along, Byron Lowe realized he could not handle it alone or with any of the people he usually called upon. Timing was crucial, but the only source he knew that could provide the required financing was a large corporation. Fortunately, Byron had over the years developed and maintained a relationship with a financial executive of a large company, one that occasionally made some real estate investments. From time to time Byron and Henry Muller had lunch at Byron's club, where Henry loved the sweetbreads. While his friend feasted on this delicacy, Byron brought him up to date on his most recent successful deals and thereby gradually established his credibility. Thus when the big opportunity came along, all that was left to do was to (have lunch and) make a formal presentation of the idea. Henry was immediately interested, and shortly thereafter the two formed a partnership. This happy alliance had come about so easily and was so mutually advantageous that it barely qualified as a negotiation; yet in effect that's what it was.

This was an ideal situation in which the real estate investor had had years to lay the groundwork for the negotiation. When you're seeking financing, you may not have even a fraction of that time. However, you can still be well prepared for the meeting with your potential lender/investor.

FOCUSING ON MUTUAL REQUIREMENTS

First, before you even begin a negotiating session, decide how much money you need and how you want it—a loan, investment of capital, or whatever. You must also determine how much you are willing to pay in interest or in the dilution of your equity participation in your business. The more clearly you have these points defined, the greater your advantage in a negotiation.

Another aspect of your homework is to understand your balance sheet (both personal and business) and know where you stand creditwise in the community. Because a banker, or any other lender (or investor) will take a look at that position, it's to your benefit to preempt their review of such data. You can get a copy of your credit report from an agency such as Dun and Bradstreet. There are also local credit clearinghouses and most trade associations have a credit-clearing service for their particular industry. After you have reviewed your report, correct any errors before you begin negotiating.

A personal balance sheet is often requested; so we sometimes have a client include one in a formal presentation, although we prefer not to in the event that it is not required. But have one in your possession, just in case.

If your business is incorporated, you might also be asked to provide a personal guarantee, a demand most entrepreneurs dislike. But if you're not willing to risk your assets to promote your business (should it not have sufficient credit to stand on its own), you can hardly expect a lender/investor to risk assets to further your goals.

> The more secure your business is in its own right the greater your advantage in a negotiation. Your task in preparing for negotiations is to equip yourself with as many advantages as possible.

UNDERSTANDING THE LENDER/INVESTOR

The more you know about the person with whom you're negotiating, the better. If it's a banker, get a copy of the bank's annual reports and institutional advertising that pertains to their commercial lending policies. These materials will give you an idea of the type of loans the bank has outstanding. If it's an investor, try to learn what his or her previous transactions have been, successes as well as failures. (A colleague could be a source of such information. Or Dun and Bradstreet might provide a financial report that would be very informative.) Such data should provide you with considerable insight as to how these people proceed, although the assumptions you make about the lender will differ dramatically from the assumptions you make about the investor.

The lender will in most cases be concerned with the security of the investment; the investor, like you, may be more willing to take a risk.

> In either case, the extent of risk is a key factor in the negotiation. The greater the risk, the greater the interest rate, or the larger the amount of equity you will have to concede.

Consider the amount of interest you are prepared to pay or equity you are willing to give up. Try to put yourself in the other person's shoes and assess how good a deal your business actually is. You must be reasonable and flexible about your expectations.

Lenders concern themselves with how the loan is to be repaid. Generally, they like to receive payment from the profits of the business. When that isn't possible, they will look to a secondary source of collateral or security. Investors probably will not require a secondary source of collateral. Though they also are concerned with the security of the investment, if yours is a new, or fairly new, business and certain losses are to be expected, they may be satisfied with the possibility of a tax shelter, which the business could provide. Should this be the case, have your financial and legal advisers construct one to meet your investor's specifications.

There are endless possibilities that may enter into a negotiation with either investor or lender. When you're dealing with a banker, the granting of a loan may depend on transferring to the bank the business previously handled by your (computer) service bureau or depositing your company's pension fund in the bank's trust department. Anticipate as many of the alternatives as possible. Regardless of what comes up during the discussion, be guided by the following admonitions:

1. *Don't* miss the subtleties of the discussion.

2. *Don't* hesitate to ask questions.

3. *Don't* indulge in "wishful hearing" (being so anxious for the other party to say what you want to hear that you miss what is actually proposed).

DEALING WITH LENDERS' JARGON

Before entering into discussions with a potential lender or investor, it will help if you are familiar with the language that is bound to be an integral part of the negotiations. A typical loan agreement, for example, is laden with technical jargon that usually centers around five issues—amount, rate, terms, collateral, and covenants—none of which is quite what it appears to be.

Amount, Rate, and Terms

The amount, rate, and terms of a loan agreement interact with one another. The latter two have a direct impact on the amount one believes one is borrowing, and the amount and the terms affect the rate. You might think you're getting a $50,000 loan, but when negotiations have been completed, you may actually have available ony $45,000. To illustrate, let's take a look at a situation we encountered when a client was seeking a $50,000 loan during a tight money period.

The prevailing prime rate of bank interest at the time was 15 percent. However, this loan package was offered by a private lender who was restricted to a 10 percent interest rate by the California usury laws then in effect. As a result, the loan became available to our client at 10 percent *in addition* to fifteen points off the top, to be paid within a one-, two-, or three-year period at the discretion of the borrower.

Computed just like interest, points represent a surcharge or an amount due simply for consummating the loan. Thus, in our client's case, fifteen points off the top are the equivalent of $7,500, leaving her only $42,500 to work with on a $50,000 loan. If she needed the entire $50,000, she would have had to borrow $58,900, paying approximately $8,900 in points.

Now let's figure the cost of that same $50,000 loan, assuming our client accepted the lender's terms and paid the points over a one-year period. The interest computation would look like this:

$$10\% \times \$50,000 \times 1 = \$\ 5,000$$
$$\text{Add points of} \qquad\qquad \underline{\ \ 7,500}$$
$$\text{Total cost of loan} \qquad \$12,500$$

This represents an actual interest rate of 25 percent:

$$\frac{\$12,500}{50,000} = 25\%$$

If the borrower extended the payment of the points over a two-year period, the cost of the loan would be computed as follows:

$$10\% \times \$50,000 \times 2 = \$10,000$$
$$\text{Add points of} \qquad\qquad \underline{\ \ 7,500}$$
$$\text{Total cost of loan} \qquad \$17,500$$

This represents an actual annual interest rate of 17.5 percent:

$$\frac{\$17,500}{50,000} \div 2\,\text{years} = 17.5$$

Now let's see what would happen if the borrower amortized the points over three years:

$$10\% \times \$50,000 \times 3 = \$15,000$$
$$\text{Add points of} \qquad\qquad \underline{\ \ 7,500}$$
$$\text{Total cost of loan} \qquad \$22,500$$

This represents an interest rate of 15 percent:

$$\frac{\$22,500}{50,000} \div 3\,\text{years} = 15\%$$

Although you can lower the rate by amortizing the points over a two- or three-year period, you actually pay more because you're buying more time. Thus it behooves you to compute the true effective cost of money, just as you must decide the amount you really need to borrow.

The amount you borrow is subject to numerous variations and may be affected by factors other than the points you pay. For instance, you may want the loan in a lump sum, to be repaid over a short term or over a long term. Or a line of credit may be called for wherein you borrow in varying amounts up to a certain limit throughout the course of the agreement. If you have a $500,000 line of credit, you needn't borrow all the funds at once. You can borrow in increments—usually in thousand dollar round lots—until you reach the limit. Each of these individual loans is represented by a separate note indicating the rate agreed upon and the date it is due.

However, the agreed-upon line of credit usually does not specify a fixed rate for each of the individual loans. The best deal you can hope for in a bank line of credit (or on a regular loan) is the prevailing **prime rate,** that is, the rate the banks charge their most credit-worthy customers (which could vary with each separate loan). For others, bank loans may also be based on the prime rate, with an addition of one to five percentage points, depending on the borrower's credit rating and the degree of risk involved.

> *Know what the market is before you negotiate.* Even with the most enviable credit rating, you cannot expect to pay 10 percent interest if prime is at 12 percent.

Another factor that many banks use to increase their rate (and that also affects the actual amount of money available for use) is the **compensating balance**. Although many banks do not choose to include this requirement in a formal agreement, there is often an understanding, or oral agreement, that the borrower will maintain such a balance. When this happens, the compensating balance is stated as a percentage of the total loan package. For example, if you borrow $100,000 and agree to maintain 15 percent in compensating balances, you must have an average of $15,000 in the bank at all times, thereby reducing the amount of money you can actually use to $85,000. Like points, compensating balances must be computed into the cost of money.

If you borrow at a rate of 10 percent, with a compensating balance of 15 percent, the *true* effective cost would be as follows:

$$10\% \times \$100,000 = \$10,000$$

$$\frac{\$10,000}{85,000} = 11.8$$

Because you would be paying $10,000 for the use of $85,000, the cost of the loan is somewhat more than the stated rate.

Another aspect to keep in mind is that the *timing* of payments and prepayment of points or interest also affect the amount of money available for use, as well as the overall cost of the loan. A **prepayment penalty** may be imposed if you pay off the loan earlier than stipulated. The fact that the lender wants a fixed rate of interest over an agreed-upon length of time is the justification for this penalty. Therefore should you have any doubt about the length of time you need the funds, consider what such an agreement may do to the cost of your money. Conversely, some banks require an **annual cleanup,** which means the borrower with a line of credit must pay up all loans at least once a year. Sometimes this has to be accomplished artificially by "borrowing from Peter to pay Paul."

Although truth in lending laws require that commercial lenders stipulate the exact interest rate they are charging, there are ways around such stipulations as you have just seen. Thus when you're a borrower, beware!

Don't sign an agreement before you confirm the rate and the amount of money available for use. Be sure you fully understand the basic terms of the agreement, your timing commitments, and the penalties to be imposed in the event of default.

Collateral

Collateral is the heart of the **security** or **pledge agreement** between lender and borrower, through which the borrower guarantees certain assets in the event of a default on the loan. Such collateral might be accounts receivable, inventory, equipment, or often one's house. The more **liquid** the **asset,** the more amenable the lender will be. However, it is only as a last resort that the average lender will accept any of these rather than the payment of the loan. Then, too, in lieu of collateral, lenders will often accept a **guarantee** provided by a relative, business associate, or friend who has a strong financial statement.

Almost all loans are protected by some kind of assets or guarantee, thereby qualifying them as secured or collaterized loans. Only entrepreneurs with the highest credit rating are eligible for a **character loan** and do not have to provide security, although they may have to purchase executive life insurance, which protects the loan in the event of the untimely death of the principal borrower by making the lender the beneficiary, or loss payee. The latter is a common demand among lenders, and with SBA loans it is mandatory. Once again, the purchase of life insurance will add to the cost of the loan; so this could be an important factor in determining whether you find the offered agreement acceptable.

Covenants

The final segment of the loan package is comprised of the **covenants** of the basic agreement, in which you consent to certain conditions and stipulations. If you do not meet these agreements, you may be in default.

Covenants vary, depending on the business and on its particular characteristics. A lender might, for example, demand that the business maintain certain ratios (usually affecting working capital and debt equity) throughout the life of the loan. Should this happen, the ratios you present with your projected balance sheet in your business plan had better be realistic because the lender will hold you to them. Moreover, you should understand the lender's exact ratio requirements and know how they are computed. In the computation of the debt-equity ratio, for example, **subordinated debt** may be considered either debt or equity (a subordinated debt is typically an officer's or shareholder's loan to the company). But it is to your advantage that the lender classify it as equity. This will probably be the case because, by definition, such debt is due and payable *after* the principal loan (under negotiation) is paid.

Your company's financial reporting procedures may also become an integral part of covenants. In agreeing to stipulations in this area, beware of the basic cost of a certified audit or other CPA-prepared report (see Chapter 3, "Audited Statements" and "Unaudited Statements") before they are incorporated into a loan agreement. Have a clear understanding of what your company's needs are as well as those of your lender or investor. In your negotiations make sure that the statements prepared will serve both your needs. For example, should you agree to furnish an audited statement simply because the bank requests it if you don't really need it to run your business? Such an arrangement can cost thousands of dollars annually and could lock you into a commitment indefinitely.

At times a lender may also insist on certain restrictions of officers' salaries or on permission for officers to borrow from the company. Be alert to such requirements, and if they are advanced during negotiations, be sure you can live with the agreement.

Loan Packages

There are almost as many different conditions for a loan as there are people, and for each demand there are alternatives.

> When you sit down at a negotiating table, make sure you understand what is being proposed and don't agree to anything you don't fully comprehend.

This same counsel may be given whether you are negotiating for a loan or for an investment, although the language used in connection with an investment differs considerably from that of a loan. The lender and the investor, after all, do have different goals.

DEALING WITH TERMS USED IN PARTNERSHIPS, JOINT VENTURES, AND CORPORATIONS

The lender expects to be repaid the full amount of the loan, plus interest; but the investor is putting up money for an indefinite time, and repayment may come only when someone wishes to buy that investment, or share, in the business. As we shall discuss further in Chapter 14, equity interest in a company may be obtained through investment in a corporation, a joint venture, or through a limited or general partnership.

Partnerships and Joint Ventures

Whether one is seeking investment in a business via a partnership or through a joint venture, the jargon is basically the same, with the agreement between parties covering five basic areas: amount; term; the parties; allocation of profit and loss; and transfer, assignment, and dissolution.

Amount The amount to be invested in a partnership is determined by the needs of the business and by the degrees of risk involved in the venture.

Term Although the term, or length of time, of the arrangement may be either indefinite or fixed, depending on the agreement of the parties, keep in mind that term has a direct bearing on the **liquidity** of the venture, (whether a party can convert the investment back into cash if and when he or she wishes). An investor who wants to liquidate may be prevented from doing so by the term of the agreement and thus suffer a loss because of early liquidation. Conversely, if the term (length of time) of the agreement is not fixed, the business could be thrown into a financial bind should a partner or investor withdraw his or her capital at an inopportune time.

The Parties Regardless of the structure of the business—partnership, joint venture, or corporation—the parties involved in the agreement are the participants in the negotiation (that is, the entrepreneur and the investors, or the co-owners or co-partners). Each party's duties, responsibilities, and benefits should be outlined in the agreement.

Allocation of Profits and Losses   The allocation of profits and losses among partners (or members of a joint venture) is usually arranged to provide maximum tax benefits to those in the higher tax brackets, which in the case of limited partners may be the reason they became involved in the first place.

As a further incentive, cash distributions may also be tailored to the needs of the (limited) partner; a company can generate tax losses while actually accumulating cash reserves. (This might occur, for example, when depreciation on a building exceeds the income of the business housed by that building.) The cash distribution can then be provided in the partnership agreement in order to give additional liquidity incentives to the investor. On the other hand, some agreements require compulsory contributions to the company if additional cash is needed, an arrangement that reduces the appeal for many investors unless the entrepreneurs have a proven track record.

Transfer, Assignment, and Dissolution   The conditions for **transfer** and **assignment** refer to the liquidity of an investment and determine whether an interest in the business may be transferred or assigned (given) to a third party. The easier it is to make such a transfer or assignment, the more liquid the partnership or venture. However, if members of a partnership or joint venture transfer their interest and the new party is not compatible with the others, it can cause problems.

> Although parties entering into negotiation will not like to contemplate **dissolution,** it is best to make arrangements for the termination of an alliance at its onset, when the principals are in the "honeymoon" stage, rather than wait for the possibility of a disagreement.

This part of the agreement might cover a variety of conditions, including asset distribution and parties' future responsibilities. Consider as many eventualities as possible. They will depend on the nature of your business and your specific partnership or joint venture arrangement because the structure of either arrangement may be tailored to fit the needs of those involved.

Corporations

Though it may surprise you, there is also opportunity for flexibility in agreements with corporations, thereby allowing room for negotiation with each individual stockholder. We refer now to the private or closely held corporation, *not* to the publicly held company with stock certificates sold over the counter or through a stock exchange.

Some of the terminology to be aware of, should you decide on attracting investors through the corporate structure, are the two classes of **stock—common** and **preferred**. Holders of common stock have a right to vote but no rights to receive dividends unless the directors deem that they be issued. Holders of preferred stock are usually given priority over holders of common stock in regard to dividends and in the distribution of assets upon dissolution of the business.

Both common and preferred stock certificates may also have **convertible features,** that is, the right of stockholders to transfer their stock from common to preferred, or vice versa, or into a loan, thereby earning interest for the note holder. Similarly, the convertible feature may be applied to a loan wherein the note holder can convert his or her loan to stock.

At the option of either the corporation or the stockholder, some stock or debt instruments (a note for a loan) may also have redemption features allowing the holder to return the stock or note to the corporation in exchange for cash.

Not only are there different classes of stock with myriad features, but there are variances in tax treatment of the two corporate forms—the **regular corporation** and the **Subchapter S corporation**. In the latter, shareholders elect to have the corporation assume the tax status of either a proprietorship or a partnership, thereby providing tax advantages to the shareholders not otherwise available to them in a regular corporation. A word of caution, though. Because the options involved become very technical and there are specific criteria to observe (as well as pitfalls to avoid) in going the route of the Subchapter S corporation, we recommend seeking professional help should your search for investors lead you in this direction.

Confronted with numerous combinations of classes of stock and accompanying features, with or without debt (loan) instruments, you and your adviser will have to ferret out the package that will be most attractive to your investors.

PRELIMINARY AND CLOSING WORK

Presumably, defining your needs, learning as much as you can about the other participant, and having a feel for the language to be used will give you the confidence you need to enter into negotiations. But successful strategy also requires a formulation of the approach to take.

Who, for example, will conduct the negotiations? Will it be you, an agent (someone other than yourself), or both? If an agent, it could be your financial adviser, CPA, attorney, or a member of your staff. You may decide to use this person to get a feel for the arena so that you avoid becoming involved in an awkward situation. The agent might do the exploratory work. You could enter the scene after the initial screening and preliminary negotiations are completed.

You must also establish where the meeting will take place. If it's to be at your headquarters, will there be a tour of the plant? If so, will the meeting be held before or after the tour? Make sure that the lender/investor is aware of the agenda and that you have determined how long the negotiations will require. If you are to be host, you may want to arrange for lunch on the premises or in a restaurant. Be sure this invitation is extended. Graciousness only reinforces good negotiations, and comfort is also important because ambience affects mood. Make certain that adequate supplies, beverages, and telephone services are on hand. Attention to such details also gives the lender/investor an idea of how thorough your organization really is.

If your meeting is at the bank and you require such equipment as a projector and screen or a conference room, inquire beforehand to make certain they can be provided.

Although you begin the relationship with a positive and flexible approach, there is always the chance that things will not work out. Thus it is wise to provide yourself with enough lead time to activate an alternate plan should the first not succeed. With this in mind, you have a right to expect a response to your financing request within a reasonable period. Discuss the matter during negotiations and don't hesitate to call if you haven't heard within the time agreed upon. If it seems appropriate, get an informal reaction to your request before you end your meeting.

Finally, when you consummate the deal, make sure it is in writing, covering all the terms of your agreement. Never depend on memory or on an oral agreement. What happens if a bank officer or other lender or investor dies, is transferred, resigns, or leaves the country? Once you understand the deal, codify it. After all, you and the lender/investor are going to have to live with one another for some time. Make certain that you both understand the terms—that you make a good marriage.

ACTION GUIDELINES

Before meeting with the other participant be sure you can answer yes to the following questions:

- Have I reviewed my credit rating and personal balance sheet, as well as that of my business?

- Have I learned as much as possible about the lender/investor?

- Have I determined what I am willing to pay in interest or concede in equity?

- Have I decided on the collateral I am equipped to provide?

- Do I understand the jargon to be used in negotiations?

Prior to signing an agreement with a lender, be sure to confirm the following:

- Amount of cash you will have available for use

- True rate of interest you will pay

- Terms of the agreement

- Collateral to be accepted

- Fine points of the covenants

Never consummate an arrangement with an investor before verifying the following:

- Amount to be invested

- Equity to be conceded

- Length of the agreement

- Division of profits and losses

- Fine points of transfer, assignment, and dissolution of your agreement

If you have chosen the corporate structure, you and your investors will have to make decisions on the following:

- Common stock certificates

- Preferred stock certificates

- Debt instrument possibilities

- Convertible features

- Redemption features

- Tax implications of a regular corporation versus a Subchapter S corporation

12

Getting Cash from the Banks

This chapter will

- Tell you how to find the right bank for your company

- Describe a bank's major concerns with loan customers

- Explain the mechanics of processing a bank loan

Most people approach a bank as if they were entering a house of worship. Perhaps it's the high ceilings, plush carpets, or the expanse of marble and granite that inhibit the outsider. Certainly one factor is that the bank, representing not only money but security and power, is viewed as both a custodian (of funds) and a pillar of the commercial community. Thus by the very nature of their job, bankers command a position that sets them apart from every potential borrower. It's an attitude that puts the customers on guard, and therefore at a disadvantage before they even begin a relationship. We hope this chapter will put the situation in perspective, because if you've decided a loan is the type of financing you want, a bank is going to be an obvious consideration as a source of funds. There are others, of course, and we'll discuss them in Chapters 13 and 14; but let's start with the banks.

CHOOSING THE RIGHT BANK

Banks probably lend more money than any other institution, and they can come up with just about any type of loan you can think of—**secured, unsecured,** commercial, consumer, **long-term, short-term,** or a **bridge**

(interim) loan or a line of credit. As far as time is concerned, however, banks tend to make more short-term loans because they, in turn, borrow more short-term funds.

So be imaginative. You might consider a combination of methods to reach your financing goal, including a bank loan, equipment leasing, factoring, or private investment, sources we'll discuss in Chapter 14.

There are also many sizes of banks. If you want success sooner than later in your attempts to raise cash, it's important that you approach a bank that will be interested in the size loan you're seeking. For example, if you're a small to medium-sized entrepreneur, you'd fare best with a small to medium-sized bank. As your business flourishes, should you find you've outgrown the bank with which you're dealing, your contact there might suggest another bank to meet your cash requirements while you retain your relationship with the smaller bank. You or your first banker can initiate this arrangement. The point is that your concerns will change as your business grows. While your business is small, you may question whether the size loan you seek represents enough of a challenge for a particular bank. When your company is larger, you may wonder whether the financing you want represents too much of a risk for the bank with which you do business. If you are able to determine this information, you will also have some idea of where your company stands in the bank's scale of customers.

Some banks can handle a wide range of customers. Just as one of your concerns is to diversify your products for the good of your company, these banks are interested in diversifying their portfolio. They wouldn't want all their customers to be the same size any more than they would want them all in the same industry.

But you also have to recognize that lending officers and lending institutions have certain predispositions and prejudices—many of which are based on their experiences. Keep this in mind and seek out those sympathetic to your kind of company and financing requirements.

You might start off by contacting the loan officer of the bank you're considering and telling him or her that before applying for a loan you would like to know what kind of business arrangement you might expect with his or her bank. While researching this subject, we polled some of our banking contacts on the matter and compiled the following questions, which should be helpful in this respect.

1.   For starters you might ask the loan officer what his or her attitude is toward new loans. Is it attempting to seek loan business or to discourage it?

2.   What size loan does the bank prefer to make?

3.   Does it concentrate on businesses within a certain size range? If so, is it the small, medium-sized, or large business? (Be sure to compare your definitions regarding size.)

4.   What auxiliary services does the bank offer (inventory, accounts receivable, or accounts payable service)? If it does offer such services, is a loan customer obliged to use them? (See Chapter 11.) Frequently there are hidden costs in addition to the fee for such services, as when a bank is getting use of accounts payable funds you could be using yourself. (See Chapter 11.)

5.   Can the banker give a customer as a reference? (In some states this would be prohibited by law.)

6.   How receptive are the bank's senior people to customers like you?

7.   Because continuity with personnel is an important consideration in any banking relationship, you might inquire about maintaining this continuity in the absence of your initial contact.

8.   What is the chain of progression for a loan application? In other words, how does it go through the bank? (With this information you can determine how far you are from the decision makers and how many times your story will have to be retold.)

9.   What is the bank's average turnaround time in granting a loan?

In addition, you may ask the loan officer any other questions you might have pertaining to availability of funds and personnel as well as servicing your needs. Pursuing such a line of questioning will give you two advantages with a potential banker. First, it will help you determine whether you want to approach that bank for a loan. Second, it will give you some insight on the most successful approach to use when you finally make your pitch for cash.

Any bank you petition for a loan is going to scrutinize you and your business most carefully before parting with its funds. Keep in mind that you are offering the bank business and that if they make the loan, you will be paying back the loan, plus interest. It's a mutually beneficial association. Thus you are well within your rights to do some scrutinizing, too.

WORKING WITH A BANK

In your search for the right bank, you may come in contact with a loan officer, branch manager, or other executive with whom you would like to associate. In fact, you might even base your choice of bank on your acquaintance with this person. This reason for selection would certainly be valid. Sometimes the fate of your loan hinges on your finding an effective and compatible person with whom to work.

The first person you contact will vary according to the bank. If you're the entrepreneur of a small business, you will typically deal with a branch manager. If you're a larger company, your first contact may be with the regional headquarters of a bank or the regional manager. In other situations, it may be the loan officer. In any case, your backgrounds are distinct opposites. Bankers are usually cautious, conservative keepers of other people's money. The large organizations for which they work represent security to the employee as well as to the depositor. And once they gain some responsibility, bankers could lose their jobs by making one big mistake. Thus they are very careful not to make any mistakes at all.

You, on the other hand, are willing to risk all for the success and growth of your business. Accountable for both your company's successes and failures, you are accustomed to making decisions quickly. If a mistake results from those decisions, so be it; you learn from such experiences and benefit by them. But, understandably, a bank must have a different attitude toward its personnel. Awareness of their situation may help you in your relationships with bankers.

The most frustrating part of your experience, the first time around at least, will be in attempting to establish some continuity with banking personnel so you don't have to repeat your story. Find the path to the decision maker as soon as possible, and make an appointment with him or her. Possibly you have a friend, CPA, attorney, or member of the bank's board of directors who may approach a bank on your behalf to find out who this person is. However, knowing a member of the bank's board can be a double-edged sword. Your friend on the board could facilitate the introductory process, but the person with whom you're put in touch is going to be extra careful in processing your loan. If your loan application fails to meet approval, he or she is going to lose face. If the loan is approved but handled inefficiently, he or she is going to lose face. Therefore you have a few elements to weigh if you are considering that route.

One way to maintain continuity is to be certain your file is properly documented when you first assemble your material (present your business plan). Then make sure it is kept current by providing updated information as needed. Whoever becomes your contact at the bank will in most cases not be the person who approves or refuses your loan, but he or she is the person who will probably make the presentation to the loan committee on your behalf.

UNDERSTANDING THE LOAN COMMITTEE

The function of the loan committee differs slightly from bank to bank. It usually acts on every loan somewhere along the line, but it could be before or after the loan is granted, according to the particular bank and its policies, the trust the loan committee places with the loan officer, or any combination of these elements. The committee's primary function is to control the diversity and quality of the loan portfolio. After determining that selection, at many banks, it submits all loan applications to the bank's board of directors, indicating its approval or disapproval on each one, in order to get the board's action. Regardless of loan size, most banks have on record some indication that the loan committee has reviewed and acted upon each presentation.

After a loan is granted, it is periodically reviewed and graded by an officer or committee. When a loan is rated as a high risk, no matter how much authority a loan officer might have, he or she cannot act independently but will have to get committee approval in order to alter any terms of the agreement. (See Chapter 11 for more on this subject.)

Considering how little control you have over decisions once you have made your "pitch" with your contact at the bank, you will want to make sure before you make your presentation that you have covered as many bases as possible.

In Chapter 1, we referred to important considerations in establishing your credibility with a potential lender/investor. In other chapters we pointed out other areas in which you must demonstrate control if you are to prove your ability as a competent boss of the business. Now we'll reinforce that concept with some of the responses we heard while polling a number of bankers for the information in this chapter.

The Bank's Key Concerns

According to our survey, the following information will command the bankers' attention:

1. Your *character, integrity,* and *overall management skills.*

2. Your company's *track record,* that is, its sales and profits. The bank will want to know exactly *how profitable your business is.*

3. Your *product and its relative importance to the market.* What kind of future does it have?

4. *Your financial statements.* These should be in excellent order because they demonstrate your control over your business. To enhance your credibility, they should be accompanied by a CPA's statement. (See Chapter 10.) The better the presentation, the less work there is for the bank, a factor that often means a lot.

5. A description of the *purpose of the loan* so the banker can determine whether your request is valid. For example, you may need money for inventory, equipment, or acquisition of a new building or another business.

6. Your company's ability to *provide data to the bank both accurately and in a timely fashion.* In order to do that, you *must* have control over your business. Moreover, bankers *hate* surprises. In most instances, you will be aware of a problem before your banker picks up on it; so your credibility will fare much better if you bring it out in the open. Be candid about the problem and even ask for assistance in solving it. The banker may be able to help if called upon early enough.

7. The *primary and alternative source of repayment.* Because the bank looks to your business as the primary source of repayment, it has to feel confident the business will succeed and be able to meet its commitments. However, if it should not, there must be a secondary source of payment, such as a redemption of hard assets for cash (the assignment of an accounts receivable to the bank, for example, in which case your customer will pay the bank instead of paying your company, or the sale of one of your buildings, which the bank would take over).

Signs of a Risky Loan

When we asked the bankers what they considered a risky or "bad" loan, they listed the following:

1. *Accounts receivable past due.* This situation indicates that cash is coming in too slowly and that a company is out of control. But it may also be a symptom of a situation that requires action other than financing. (See Chapter 7.)

2. *Accounts payable stretched way out.* In other words, a company is paying its bills or meeting its obligations too slowly. This usually means the company is not in as good shape as it should be.

3. *Poor inventory operation.* An evaluation of the company's inventory reveals there are back orders, work in process, and finished goods that are out of the normal sequence for a healthy inventory turnover.

4. *Deterioration of debt-equity ratio.* A company that is already top-heavy with debt is going to be hard put to get a loan that will only add more debt.

5. *Withdrawal of large profits* by the company's officers. If the principals of the company don't care enough to invest in its equity, why should an outsider contribute to its finances?

6. An *attempt to borrow short-term funds when long-term funds are* actually *needed,* or *attempting to borrow long-term funds when the company* really *needs* to increase *equity.*

7. *Insufficient financial data.* This makes it impossible for a potential lender, and even for the boss of the business, to know the company's true status.

8. *Poor credit rating* for principal company officer(s). The bank assumes that if you haven't been honoring your personal commitments on time, you're not likely to do any better with those of your company. But, once again, extenuating circumstances can be considered.

9. *Personal problems with executives.* Such problems as divorce, serious illness, or death indicate company leadership is shaky and will cause a bank to hesitate, delay, and require reassurance before granting a loan.

At this point you may be ready to throw in the towel, concluding that getting a bank loan requires more effort than it's worth. But if you think about it, you'll agree a bank or any other potential lender has good reason to hesitate if any one of the listed conditions is present. If any of these situations exist, the lender would have to take more of a risk than is reasonable. And why should he or she? Would you—unless, possibly, the borrower is a good friend or a family member?

Now that you know just what the bank considers red flags on a potential loan, you can do something about them. Poor inventory control, long overdue accounts receivable, or a top-heavy debt-equity ratio aren't good for the health of a company under any circumstances; so even if you aren't seeking financing, they shouldn't exist.

> Recognize your problems and start to get your house in order. Then go after your loan.

DEALING WITH MORE THAN ONE BANK
Approaching Banks

In most cases you can approach more than one bank at a time.

> If you've had foresight in anticipating the need for a loan, you should have more than one bank lined up as a potential resource. But don't approach two banks of the same size simultaneously, and certainly don't approach five or six banks at once.

Sensible competition is an accepted procedure, as long as it's not overdone. Usually if someone has been approaching you for your company's banking business, give her or him a shot at the loan. You can also approach any other bank you might select. But in every city—from New York to San Francisco—the banking community is small. Therefore rather than have a bank find out by accident what you're doing, be open and above board. Let the banks know you're shopping around, particularly if this is a first-time loan. Should you not do so, any of the credit clearinghouses are apt to "drop" the news, and that could be embarrassing. But if you already have a relationship with a bank and are sending out feelers with the thought of making a substitution, better to do so discreetly rather than come right out and tell the bank with whom you're associated that you're looking for a better deal.

Participation and Split Borrowing

Earlier in this chapter we mentioned **participation** when referring to a situation in which you have a relationship with one bank for a loan or a line of credit but your company has grown and you want to extend that credit. Your bank may not be able to do so without bringing in another bank as a participant. This type of arrangement is common, with one bank running the show and coordinating it with the approval of all involved. It usually works smoothly.

In **split borrowing,** a business might borrow money from one bank and, without the first bank's knowledge, get another loan from a second bank. This creates a risky and undesirable situation. No one knows what the other parties are doing, and the company's financing program cannot be smoothly coordinated. If your business should encounter financial difficulties, each bank, unaware of your other commitments, may **call its loan,** creating too heavy a load for your business to carry. At that point, forced disclosures of what you have done could be not only embarrassing but fatal to your business.

WAITING FOR THE REPLY

In most cases, two weeks is a reasonable length of time in which to expect an answer to your loan request. However, even before that much time elapses, don't hesitate to call your contact at the bank. Inquire whether everything is in order or whether you might provide the bank with additional information. In this way you may get a feel for what the answer is likely to be.

Chances are you're going to get that loan. But if you don't, try to determine why it was denied. It may have nothing to do with you or your business; it may be the result of a change of policy at the bank. Assuming your presentation is in good shape, approach another bank or one of the other sources of financing we list in the next two chapters.

ACTION GUIDELINES

Ask the following questions to help select the best bank for your company:

- Why am I interested in this particular bank(s)?

- Do I have a compatible contact(s) at any of the banks I'm considering?

- Do I have a friend, business associate, or CPA who can make an introduction?

- Where would I fall in the bank's line of customers?

- Is the bank(s) amenable to my company's business?

- Does my company offer enough business to warrant the banks' continuing attentive service?

You will help assure your company of a bank loan if you can answer yes to the following questions:

- Have I attempted to contact the person(s) who makes the final decisions on loan applications?

- Have I carefully responded to all bank inquiries?

- Have I provided adequate and timely information about the organization, management, product, and financial condition of my company?

- Am I certain my company has satisfied a bank's typical concerns?

- Am I sure my company has a good risk rating?

- Have I covered all bases by approaching more than one bank?

13

Getting Cash from Uncle Sam

This chapter will

- Describe loans available through the Small Business Administration

- Explain the criteria on which the SBA grants loans

- Discuss the mechanics of working with the SBA

- Describe financing opportunities available through SBICs

- List the advantages and disadvantages of SBIC financing

- Provide other sources of government financing

When you contemplate raising cash, the federal government may not come readily to mind as a source. But Uncle Sam could well be your answer— if you've struck out with other sources of financing and if your business meets the established criteria. Recognizing that our capitalistic system is based on the entrepreneur, the government has devised two ways to give financial assistance to certain businesses: the Small Business Administration (SBA) and small business investment companies (SBICs) which, though privately owned and operated, are licensed by the SBA. Both are often overlooked by the veteran business person as well as the novice.

SMALL BUSINESS ADMINISTRATION

The SBA was established to assist smaller firms in getting started or to enable them to expand, grow, and prosper. Unfortunately, its name can be misleading; its funds are not necessarily restricted to the "small business." For CPAs, bankers, and everyone else working with entrepreneurs, defining the term has been a challenge, but the SBA has its own definition. What the SBA considers a small business many would view as medium sized.

What Is Small?

According to the SBA, a small business is independently owned and operated, not dominant in its field, and meets the following employment or sales standards:

1. A *retailing and service business* is small if annual sales or receipts are between $2 million and $8.5 million, depending on the industry. In some instances the SBA applies other criteria to this category; so to determine whether your business qualifies, check with your nearest SBA field office (listed in Appendix F).

2. A *manufacturing business* is small if average employment in the preceding four calendar quarters did not exceed two hundred fifty, including employees in any affiliate.

3. A *wholesaling business* is considered small when yearly sales range from $9.5 million to $22 million, again depending on the industry.

4. A *construction business* is considered small when annual sales do not exceed $9.5 million averaged over a three-year period.

If you have some question as to whether your firm fits these size specifications, contact your nearest SBA field office.

Approaching the SBA

Once you've determined that your business is the right size, the route to the SBA is through the banks. This fact holds true for both lending instruments traditionally used by the SBA—the **guaranteed loan** and the **direct loan.**

Because it is a public agency using taxpayers' funds, the SBA will refuse financing if you can obtain funds from a bank or private resource at reasonable terms. In view of this regulation, you must first apply for a loan from a local bank or other lending institution. If the bank turns you down, you may ask that it consider granting the loan with an SBA guarantee, in which case the bank, not you, requests SBA participation. The bank, acting as an agent or intermediary for the SBA, usually processes the loan and presents it to the agency. The SBA then acts as guarantor to the bank, guaranteeing 90 percent of the loan up to a maximum of $500,000 if the borrower can meet two out of its ten specified objectives or up to a maximum of $350,000 if these objectives cannot be met. The bank is liable for the other 10 percent of the loan, a minimal risk and one it is willing to take for a business it believes may have a better than average chance of succeeding. The SBA objectives are the following:

1. Construction of medical facilities, the need for which has been certified by the appropriate local authority

2. Conservation or production of energy

3. Creation or preservation of jobs

4. Performance of a specific government contract

5. Stimulation of the economy in areas of unemployment

6. Conservation of natural resources

7. Improvement of mass transit facilities

8. Economic development in depressed urban or rural areas

9. Assistance to broadcasting and cable TV operations

10. Revitalization of SBA-designated neighborhood business areas

Because the guaranteed loan allows the SBA to make maximum use out of limited funds, approximately 90 percent of the agency's financing is made available in this way. But should the bank refuse to grant a loan under any conditions—even with an SBA guarantee—you have the alternative of applying for an SBA direct loan (the amount of funds available through this means is contingent on current economic conditions and administration policies). In this case you would accompany your application with a business plan and letter(s) of declination (for the loan) from the required one or two banks, whichever applies in your area.

> If your business is in or on the fringe of a city of more than two hundred thousand people, you must approach and be refused by two banks before applying for a direct SBA loan.

One of these letters must be provided by your principal bank (the bank in which you have your company's checking account). There is less money (and sometimes none at all) available for direct loans; so the usual maximum is $150,000, a figure that changes from time to time depending on availability of funds.

But when they are available, direct loans usually involve a lower interest rate than guaranteed loans. Just as with any other lending arrangement, however, you must demonstrate your credibility or your ability to run a profitable business.

Advantages for Special Groups

Because of its responsibility to the general public, the SBA has as many requirements as it has restrictions, and for all of its nineteen lending programs there are explicit criteria with which a company must comply if it hopes to qualify for SBA assistance. One of its basic regulations, for example, is that any recipient of SBA funds agrees to prohibit discrimination based on race, color, religion, national origin, sex, or age in either employment of or service to the public.

The agency gives special consideration to loan applications from persons within certain categories, including veterans, the handicapped, and the economically or socially disadvantaged. In recent years the agency has made special efforts to assist minority groups, offering economic opportunity loans (EOLs) geared especially to blacks, Hispanics, Native Americans, and Orientals. Theoretically, the SBA does not assign women to the category of a minority. However, women are offered some relaxed credit requirements, and within some SBA branches there are specific considerations for women, particularly regarding debt-equity ratios, experience, education, and credit ratings.

If you fall into any of these groups, keep the SBA high on your list of financing sources.

There are other advantages, too, for minorities, as illustrated by the experience of a client we helped in establishing a new business. The San Francisco Wrecking Company is comprised of two partners, both of whom are members of minorities. One is black, the other, Oriental. Because they were starting their own company, they had no accounting system; so the first item on their agenda was to establish a series of control reports and functions, the preparation of which could be handled for the most part at minimum cost by their original skeleton crew. The next step was to establish goals to determine the amount to be borrowed. Then, rather than have this partnership lay out more of its meager capital for professional fees, we contacted a nonprofit organization and asked its personnel to help assemble the appropriate data. This was accomplished on a nonfee basis, and although the assisting agency could not have provided the staff to create an accounting system, it did have personnel familiar with follow-up procedures. Interviewing the clients, working with them in organizing the data, and coordinating the entire project was completed in four months. Not bad, considering it was a new company, and its efforts to raise cash culminated in a successful SBA loan.

Throughout the country, there are many such nonprofit organizations funded by the federal government to assist minority entrepreneurs in seeking financing and controlling their businesses. Banks are always happy to give referrals to them. Their assistance is usually restricted to minority groups; so if you fit the description, make use of it. A word of caution, though. Because the professional personnel who service these clients donate their time, their tours of duty are limited and turnover is high. Therefore continuity may be a problem and the lack of it could extend the time required to complete your project.

Drawbacks to Working with the SBA

Unfortunately, processing doesn't always advance as quickly or as smoothly as it did in the case of the San Francisco Wrecking Company. Scientific Distributing Company, another client, had a problem when the bank guiding management through an SBA-guaranteed loan took so long that the company was forced to go to another bank. Oddly enough, the other bank put together a loan package that didn't require an SBA guarantee; so the time expended in negotiating the final deal was minimal.

Assuming that your data is complete and effectively prepared, the speed with which your loan is processed depends on the personnel at the SBA and at the bank with which you are working.

Remember, you're the customer; and when you get your loan, you're the one who pays for it—regardless of who may guarantee it. So don't accept second-rate service from either the banks or the SBA.

Most of the people you'll be dealing with are professionals, but they do have an enormous volume of data to follow and any company can get lost in the shuffle. There are a lot of forms to contend with when you're working with a government agency. And, red tape being what it is, it *can* take a long time to get an SBA loan processed. In spite of these drawbacks, it may still be worth your while to go this route.

Keeping Faith with the SBA

You'll have to stay on top of the situation and follow through on the progress of your loan, keeping your contacts aware that you're still alive and very much interested in completing negotiations. And just as with a bank or any other creditor, it's essential that you maintain good communication with the SBA. You *must* keep your SBA contact informed of any moves or changes in your company. This was very sharply impressed upon us when one of our clients failed to do so and nearly went under because of it.

With some initial difficulty, we had helped this company obtain an SBA-guaranteed loan. Sometime later the principals were having problems maintaining their agreed-upon payments to the bank. Although the company's future began to brighten several months after problems set in, the bank opted to cash in on its guarantee, not because the bankers no longer had any faith in the company but because bank policies had changed and its representatives felt they would be better off with 90 percent of their money at once than with 100 percent of it later.

Our client was unaware of the reason for the bank's decision. When the bank turned the administration of the loan back to the SBA, our client failed to communicate with the SBA regarding his company's status. When he felt that the SBA and all the authority it represented was breathing down his neck, his way of coping was to ignore the situation. Not understanding the company's paranoia and concerned by its lack of payments, the SBA called the loan, or asked for payment in entirety. Not having any portion of his payment, let alone the entire principal, our client felt his company was doomed. It was at this point that we learned of the situation and persuaded him to arrange for a meeting with the agency.

Ironically, the people at the SBA could not have been more cordial. After we described the transition and turnaround our client's company was experiencing, we provided projections of sales and profitability and explained about the misunderstanding the company's president had had of the situation at the bank. We also pointed out his own problems in communicating. In addition, we brought along the company's new administrator and assured the SBA that this was the person with whom they would maintain contact in the future. The SBA granted the company a grace period on payments and awarded more in terms of flexibility than the company would ever have dared to hope. All that was requested in turn was that the agency be kept apprised of what was going on. The promise was made and kept. Moral: This branch of the government does have a heart. Just level with your contacts. After all, the SBA was established to help the entrepreneur, not to put anyone out of business.

Other SBA Services

The Small Business Administration publishes a wealth of materials on just about every business you can think of as well as on almost every aspect of running a business. A list of its publications is available from your nearest SBA field office. The agency also maintains a management assistance and counseling program staffed by professionals and by volunteer organizations, such as SCORE (Service Corps of Retired Executives) and ACE (Active Corps of Executives).

Through its Small Business Institute, the SBA contracts with business schools to send students (usually those in graduate programs) to help firms in trouble, and the agency co-sponsors management training programs with universities, colleges, other educational units, trade and professional associations, chambers of commerce and local business organizations. Its prebusiness workshops are geared for persons contemplating entrepreneurship or those who have been in business for a year or less.

For veterans and minorities, there are additional SBA benefits, which include an advocacy program and procurement assistance. Through the latter, the agency cooperates with various government departments in order to set aside prime contracts for small business, and with big prime contractors it subcontracts to small business.

SMALL BUSINESS INVESTMENT COMPANIES

If you've had loans from a bank or the SBA and have exhausted those sources of financing, perhaps you need an investment or long-term capital. Or you may need the capital *before* you can apply for a loan in order to improve your debt-equity ratio. In any of these cases, Uncle Sam may help again, indirectly, through a small business investment company.

Though privately owned, an SBIC is licensed by the Small Business Administration and is controlled by that agency in respect to the size of the investment it can make (and thus the percentage) of a company that it can own. SBICs fall within the category of **venture capitalists**—companies that place capital into somewhat risky businesses. But when they are successful, the SBIC (or venture capitalist) enjoys an extremely attractive return by sharing in the profits as a company grows and prospers. An SBIC must comply with SBA regulations and may get part of its funding from the Small Business Administration.

How an SBIC Can Help

Generally, you would approach an SBIC if your company has been around for a while and you need capital. If your company qualifies for SBIC financing and a deal is made, the SBIC would probably provide your company with one of the following "equity type" investments:

1. A **loan with warrant.** In return for a loan, you would issue a warrant, or statement, authorizing the SBIC to purchase common stock in your company, usually at a favorable price during a specified period of time.

2. **Convertible debenture.** In return for lending you cash, the SBIC would receive a debenture (certificate) so that it might either accept repay-

ment of the cash (loan) or convert the debenture into an equivalent amount of common stock in your business.

3. **Common stock.** The SBIC would make an outright purchase of common stock, which gives it a share of your business.

In addition, some SBICs make straight long-term loans with no equity features involved. Some sort of security is always required for these loans, but the SBIC may take a second mortgage, personal guarantee, or other collateral that is not always acceptable to banks or other conventional lending institutions. An SBIC will often subordinate its loan to other loans made by a business, thereby strengthening the company's credit with banks or other lenders.

What an SBIC Considers Small

Governed by regulations established by the Small Business Administration, an SBIC also has certain guidelines for the size company in which it may invest or to which it may lend money. Generally, a company is considered the appropriate size for SBIC financing if it meets the following criteria:

1. Its assets (material items owned by the business) do not exceed $9 million

2. Its net worth (or equity) does not exceed $4 million

3. Its average net income after taxes for each preceeding two years does not exceed $400,000

When determining the size of a business, other factors considered relate to the size of any affiliates, including a parent company that can control the firm, and any other companies controlled by the parent company. Firms operating under franchise agreements are considered small businesses if they have the right to profits and responsibility for any losses resulting from the operation.

Considerations for Special Groups

In keeping with the SBA's consideration for special groups, an integral part of the SBIC program includes small business investment companies, formerly called MESBICS, that provide long-term loans and/or capital investment to applicants who qualify as economically or socially disadvantaged. Although there is no precise definition for the term *economically or socially disadvantaged*—allowing for flexibility in interpretation—such persons often include blacks, Native Americans, Eskimos, Aleuts, Mexicans, Puerto

Ricans, Cubans, Filipinos, and Orientals. Other factors that affect the determination of economic or social disadvantage are income level, location (such as urban ghettos or depressed areas), education, physical or other special handicaps, and being a Vietnam era veteran.

Typically, members of these groups applying for SBA financing receive the following advantages:

1. Special attention when the application for a loan or investment is processed

2. Limits on the interest rate that may be charged, which differ from limits on loans to other SBIC borrowers

3. Greater restrictions on the degree of SBIC ownership in their companies

Working with an SBIC

SBICs invest in all types of businesses, ranging from manufacturing and service industries to construction, wholesale, and retail firms. But they are *very* selective and only one out of ten applications received is seriously considered. In addition to using criteria similar to that of the Small Business Administration, the SBIC scrupulously evaluates a prospective investment on the basis of the company's credibility. In this regard, both a proven product and a proven individual are important. Size is often a dual factor in that a company must be "small" enough; yet some SBICs will not consider investment in a business with less than $1 million in sales. This relates back to the proven product. Other SBICs will consider investments only in particular fields or in those industries in which they see potential.

Once an investment is made, an SBIC usually takes some role in management, though often only a passive one, such as a seat on the board. Others participate more actively, possibly as a consultant in their areas of expertise.

Whether its role is active or passive, the SBIC will have a watchdog keeping close tabs on its investment, particularly on a company's accounts receivable and inventory positions.

The SBIC is in business to make a profit—just as you are. Thus if you go this route, you will have to pay the price of someone looking over your shoulder. Yet keep in mind the advantages of this situation. If your company has an SBIC for a "partner," new problems may be recognized quicker and dealt with more effectively than they would be otherwise.

An SBIC might also require that your company produce regular financial statements or progress reports, both procedures that a good manager should enforce in any case.

With its careful monitoring, an SBIC can recognize when a company is severely out of control. In such cases, it usually recommends remedial action, which may require new management. Additional capital is often necessary, and this could result in further dilution of your percentage of ownership in your own company. These are some of the possibilities to weigh if you contemplate SBIC financing.

Choosing an SBIC

There are many sources of referral. Your attorney, an investment counselor, an investment banker, your CPA, or your banker may have associations with SBICs. Because many banks have interests in SBICs, there is frequently a relationship between the two, and you could get both capital and a loan through the same channel.

Your local SBA office might also be helpful in locating an SBIC. Although they are not allowed to recommend one over another, they will provide a list and may be able to tell you what types of investments the different SBICs have been making.

In selecting an SBIC, there are some important factors you should keep in mind:

1. The kinds of investments a particular SBIC has been making

2. The amount of money the SBIC has available for investment

3. Whether the SBIC will be able to assist in additional financing later, if needed

4. Whether the SBIC has contacts that would be helpful in a possible future public offering

5. The management services the SBIC offers

Unless you and your company have already established a firm relationship with an SBIC, your initial presentation will have much to do with your success in getting financing.

As with any other lender/investor, you will have to establish credibility by convincing your potential source of cash that you have a viable product and are capable of running a profitable business. The generally accepted approach for accomplishing this task is through a well-designed business plan.

OTHER GOVERNMENT SOURCES OF FUNDS

If your company is large enough to employ a substantial number of people (though sometimes as few as fifty), you'll find there are also public funds available through redevelopment agencies on the national, state, and local levels. Looking to companies that will provide jobs and bring in business, these agencies are interested in the economic well-being of underdeveloped or depressed areas and the revitalization of urban ghettos.

We've known a number of firms to benefit from this seldom thought-of source of funds, which is available not only to big business but to relatively small firms as well. The type of assistance they've received has ranged from tax concessions to direct loans, loan guarantees, outright grants, or combinations of these. It has helped to establish plant facilities, open branch plants, or buy equipment. However, like other government funds, the sources, availability, and eligibility requirements change frequently. Thus we suggest you assess your situation and apply to the appropriate agency for the area in which your business is, or will be, located if you think you may qualify for such funds.

ACTION GUIDELINES

Your eligibility for an SBA loan may depend on the following:

- Your sales volume
- The number of people you employ
- The availability of standard bank loans
- The availability of a loan from other sources
- The availability of loans at reasonable terms
- The number of SBA objectives with which your company complies
- Whether you are economically or socially disadvantaged
- Whether you are handicapped or a veteran

Assuming that your business meets the size specifications, if you can answer yes to the following questions, you may want to consider SBIC financing.

- Has my company been in business for a while?
- Do I need long-term or growth capital?
- Does my business demonstrate excellent growth potential?
- Have I exhausted my credit with the banks and the SBA?
- Do I have an acceptable debt-equity ratio?

14

Other Options for Raising Cash

This chapter will

- Familiarize you with more sources for raising cash or meeting your company's need

- Show you how to weigh the advantages and disadvantages of these options

- Prepare you to select or combine two or more possibilities

The more options you have when you need to raise cash, the better able you'll be to meet your company's financing needs. There are sources other than the bank, the SBA, and SBICs. Ideally, you'll maintain contact with several and do business with more than one.

If you anticipate your financing needs and don't wait until you're desperate, you can shop around and be more selective in regard to both source and arrangements.

You may even establish some viable contacts before you need them. If it's feasible, *get your promise for future financing in writing*, even if you have to pay a **standby fee** (a price paid to a lender to have funds available should you need them). It will save you time and energy when the need arises. The usual standby fee is .25 to .50 percent of the anticipated total commitment.

If at first you don't succeed, keep trying. Even if a number of sources refuse you, if your company is well managed and its outlook is good, you should be able to find an interested lender/investor.

PRIVATE INDUSTRIES

Giant corporations like Ford, General Motors, and any number of private companies—with insurance companies high on the list—have large amounts of surplus funds that must be put to work. ("Private" here refers to privately owned, as opposed to government owned. We do not mean to imply that it cannot be a publicly held company.) Thus these companies have established **finance companies** within their organizations to invest this capital in other businesses. Typically, however, they will work only with well-established firms seeking at least $250,000 because it takes as long to process a $50,000 loan as it does one for $250,000. Thus the smaller loan is considered hardly worth the trouble. These boundaries might preclude applications from a new business, but if yours is an established firm and if your business requires and can support a sizable loan, this is a source you should keep in mind. These companies also have pension funds they must invest.

Many finance companies established by larger corporations have branch offices in major metropolitan areas. As a general rule, though, you would not approach the company yourself but proceed through an intermediary. An application for a loan (or investment) by private industry can often be made through an investment banker or broker who works on a commission basis, getting paid only when and if his or her efforts are successful. This person usually puts together a business plan for your company.

If the presentation is successful, the broker or investment banker's fee is pretty hefty—anywhere between 1 percent and 5 percent of the loan. For this reason, brokers, too, prefer to work with established companies that can afford them. Because they operate on contingency only, they will usually not consider working on a loan of any less than $2 million to $3 million. Because such restrictions rule out many businesses, you may have to consider other approaches to private industry funds, making inquiry through an investment banker (even if you know he or she won't be interested in your account), your bank, or your CPA. In some cases an insurance agent has steered an entrepreneur in the right direction.

Every case is unique, but you should at least know of this source of funds. Depending on your situation it could be well worth your while to pursue because private industries charge lower interest rates than a bank and are often willing to provide medium- to long-term financing, in contrast with the bank's emphasis on shorter lengths of time.

COMMERCIAL FINANCE AND/OR FACTORING COMPANIES

Another source of funds for businesses of all sizes are the commercial finance and/or **factoring operations,** which are often one and the same organization, although they offer different approaches.

> The major distinction between the two is that the finance company lends money against accounts receivable or inventory—and sometimes equipment—as security. The factoring operation purchases your accounts receivable at a negotiated discount rather than make a loan.

In the latter situation, the customer is instructed to pay the factoring operation directly, a procedure that could alleviate a lot of credit problems. However, you should have a choice as to whether you engage in this arrangement with or without recourse, that is, whether your business or the factoring company assumes the risk for customers who fail to pay.

Because finance and factoring companies may not be as concerned as a bank about your organization's overall financial condition, you will pay somewhat higher rates, most often five to nine points above the bank's prime. But this could be offset by a number of advantages. For one, you won't have to comply with compensating balances, a contingency often accompanying bank loans. Moreover, many finance and factoring companies are expert within certain industries and through their attendant credit services can provide specialized screening of customers via accounts receivable. This can save you substantial bad-debt losses. Another advantage is that you typically would not need a formal presentation or business plan to conduct business with a finance or factoring company. Your accounts receivable alone should suffice for a cash advance, and the transaction is usually expedited a lot faster than by other sources of funds.

STOCK SALES

Accepting the idea of selling stock in your business may require putting aside a lot of preconceived notions, but when it's capital you want, this route could be a lot easier than you think. Selling stock to the public, of course, conjures up images of corporations, and indeed you would have to incorporate. However, a corporation doesn't necessarily spell "Big Business." Even an individual, or sole owner of a company, can incorporate and frequently does so for tax purposes.

> Incorporating simply means that your company, in the eyes of the law, becomes an artificial entity, invisible and intangible.

The corporation, in effect, is a fictitious "person," adopted as a device whereby an individual or group of individuals may act only through directors, who are elected by owners or shareholders and who guide its policies and elect its officers. The latter, in turn, select the corporation's administrative agents and employees.

The laws in each state vary greatly; so we won't cover the specific regulations on selling stock in every area. Wherever you're located, you will need the services of an attorney and a CPA. Depending on the amount of cash you want to raise and on whom you will be approaching, many states allow companies to offer stock through circulars or brochures, as opposed to a public offering made through an underwriter, which must comply with requirements of the Securities and Exchange Commission. (Circular offerings are official descriptions for the presentation of a stock, the requirements of which are usually governed by a state regulatory body.) This route at least makes the procedure easier and less expensive. In fact, we have seen successful stock offerings for as little as $100,000 processed for minimal costs.

One method of keeping down the fees involved is by offering stock in exchange for services to the professionals you hire (such as your attorney or CPA). We know of cases in which the professional was paid from the proceeds of the sale of stock. There are myriad ways to go about it. Just be sure to get competent help because the regulations are tricky. We don't recommend that you make this a do-it-yourself project.

It's true that you will have to give up a portion of your business to go this route. However, a percentage of something is better than nothing at all, and you probably can retain a controlling interest (over 50 percent of the stock). Talk to your professionals about the advantages and disadvantages of selling stock.

LIMITED PARTNERSHIPS

Just as with the sale of common stock, offerings of **limited partnership** interests are usually governed by a state regulatory body, and, again, an offering circular or brochure must be prepared. Thus we again caution you to obtain the services of a competent attorney and CPA. If time is an important factor, you will probably find that a limited partnership is quicker to process than a stock offering. No doubt you will also find that, at its onset, the limited partnership is more advantageous than a sale of common stock because the terms under which you invite prospective investors to share in your business are typically more flexible than those required for a corporation and are thus easier to negotiate. Later, as your company grows, you may have to alter the structure of your business, depending on how it evolves and its subsequent requirements.

For the investor, the limited partnership has the appeal of a tax shelter because losses incurred by the business may be passed along to the partners and taken as deductions on their personal tax returns. Limited partners must be made aware that when the business does become profitable, profits are likewise personally taxable. This contrasts with a corporation (other than a Subchapter S corporation), in which losses may be passed along to the stockholders only through the failure of the company.

In Chapter 2, we presented the case history of Grautmann-Brock Associates, whose founders raised capital through a limited partnership arrangement, the only practical option open to them at the time. Both advantages and pitfalls were outlined to the investors, and after the company became profitable, the principals needed to retain in the business a substantial portion of accumulated earnings as operating capital. As a result, the limited partners would have been taxed on profits that were not going to be distributed. In order to protect them from that fate, the partners opted to enter into a tax-free reorganization, forming a corporation, with the limited partners becoming shareholders.

It may sound complicated, but it's actually not that involved. However, it is essential to have experienced professionals handle such proceedings because an error in detail could cause disastrous results, taxwise, for both a company and its investors.

GENERAL PARTNERSHIPS

If capital is your goal, a **general partnership** is another investment alternative, and it might solve additional problems, as well as meeting your financial needs.

> With its range of possibilities for pooling resources, a partnership could provide your business with an ideal balance of talents, skills, and other expertise.

In some cases, one partner contributes knowledge and experience and another puts up the capital.

In the case of one of our clients, a three-person partnership, each makes a unique contribution to the business in addition to her equal share in its capitalization. Pfeiffer, Feigen, and O'Malley formed their partnership to open a shop selling museum-quality art and handcrafts. Pfeiffer brought her administrative talents to the firm; Feigen is a superstar when it comes to sales; and O'Malley has a relentless nose for ferreting out a quality product—an ideal partnership. To top it off, these women like each other—an important factor for working or involved partners in any business. If a good marriage is made in heaven, then even more so is a successful partnership. To make it work, there must be the right mix of personalities and temperaments, the right chemistry, respect, and harmony. If there isn't, you're better off with *any* other arrangement, regardless of the financial incentives.

A partnership needn't be based on equality in order to be workable. You can have an arrangement with an uneven distribution of profits or loss or one where one partner works in the business and draws a salary while the other shares in the profits only in relation to his or her capital contribution. As in other situations, there are as many possibilities as there are people.

JOINT VENTURES

Though in many ways similar to a partnership, a **joint venture** is even more informal than the most informal partnership. In a partnership, the persons involved associate as co-owners for the profitable advancement of their business. In a joint venture, co-ownership exists merely for a given, limited purpose, without the usual powers, duties, and responsibilities that accompany a partnership. Although there are often more, usually only two parties engage in a joint venture, in contrast to a partnership, in which there may be many persons involved.

In a joint venture one of the principals, and sometimes both, is a passive member of the relationship. That is, two parties forming a joint venture may make equal contributions to the relationship and then hire an administrator to run it. Such was the case with a garment manufacturer we know who formed a joint venture with a retail chain. The manufacturer contributed the product and the retailer, the sales expertise. Then they hired an administrator to run the operation. We also know a steel supplier who formed a joint venture with the manufacturer of precision tools and a builder who formed a joint venture with a doctor, who contributed the capital for the manufacture of prefabricated homes.

If you have an ability or product, find the company or individual who can supply the missing link. It may be capital; it may be expertise; it may be raw materials. There's nothing wrong in accepting raw materials in lieu of capital, particularly if it is the right contribution for you.

Even a corporation can form a joint venture with another corporation. Should you entertain this possibility, be sure to seek counsel first to determine the legality of the arrangement in your state.

VENTURE CAPITALISTS

The major difference between private venture capital firms and small business investment companies is that private firms have no affiliation with the federal government. Otherwise venture capitalists operate the same way as SBICs in that they may provide either investment or a long-term loan. In return, the venture capitalist will take some role in management, either through a seat on the board or as a consultant. When they do make a loan, it is on a highly secured basis and bears a very high interest rate.

For the most part, venture capitalists work with high-risk operations (many of which are high-technology companies) that show a potential for rapid growth in both sales and profitability. Even though a venture capital firm may back a fledgling company that is undercapitalized, it still expects a proven product and/or individual. In other words, the business must indicate a *very* good chance of success.

Should you wish to pursue this avenue of financing, your attorney, your investment counselor or broker, or your CPA should be able to put you in touch with venture capitalists. You may also get a listing from the National Venture Capital Association, 2030 M Street, N.W., Washington, D.C. 20036.

YOUR CUSTOMERS

At times even customers can and do solve an entrepreneur's financing dilemma, particularly when the entrepreneur has a unique product or service the customer wants or needs.

One of our clients was in just such a position after developing a unique software product for use in data-processing installations. Even though it had been marketed for some time, the product was still in a semideveloped state and required frequent servicing. Thus clients using the software not only depended on the company to maintain their product but also looked forward to the development of additional products for use in their computer installations.

Strapped for funds and attempting to get financing, our clients explained their situation to some of their customers. Their story fell on receptive ears, and because of its unique position in the market, the company was able to arrange for short-term loans with these customers. Shortly thereafter our clients obtained conventional bank financing and soon repaid the first loans.

Not all experiences of customer financing have gone so smoothly.

Another of our clients put up a considerable investment to form a corporation for the sale and construction of swimming pools. His partner and fellow stockholder was an experienced and talented salesman, a background he put to use in preselling over one hundred pools. He had the foresight to collect substantial down payments on the presales. Excavation began immediately upon payment. Unfortunately, this gentleman did not have his production crew assembled to complete the pools before the advance money was spent. The result was one hundred irate customers each of whom had a huge hole in the backyard. Suits ensued, and then an indictment (on charges of fraud) by the district attorney. The second partner, who subsequently became our client, had to honor many of his partner's commitments. The whole thing was a very muddy business.

We mention this vignette to make you aware of some of the pitfalls involved in using your customer as a source of funds. However, if you can utilize this kind of opportunity and combine it with other funds to accumulate the necessary financing, so much the better. Just proceed cautiously and have your business well under control—and be sure you can follow through.

SUPPLIERS AND LANDLORDS

When we suggest your suppliers as a source of financing, we refer not only to those who furnish you with raw materials but to anyone who provides you with services, such as the professionals you retain for counsel, your CPA, and your attorney. Sometimes you can trade services for your product. If you need equipment that in turn requires a tremendous amount of cash, many suppliers of such equipment have built-in programs for their customers, typically requiring somewhere between 15 and 20 percent of the total cost as a down payment, with the balance on extended terms. It's buying on time, of course, but it's also a form of financing.

Another possibility is a dating program with your suppliers. We don't mean romancing them, but rather paying on extended terms as part of your agreement to purchase certain products. For example, manufacturers of seasonal merchandise, like Christmas items, clothing, specialty candies, and toys, often have proposals through which they sell their products preseason. This is mutually beneficial because it allows the manufacturer to equalize his or her production schedule and you, the customer, to get the merchandise you need with payments scheduled for your convenience.

Your landlord could also be a possible source of funds. For example, assume that he is having difficulty renting a particular facility or for some reason is especially interested in keeping your business as a tenant. It's possible that you can negotiate several months free rent from him if you opt to enter into a lease arrangement. Or you may combine those free months with some extensive leasehold improvements he might be willing to furnish. Although it's a device that may not pop readily into mind when you think of raising cash, remember you're buying time when you obtain financing.

GUARANTORS

Often, too, one may have a friend or relative, a supplier or customer, who cannot actually provide the needed cash or product but is willing to come forward with a guarantee. A classic example of this type of arrangement was experienced by a painting contractor we knew who subsequently became a client. About to start a major project, he had been having difficulty getting financing and he knew he would have a rough time meeting his payroll. Thus he confided in a builder who wanted to use his services. With the utmost confidence that the painter would honor his obligation, the builder escorted him to the bank and arranged to guarantee a loan for enough funds to carry him through the project. The bank was happy with this arrangement and the builder wasn't out any cash.

LEASING AND SALE-LEASEBACK

For others, leasing may be the answer to financing problems. Although it doesn't put cash in your pocket, it may enable you to get equipment or building facilities. This instrument may take the form of strictly an operating lease, in which you never actually own the equipment or property, or it may be a financing transaction in which at the end of a period of installment payments you make an additional payment and own the asset.

One of the advantages of an operating lease is that the transaction does not appear on your balance sheet and therefore has no effect on your debt-equity ratio (leaving it intact for other possible financing). The disadvantage is that you may never have an opportunity to purchase the asset involved, and it could appreciate over the years. A financing transaction does appear as debt on a balance sheet. This fact should be one of your considerations in contemplating this course of action.

Limited to assets with a long and serviceable life, leasing as a solution to financing problems tends to be more expensive than a loan from a bank or other conventional source. Still, it is not that hard to come by; so keep it in mind if you strike out on other options.

BUSINESS PURCHASE

The idea of buying a business may at first sound like a strange vehicle for financing, but if you're not yet in business for yourself, or if you want to expand or diversify by acquiring another business, this can be a good method. An added advantage is that someone else has done the groundwork it takes to establish and run a business and has made all the initial mistakes for you.

There are other advantages, too, in buying an already established business. Because the company may have been around for a quarter of a century, your customers are not going to regard you as a novice entrepreneur. You may also use the age of the business as a basis for either establishing additional credit or for maintaining the contacts the business already has, such as with suppliers. It certainly has to be to their advantage to continue an association with a valued customer.

To examine just how some of these benefits could work for you, let's take a look at a hypothetical business you might buy for yourself. Suppose there is a company for sale for $250,000. This includes not only the inventory, but the accounts receivable, furniture, fixtures, and so forth. It also includes the purchase of a long-term lease in a highly desirable area, an important consideration because the owner has been running a profitable business in that location for over twenty-five years. According to the terms of sale, the present owner asks for 20 percent down, with the balance to be paid in installments of 10 percent per year for the next eight years, at the prime rate of interest. This arrangement would provide you the necessary financing that would otherwise have had to come from a third party.

> As with everything else, however, there can be problems; and when you find a business in which you are seriously interested, you must have a financial expert thoroughly review the company's books of account and other records.

Because the facts are not always what they appear to be, it often takes an experienced eye to pick out the flaws.

After your financial expert has determined that the business is indeed a good buy, it's time to have an attorney review with you the entire series of negotiations on which you intend to make your offer. It might be to your advantage to buy the assets rather than the company (with its liabilities). Or maybe the reverse will give you a tax advantage. And you may need to get outside appraisals of the accounts receivable, as well as of the inventory. After all, buying someone else's problems is not what you have in mind. Usually, though, when there is a business for sale, the seller puts together a circular or brochure, a written description very much like a business plan. You and your professional advisers must review the business plan in depth. In this case you are the investor; so make sure the seller can establish credibility with you.

FRANCHISING

Somewhat related to the concept of financing through buying a business is the possibility of a **franchise.** Interest in this option is usually limited to those about to become entrepreneurs for the first time. Moreover, the area is so vast and there are so many disadvantages as well as advantages in going this route that we will limit our discussion of the subject. It is important to know, though, that many franchisers provide up to 65 percent to 75 percent of the financing you may require for a business, in addition to maintaining educational programs that give you background and information on sales and providing prepackaged control and accounting systems to help with inventory, purchasing, and accounts receivable.

But for every consideration in favor of this type of operation there tends to be a corresponding concern; so we urge you to protect yourself with expert financial and legal counsel should you consider a franchise. Under the guise of being your own boss, you could wind up with a *lot* of expenses and too many obligations to the owner of the parent company. Weigh a franchise *very* carefully.

ACTION GUIDELINES

There are many sources of cash besides the SBA, SBICs, and the banks. If your business needs money, ask yourself the following questions:

- Can I look to any previously established contacts?

- Have I avoided becoming discouraged by refusals?

- Am I considering creative combinations of some of the following sources for raising cash:

Through Investment	*Through Loans*
Friends, relatives, colleagues	Banks
SBICs	SBA
Private industry	SBICs
Venture capitalists	Private industry
Selling stock	Finance companies
Limited partnerships	Venture capitalists
General partnerships	Friends, relatives, colleagues
Joint ventures	Customers
	Suppliers
	Guarantor assistance

Other Means of Making Cash Available

Factoring

Customers (by arranging special terms)

Suppliers (by arranging special terms)

Landlords

Leasing

Sale-leaseback

Buying a business

Franchising

APPENDIX A

Sample Business Plan

This business plan illustrates the recommendations of Chapters 9 and 10. Because it represents only one business, it cannot incorporate all suggestions set forth in those chapters.

Designs First Limited
Business Plan
19XX–19XX

CONTENTS

Prose Section

Business Purpose or Objectives and History

Founded in 19XZ as a sole proprietorship by its present owner, Robert First, Designs First Limited began operations with design and distribution facilities located at 1002 Frontera Street in San Francisco and manufacturing handled in the Far East. Its purpose, to become a leading U.S. producer of popular contemporary designs in misses dresses, is an objective long since achieved.

Offering medium- to lower-priced yet quality products with wide geographical appeal, the company has acquired an impressive list of customers among women's specialty shops and department stores located all over the United States.

Lead off with your strong points

Bearing a name that has become synonymous with contemporary design, the company has earned a reputation for

- Exemplary quality control
- Dependable service and delivery, making it a reliable resource for its customers
- Competitive prices, which may be attributed to astute purchasing techniques, long-standing vendor relationships, and a keen sensitivity to market conditions

- Consolidation and coordination of shipments, thereby minimizing freight, packing, and handling costs

- Terms of sale that allow a large number of customers favorable payment terms

State your
goals . . .

Although this reputation serves as an impetus for the continued growth of the company, management recognizes that, with its present facilities, Designs First cannot continue to serve an expanding market. Warehouse improvements are essential if the company is to continue to flourish. Along these lines, management envisions making several investments that would provide more space and coordinate the physical layout of the plant with computer programming, thereby facilitating inventory control as well.

And why you
prepared the plan

Thus the purpose of this presentation is to generate enough capital for warehouse improvements for a more effective operation, which would enable the company to continue offering popular priced goods while maintaining an above-average pretax profit.

Having decided early on in its history to occupy a place in the lower-priced markets, Designs First Limited earns a gross profit ranging from 35 to 37 percent, compared with an industry average of 38 to 40 percent. This lower than average gross profit is offset by a lower than usual overhead and by a large volume of customers seeking lower-priced goods. In turn, this provides the company with security in the marketplace and reduces business risk considerably.

Provide the history
of your company

Incorporated in 19X5, Designs First has been in operation for nineteen and a half years, during which time it has recorded a loss for only one year—19X2—a condition that reflected the effects of a year-long nationwide recession.

At the end of the first five years, total sales were about $1,400,000 a year. Next year's sales are expected to exceed $8,500,- 000, a compounded increase of 15 percent per year within the fourteen-year period.

Because of numerous buyer contacts on both the East and West Coasts, Design First's sales efforts during its first five years were concentrated in these areas. However, as contacts grew, along with awareness of the product, sales efforts were initiated and were well received across the states in between. Today the product is sold to five hundred customers located in some thirty states throughout the country.

Give the present status of your efforts

Management

Design First's management philosophy is based on the tightly knit integration of abilities of each member of its executive staff, along with its outside advisers or consultants.

This system has as its core a four-person team, three of whom serve on the company's board of directors, along with five consultants. These outside advisers/board members serve as management's support group and are retained on a yearly basis, actively participating in company direction and performance. A direct benefit of this integrated unit is a level of experience and objectivity not otherwise possible in a company of this size.

Describe your management structure . . .

Control of the company through its systems is a basic function of management and is described in detail in the ''Administration/ Operating Controls'' section of this plan. The frequency of budget review, analysis of pricing structures, efficiency of manpower, and effectiveness of marketing strategy are the key to accomplishment in all management and fiscal endeavors. Of prime importance in Design First's organization is the awareness

And how it exercises control

on the part of all personnel of the status and progress of the company so that a teamwork approach toward objectives becomes a realization. Company objectives are formulated and executed through this teamwork.

Following is a brief resume of the company's key personnel and outside consultants.

Robert First—President, Chairman of the Board of Directors

List the key people in the company

A veteran of thirty—five years in the apparel industry, Mr. First was for ten years top salesman for the prestigious firm, Beste Dresses. Having been advanced to sales manager of that company, he occupied the post for one year before deciding to open his own business in 19X4. Throughout Design First's history, he has acted as the company's director of sales, with the bulk of administrative responsibilities delegated to his executive vice—president.

Reuben Ellis—Executive Vice—President, Member of the Board of Directors

Give their backgrounds

Having joined Designs First Limited seven years ago, Mr. Ellis has assumed all duties of administrative officer of the company. Prior to his current affiliation, he practiced as an attorney, serving a number of clients in the apparel business during his fifteen years with a private firm. In connection with his efforts to supervise the coordination of the company's product with the Far East, Mr. Ellis travels abroad an average of four times a year.

Cybille Young—Designer, Member of the Board of Directors

A top graduate of the West Coast School of Art and Design, class of 19X3, Ms. Young began her career with the large sportswear manufacturer, Regnis Sports. During her three years with that company, she had a notable effect on both Regnis' product and business volume. Ms. Young chose to move to a smaller firm, where her talents would not only have a significant impact on the company's place in the industry but would afford her some influence on company policy. Over the past seven years, the name Cybille Young has become synonymous with Designs First Limited.

As reinforcement of her efforts, Ms. Young periodically counsels with Jonathan Trebley of New York, fashion consultant for many prestigious apparel manufacturers. Along with Mr. Ellis, Ms. Young is responsible for coordinating the product between San Francisco and the Far East. Thus she travels abroad several times a year.

Describe their related outside activities

Oliver Smythe—Bookkeeper/Office Manager

Mr. Smythe joined Designs First fifteen years ago upon graduation from San Francisco Community College. His prime responsibilities include preparation of monthly financial statements, credit, collection of accounts receivable, and preparation of the annual budget. He also supervises an accounts payable and accounts receivable clerk.

Discuss their duties and responsibilities in your company

Linda Artulian—Attorney, Member of the Board of Directors

A partner in the San Francisco law firm of Winde, Artulian, Freund, and Strong, Ms. Artulian has served as Mr. First's personal legal counsel for the past twenty-two years and has been the company's legal counsel since its inception.

Aaron Grieff— Certified Public Accountant, Member of the Board of Directors

Prior to establishing his own firm in 19XX, Mr. Grieff served as treasurer and financial vice-president of the apparel firm of Creeway Industries, member of the New York Stock

Include your outside consultants

Exchange. Mr. Grieff serves as general counsel to Designs First Limited.

Stephen Peete—Insurance Consultant, Member of the Board of Directors

Highlight their accomplishments

A chartered life underwriter, Mr. Peete has been an affiliate of Manhattan General Life Insurance Company for the past sixteen years and a million–dollar producer for the past ten years, as well as top producer in the nation for three of those years. He has been affiliated with Designs First Limited since the company's inception.

Asa Fruge—Executive, Member of the Board of Directors

Mr. Fruge has been chief executive officer of Radnor Department Stores of California for the past eleven years. Prior to this affiliation, he served in managerial and executive capacities for several major department stores throughout the United States.

Jonathan Trebley—Fashion Design Consultant, Member of the Board of Directors

A graduate of the Fashion Institute of Manhattan, Mr. Trebley was formerly chief designer of Scintillant Knitwear and, prior to that, a designer for Phoebe Street, a large coordinated sportswear manufacturer. He now acts as fashion consultant to a number of manufacturers in the New York area, as well as to Designs First.

Product

Describe your product

Designs First Limited produces four lines of merchandise a year: the holiday/cruise line, a spring line, a summer line, and a fall line. Each is offered in sizes ranging from four to fourteen, a scope which includes the needs of the woman with the smaller figure who is unable to wear what is generally known in the business as a petite line. This market was generally overlooked in this country when the

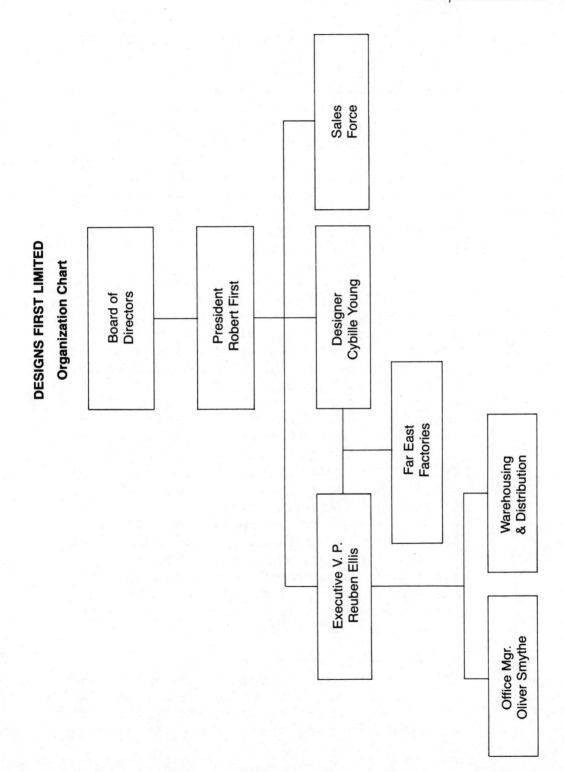

DESIGNS FIRST LIMITED
Organization Chart

Board of Directors

President Robert First

Sales Force

Designer Cybille Young

Far East Factories

Executive V. P. Reuben Ellis

Warehousing & Distribution

Office Mgr. Oliver Smythe

company began; so Designs First was a pioneer in the field. Even today, as the company pursues a pattern of controlled growth, Designs First is one of the few manufacturers to give prime consideration to this customer. Because the woman with the smaller figure will presumably always be around, Designs First views its customer approach as a policy that assures continuing support in the marketplace.

Give the history of its development

Although it began as a manufacturer of one-piece dresses, thereby appealing to only one classification of buyers, during its second year in business, Designs First began diversifying to include blouse and skirt combinations that may be worn separately or together, a line with which its sales reps may also approach the buyers of separates and casual wear. Today, a typical complete line of Designs First merchandise includes an average of fifty garments, each of which is offered in twelve to twenty colors.

In recognition of the potential shading (color) problem inherent in a separates line, the company coordinates its dye lots—a project now controlled in part by computer, that is, by segregating shade lots according to size in specific areas of the warehouse (see ''Plant and Facilities'').

Provide an overview of production

A prototype of every garment offered to Designs First's customers is developed in this country for manufacturing in the Far East, where labor is cheaper. Free-lance agents in the Far East supervise strict quality control, their efforts augmented by periodic visits from the company's managerial staff.

Selling and Marketing Strategy

Discuss the structure of the sales force . . .

Designs First maintains a showroom in each of the following cities: New York, San Francisco, Dallas, Los Angeles, and Chicago. Ten salespersons, who work for the company directly out of these showrooms, and five representatives, who carry other compatible lines as well, make up the company's sales force. All are directly responsible to the president of the company, who monitors the sales force through detailed itineraries and weekly call reports. He maintains continuous control and obtains feedback from the company's more than five hundred customers by this method. In addition, the president/director of sales makes four trips annually around the country to visit key customers and maintain close contact with salespersons and sales representatives.

The sales force is also invited to headquarters twice a year (all expenses paid) to be introduced to the company's two major lines (spring and fall). All members of the sales force work on a commission standard to the industry—6 percent of shipped goods. This remuneration is supplemented by biannual selling contests with vacation trips as awards.

And explain how it works

Designs First ships about 92 percent of all orders received (the other 8 percent being canceled), comparing favorably with an industry average of 88 percent.

About sixty days elapse between order and delivery, with terms of sale at 8 percent, due ten days e.o.m. An average of forty-four days elapse between delivery of product and collection of receivables—also an excellent record in the apparel industry. This holds true in spite of dating programs with major customers whose purchases exceed $50,000 a year.

Describe your collection record

Although current warehouse facilities limit the company's sales growth potential, management believes that the contemplated facilities expansion will facilitate realization of the company's projected sales growth (as indicated in ''Profit or Loss Statement'').

Competition

Cite your
advantages over
competitors

Although the entire apparel industry is extremely competitive, it is also very fragmented, with a large number of small manufacturers. The particular advantages enjoyed by Designs First, however, are its tenure and its reputation as a reliable resource for both quality control and delivery. In addition, the company offers the retailer a better than average potential markup because it maintains a gross profit that is two to three points below the rest of the industry. Designs First Limited has always been aware of the consumers' need for a quality product at reasonable cost, and the company will continue to meet that need.

Plant and Facilities

Tell where your
products are
manufactured . . .

All products are manufactured in contract facilities in the Far East, every one of which is operated by reputable contacts with whom the principals of the company have been associated since before the inception of Designs First Limited. Throughout their nearly twenty-year association with these colleagues, management has been totally satisfied both in terms of quality control and reliability of delivery. Because the manufacture of apparel products in the Far East is common to many similar companies, the distance factor has not and is not anticipated to present any major operating problems.

And where they're
stored

Warehouse and administrative facilities are located in the company's original headquarters and consist of fifteen thousand square feet, about two thousand of which are allocated for administrative and design offices and showrooms. The location was chosen because it was economically reasonable and situated in the area with other apparel manufacturers, thus convenient for both suppliers and buyers visiting similar businesses and headquarter-located showrooms.

At this time the company's warehouse is antiquated. If it is not modernized, sales projections for both the near and long-term future will be limited. To increase the efficiency of this facility, it is necessary to elevate the roof, thereby providing additional storage space, and to add bin storage, racks, and automated cars and rails, which will facilitate the selection of garments from storage.

With its present facilities, the company is able to ship between $8 million and $10 million worth of goods a year. With the expansion, this figure should be increased to $15 million worth of goods annually.

As an alternative solution to the warehouse capacity problem, management has considered employing an additional shift. However, it was concluded that this would be unfeasible both because the location is virtually deserted after the traditional workday and because the remuneration that would have to be offered a second shift would eliminate the advantages.

Labor Force

In addition to its administrative and design staff, the company's labor force consists of a pattern and a sample maker, a full-time warehouse supervisor, and a full-time warehouse worker. At seasonal peaks, the warehouse staff is supplemented by as many as five shipping employees. With the company situated in a major city like San Francisco, securing temporary help presents no problem.

Although Designs First has a nonunion shop, the company pays union scale wages. A major medical plan for full-time personnel, participation in the company's pension plan, and a Christmas bonus complete the fringe benefits offered. This package seems acceptable to the small staff and compares favorably with compensation offered by companies of similar size

---

Describe needed improvements ...

And their projected results

List rejected alternatives

Outline your work force

Describe pay scales and fringe benefits

in the area. To date, the company's labor force has not been approached by a union.

Administration/Operating Controls

Board Meetings

Tell what
happens at board
meetings . . .

    The basis of each board meeting (held quarterly) is the presentation of a financial report (for example, the financial highlight report; please see Exhibit A) and a comparison of that report with the operating budget for the same quarter. Any deviations from target are discussed, and proposed solutions are examined. A sales report usually follows the financial presentation, with problems related to that department then reviewed. Reaction to product, adherence to goals, new directions in any area, and evaluations of production efficiency are other matters of business typically handled by the board.

Staff Meetings

And staff meetings

    Each week the operating management staff—the president (director of sales), executive vice-president, designer, and bookkeeper/office manager—meet to discuss all key operating functions, which include, but are not limited to, sales forecast, cash forecast, purchase order reports, accounts receivable and accounts payable positions, and financial data.

Order/Booking Data

List the reports
you receive . . .

    Realizing the importance in the fashion industry of quickly determining a trend in order to schedule bookings (billing alone does not provide complete answers in analysis of the business climate), Designs First receives a service bureau's weekly summary of all customer orders received, enabling the company to trail a trend quickly, recognize windfalls, and determine an order increase or decrease (comparing target to orders received) and a dollar value per order. (Please see Exhibit B.)

Order Backlog

As an adjunct to the booking data, a computer report of all customer orders expedites the order process system. (Please see Exhibit C.)

Sales Forecast

A detailed summary of the company's annual sales forecast, a monthly sales report, shows new sales or booked sales that are scheduled for billing that month. Through a monthly review of the report, it is possible to adjust the sales forecast. Because the report is related to other information discussed at staff meetings, appropriate revisions in the cash flow, material control, and purchasing reports can be made as well. In addition, the report serves as a trigger; that is, if it is determined that certain orders are not being filled, management expedites the delivery of merchandise. (Please see Exhibit D.)

And their function

Cash Forecast

The cash forecast is a monthly report divided into weekly segments and then reviewed weekly in order to determine whether projections are on target. Any problems encountered are discussed in terms of solutions and adjusted accordingly. (Please see Exhibit E.)

Tell how frequently the reports are compiled . . .

Purchase Order Report

The purchase order report is maintained weekly and permits determination of the number of dollars committed, both current or for scheduled deliveries. It also reflects the number of garments received as of the day of the report. (Please see Exhibit F.)

Accounts Receivable Aging Report

Provided by the computer service bureau, the receivables recap is a running report of the year-to-date accounts. This report is supplemented by the company's weekly update so that any potential problem may be discussed at the weekly staff meeting. When it is determined that an account is extended beyond a reasonable period, appropriate action is taken. (Please see Exhibit G.)

Accounts Payable Aging Report

An aged accounts payable report provides management with a breakdown of all suppliers to whom money is owed and lists any past-due payables and the reason for the delinquency, if any. (For example, the company may not have received some merchandise ordered and therefore is disputing the claim.) This report also tells management whether it is availing itself of any specific trade or cash discounts. (Please see Exhibit H.)

Daily Management Report

And say who compiles them

Prepared by the bookkeeper/office manager on a daily basis, the report summarizes the cash, accounts receivable, and accounts payable positions and any other commitments. In addition, it provides a flash report of orders received for that day, which is added to the previous total in order to provide a year-to-date report, thus enabling management to determine whether it is approaching its targets. (Please see Exhibit I.)

Insurance Program

Describe your insurance plans . . .

In line with good business practices, the company maintains product liability insurance, extended employee benefits through its hospitalization program, and complete general insurance, including full-coverage liability insurance and theft and fire coverage, all of which are reviewed by management at least once annually.

Employee Pension Plan

And retirement program

The pension plan was introduced in 19X8 to offer the company's staff and labor force a retirement program that enabled Designs First

Limited to compete effectively in the labor market. Today, after contributions have been made for over eight years, the fund has grown to more than $750,000. It is managed by a team of management, staff, and the trust department of the First Bank of West Bay.

Financial Section

Introduction

The development of a long-range plan is an integral part of Designs First's management planning and control system. It is designed to serve a twofold purpose—first, to establish internal targets; second, to transmit limited yet important information to select persons outside of Designs First who are concerned with the company's present and future performance.

Explain the function of your planning

The three-year plan (described through the statements herein) is the result of several months of work on the part of management, all of whom look forward to the challenges ahead with great enthusiasm.

In summary, the forecast for 19X6 is based on an anticipated volume of $11,500,000, compared with a 19X1 volume of $6,430,000, or a compounded annual growth of 13 percent. Profits after taxes by 19X6 are projected to be $1,190,000, compared with 19X1 profits of $712,000, or an 11 percent compounded annual growth rate.

Give an overview of your planning

The major assumptions used in preparing the projections are followed by the specific statements to which they apply (that is, the statement of profit or loss and the cash forecast), with each of these showing the next three years projected (19X4–19X6) compared with the past three years actual (19X1–19X3) in summary form. The pertinent ratios also accompany the balance sheet, which follows the three statements.

Assumptions Accompanying the
Profit or Loss Statement

Sales Assumption

Explain sales trends . . .

The trend in sales has not always been upward. In 19X2, the entire industry was affected by the nationwide recession, and the company has always followed trends, despite the fact that accomplishments in sales growth have consistently been better than industry averages (Source: Apparel Manufacturers Trade Assoc.). Recovery from the recession in 19X3 brought the company back to a more typical growth pattern. The forecasted annual growth rate correlates with projections of the Apparel Manufacturers Trade Association. The

And other factors affecting sales

company is planning a major sales promotion in 19X4, which is projected to accomplish a better than average sales growth rate for that year. The company has employed similar campaigns in prior years, most notably in 19X6, when a sales growth rate over 19X5 in excess of 35 percent was experienced.

Gross Profit Assumption

Give your profit range . . .

Typically, merchants in our industry earn 38 percent to 40 percent in gross profit; we have earned and project to earn in the 35–37 percent range. This situation results from an early policy decision to opt for the lower-priced markets. However, to offset the disadvantage of earning a lower gross profit, we attract a wider than average range of customers who continuously seek lower-priced goods. This in turn provides our company with stability in the marketplace and thus reduces our business risk considerably. In 19X2, the

And explain any disparity with industry averages

company had some abnormal markdowns on merchandise that was purchased with an anticipated sales volume that failed to materialize in light of the recession previously mentioned. To reduce our risk in the future, we have invested in a computer to help in allocating and forecasting inventory. This should reduce markdowns considerably in 19X3, enabling the company to experience an additional 1 percent gross profit margin.

Selling Expenses Assumption

This category has consistently varied in direct proportion to sales volume. However, in 19X4, as stated in our sales assumption, we are planning a promotional campaign budgeted at $25,000. This additional cost is expected to yield a higher sales volume in future years, thereby justifying the extra expenditure.

General and Administrative Expenses Assumption

The basic overhead costs for the kind of business that we operate are nominal, primarily because of the low gross profit generated. Although we provide basic services to our customers, they do not in turn expect too many frills with the low prices they are paying for our goods. There are no major increases budgeted in salaries, which account for over 90 percent of total general and administrative costs. However, with the added sales volume, we expect to increase staff to cover the additional burden of handling increased volume.

Discuss your overhead costs

Pretax and After-Tax Assumption

Income generated by our company is in excess of industry standards by an average of 2 percent of sales. We attribute this result to maintaining tight control over overhead, which is necessitated by the lower than average gross profit our business generates. In 19X6, we plan a major warehouse project and therefore have forecast expenditures of over $3 million in capital equipment and improve-

Explain how your plans will affect your tax situation

ments, of which $150,000 is eligible for a 10 percent investment credit. We have therefore reduced the provision for federal income taxes accordingly.

Assumptions Accompanying
the Cash Projections

Cash Collections Assumption

Although average days outstanding of accounts receivable were extraordinarily high in 19X3 (due in large part to the recession), we are projecting a more bullish experience for the years 19X4 through 19X6 (that is, decreasing the average number of days outstanding to approximately forty-three from an average forty-four days). This compares favorably with an industry average of forty-five days outstanding.

Stress your company's accomplishments

During the latter half of 19X3, we overcame many of the problems associated with the 19X2 recession. Moreover, to increase the collection cycle further, the company has implemented a control system facilitated by the new computer purchased in 19X3.

The company has projected additional debt, both short and long term, to cover any cash shortages.

Cash Disbursements Assumption— Raw Materials and Labor

Outline your relationships with suppliers

The company has experienced excellent relationships with its suppliers and has negotiated favorable terms on future purchases of raw materials. These terms include not only time extensions on payments but also special warehousing on select items. The latter will enhance the company's inventory turnover because it will not have to stock certain key raw materials for more than thirty days.

Provide your inventory turn

In the past the company has experienced a turn of approximately 2.5 and is projecting an

PROFIT OR LOSS OR INCOME STATEMENT

	Past Three Years Actual							Next Three Years Projected					
	19X1		19X2		19X3			19X4[a]		19X5		19X6	
	$	%	$	%	$	%		$	%	$	%	$	%
Sales	6,429,330	100	4,058,510	100	7,010,970	100		8,500,000	100	9,900,000	100	11,500,000	100
Cost of Sales	4,181,160	65	2,923,040	72	4,427,140	63		5,440,000	64	6,340,000	64	7,360,000	64
Gross Profit	2,248,170	35	1,135,470	28	2,583,830	37		3,060,000	36	3,560,000	36	4,140,000	36
Selling Expense	514,340	8	556,680	13	570,880	8		935,000	11	850,000	8	920,000	8
Gen. & Adm. Expense	576,550	9	682,670	17	717,390	10		805,000	9	975,000	10	1,100,000	10
Total Expenses	1,090,890	17	1,239,350	30	1,288,270	18		1,740,000	20	1,825,000	18	2,020,000	18
Pretax Profit	1,157,280	18	(103,880)	(2)	1,295,560	19		1,320,000	16	1,735,000	18	2,120,000	18
Prov. for Federal & State Taxes	445,200	7	—	-	619,000	9		630,000	8	840,000	9	930,000	8
Net Income	1,712,080	11	(103,880)	(2)	676,560	10		690,000	8	895,000	9	1,190,000	10
% Annual Growth Rate													
Sales	16.9%		(36.9%)		72.7%			21.2%		16.4%		16.2%	
Pretax Profit	16.8%		(108.9%)		1347.2%			1.9%		31.4%		22.2%	

[a]The projections for 19X4 represent the operating budget.

increase to an average turn of about 3.25 over a three-year period. This will be accomplished not only as a result of the aforementioned relationship with suppliers, but also through the coordination of that arrangement with decreasing inventory levels programmed and controlled by the computer purchased in 19X3.

Overhead Expense Assumption

For the overhead expense assumption, please see the selling expenses and general and administrative expenses assumption accompanying the profit and loss statement.

Ratios Accompanying the Balance Sheet

Current Ratio

Relate the history of your current ratio to your projections

The company has consistently maintained a current ratio of almost 2 to 1 in all years other than 19X2, when the country was in a mild recession. As a result of the recession, our accounts receivable were at an all-time high, and to meet our obligations to suppliers, we had heavier than usual bank loans, thus temporarily increasing our current debt load. We project a lower than industry average in 19X6, when we anticipate additional loans on a short- and long-term basis in order to finance the new warehouse facility. Our projections allow for the expectation that this condition will extend only through the end of 19X6, when additional profits from the new facility will further enhance the company's profitability and hence its cash position.

Quick Asset Ratio

The same factors that affected the current ratio also apply to the quick asset ratio. (See current ratio for explanation.)

Sample Business Plan **223**

CASH STATEMENT

	Past Three Years Actual			Next Three Years Projected		
	19X1	19X1	19X3	19X4	19X5	19X6
CASH RECEIPTS						
Collections-Accts. Rec.	$6,403,370	$4,235,070	$6,582,550	$8,337,080	$9,799,780	$11,229,100
Depreciation	177,150	185,000	225,000	275,000	300,000	400,000
Long-Term Debt	–	–	1,000,000	–	–	1,500,000
Notes Payable–Banks	–	150,000	1,000,000	100,000	–	300,000
Other	–	–	10,050	–	–	–
Total Cash Receipts	6,580,520	4,570,070	7,817,600	8,712,080	10,099,780	13,429,100
CASH DISBURSEMENTS						
Raw Materials & Labor	4,364,860	2,631,550	4,581,920	5,695,290	6,339,370	7,168,660
Overhead Expenses	938,890	1,179,350	1,382,420	1,688,800	1,906,000	1,940,000
Fixed Asset Expenditures	452,150	600,000	1,000,000	400,000	650,000	3,000,000
Repayment of Note Payable to Bank	200,000	–	200,000	–	200,000	–
Repayment of Long-Term Note	116,000	116,000	116,000	216,000	216,000	216,000
Other Income–Other Charges–Net	17,500	2,250	–	–	100,850	91,400
Income Taxes	445,200	–	619,000	630,000	840,000	930,000
Total Cash Disbursements	6,534,600	4,529,150	7,899,340	8,630,090	10,152,220	13,346,060
Net Cash Overage or (Shortage)	45,920	40,920	(81,740)	81,990	(52,440)	83,040
Cash–Beginning of Period	255,500	301,420	342,340	260,600	342,590	290,150
Cash–End of Period	$301,420	$342,340	$260,600	$342,590	$290,150	$373,190
Average # of Days of Accounts Receivable (Industry Average– 45 Days)	38	45	50	46	42	42

Describe how projected improvements will affect turnover rate

Debt Equity Ratio

The company takes pride in maintaining its debt level within the benchmarks cited by the industry. It plans to continue this policy in order to sustain its excellent relationship with its banks and other creditors.

Inventory Turn Ratio

The company maintains an inventory turnover that has surpassed industry averages (2.5) in all prior years with the exception of 19X2, when its average inventory level was approximately $200,000 in excess of projections. This higher inventory level was caused by the recession, which reduced projected sales far below expectations.

The positive trend continued, however, in 19X3, as noted on the accompanying balance sheet, when the company achieved an inventory turn of 2.85.

Give your debt-equity ratio

With the advent of a computerized purchasing system and improved warehouse facilities, the company expects further improvement in its turnover to a rate of 3.5 by 19X6, which, when measured with industry averages, represents a reduced investment in inventory of approximately $1 million over the next three years.

Financial Requirements

Designs First Limited has enjoyed an excellent working relationship with the First National Bank of West Bay, its principal bank, which has provided the company with its working capital needs for the past twelve years.

Tell how much you need . . .

At this stage of its development, however, it is not working capital that the company requires but a long-term loan of $3 million in order to remodel and update its warehouse.

And how you'll use it

With improved facilities, the company should not only be able to sustain the 13 percent growth rate it has experienced in the

BALANCE SHEET

	Past Three Years Actual					Next Three Years Projected		
	19X1	19X2	19X3			19X4	19X5	19X6
ASSETS								
Cash	$ 301,420	$ 342,340	$ 260,600			$ 342,590	$ 290,150	$ 373,190
Accounts Receivable	912,760	736,200	1,164,620			1,327,540	1,427,760	1,698,660
Inventory	1,519,600	1,353,110	1,555,540			1,813,330	2,012,700	2,102,860
Prepaid Expenses	55,000	47,500	60,250			60,250	100,750	151,500
Total Current Assets	2,788,780	2,479,150	3,041,010			3,543,710	3,831,360	4,326,210
Fixed Assets	2,577,900	3,177,900	4,177,900			4,577,900	5,227,900	8,227,900
Depreciation	648,900	833,900	1,058,900			1,333,900	1,633,900	2,033,900
Fixed Assets—Net	1,929,000	2,344,000	3,119,000			3,244,000	3,594,000	6,194,000
Other Assets	70,500	80,250	57,450			57,450	117,800	158,450
Total Assets	$4,788,280	$4,903,400	$6,217,460			$6,845,160	$7,543,160	$10,678,660
LIABILITIES & CAPITAL								
Notes Payable—Banks	$ 150,000	$ 300,000	$ 100,000			$ 200,000	$ —	$ 300,000
Accounts Payable	857,800	982,800	1,030,450			1,132,950	1,432,950	1,714,450
Accrued Expenses	243,850	303,850	209,700			260,900	179,900	259,900
Current Maturities of Long Term Debt	116,000	116,000	116,000			216,000	216,000	250,000
Total Current Liabilities	1,367,650	1,702,650	1,456,150			1,809,850	1,828,850	2,524,350
Long Term Debt	464,000	348,000	1,232,000			816,000	600,000	1,850,000
Total Debt	1,831,650	2,050,650	2,688,150			2,625,850	2,428,850	4,374,350
Common Stock	500,000	500,000	500,000			500,000	500,000	500,000
Retained Earnings	2,456,630	2,352,750	3,029,310			3,719,310	4,614,310	5,804,310
Total Capital	2,956,630	2,852,750	3,529,310			4,219,310	5,114,310	6,304,310
Total Liabilities & Capital	$4,788,280	$4,903,400	$6,217,460			$6,845,160	$7,543,160	$10,678,660
					INDUSTRY AVERAGES			
	2.03:1	1.46:1	2.09:1	Current Ratio	1.80:1	1.96:1	2.09:1	1.71:1
	.88:1	.63:1	.98:1	Quick Asset Ratio	.95:1	.92:1	.94:1	.82:1
	63%	72%	76%	Debt Equity Ratio	80%	62%	47%	69%
	2.75	2.15	2.85	Inventory Turn	2.50	3.00	3.15	3.50

past but to exceed it, with a predicted average growth rate of nearly 18 percent over the next three years. Moreover, it is anticipated that the income produced from streamlined warehouse facilities will be equivalent to earnings of 21 percent on the company's contemplated investment. (Please see the net present value calculation and projected earnings of the company.)

Describe how you'll pay off the debt...

Based on the additional projected earnings of the company that should result from improved warehouse facilities (see the net present value calculation), along with the company's ongoing earnings capacity, management anticipates that Designs First will be able to repay indebtedness in the amount of $2,400,000 over the next fifteen years at the rate of $390,000 per year, including the assumed interest rate.

And explain any timing problems

Such a program, however, is based on the expectation that improved facilities will be completed by May 19X4, in time to meet the demands of the 19X4 fall season. Hence the company must conclude the proposed financing plan by December 19X3, in order to finalize negotiations with the building contractors by January 19X4.

SOL POSTYN

CERTIFIED PUBLIC ACCOUNTANT

December 30, 19X3

Mr. Robert First
President
Designs First Limited
1002 Frontera Street
San Francisco, California

Dear Robert:

I have prepared the accompanying financial projections concerning your company for the year ending
August 31, 19X3.

I believe the projections reflect assumptions about
future events based on present circumstances and
available information, but I am not expressing an
opinion on whether those assumptions are either reasonable or comprehensive.

Projections are inherently subject to varying degrees
of uncertainty and their achievability depends on the
timing and probability of a complex series of future
events, both internal and external. Accordingly, I am
not expressing an opinion on the realization of the
projections or on the probability that the actual
results for any period may or may not approximate the
projections.

Cordially yours,

Sol Postyn

SP:bcs

NET PRESENT VALUE OF PROPOSED PURCHASE OF WAREHOUSE AND WAREHOUSE IMPROVEMENTS

	PROJECTED STREAM OF CASH FLOW				DISCOUNTED CASH FLOW
Year	(1) Projected Reduction of Warehouse Expenses (A)	(2) Depreciation (B)	(3) = (1) − (2) Taxable Income	(4) = (3) × 48% Income Tax (C)	(5) = (1) − (4) Net Cash Flow After Taxes	(6) Present Value of Net Cash at 16% (D)
1	$178,900	200,000	(21,100)	(10,100)	189,000	162,918
2	446,200	200,000	246,200	118,200	328,000	243,704
3	504,900	200,000	304,900	146,400	358,500	229,798
4	474,600	200,000	274,600	131,800	342,800	189,225
5	442,900	200,000	242,900	116,600	326,300	155,318
6	420,750	200,000	220,750	106,000	314,750	129,047
7	420,750	200,000	220,750	106,000	314,750	111,421
8	420,750	200,000	220,750	106,000	314,750	95,998
9	420,750	200,000	220,750	106,000	314,750	82,779
10	420,750	200,000	220,750	106,000	314,750	71,448
11	420,750	200,000	220,750	106,000	314,750	61,376
12	420,750	200,000	220,750	106,000	314,750	52,878
13	420,750	200,000	220,750	106,000	314,750	45,639
14	420,750	200,000	220,750	106,000	314,750	39,343
15	420,750	200,000	220,750	106,000	314,750	33,993

Net present value of operational results $1,704,885 (E)

Residual value of warehouse   1,300,000 (F)

Total cash inflow   3,004,885

Less discounted value of stream of cash outflow
on purchase and financing of warehouse project   2,033,837 (G)

Net present value of warehouse project $ 971,048

KEY ASSUMPTIONS

(A) Projected Reduction of Warehouse Expenses

It is estimated that the company will save approximately $.45 per garment over the projected useful life of the warehouse. This will include storage, handling, payroll and inventory taxes, easier access to product, increased shipping ability and hence increased inventory turnover.

(B) Depreciation-15 year straight line

(C) Effective incremental tax rate is estimated to be 48%.

(D) Assumes present cost of money at 16% for short-term funds.

(E) Property is expected to increase in value at the rate of 10% per annum. At the end of the 15th year, it is expected that it may require $500,000 of renovations. The residual value has been discounted at 16%.

(F) Assumes cost of money at 14% for long-term funds. Total purchase price $3,000,000; 20% down payment; 15 year amortization schedule.

(G) Purchasing the facility gennerates a Net Present Value (NPV) of more than twice the NPV of leasing the facility.

CONCLUSIONS

Please note: *The rate of return or the interest that is equal to the operating income that the investment will yield plus the increased value of the property at the end of 15 years plus returning the original cost of the investment is slightly more than 20%. Thus if funds presently cost 16% the investment is worthy of consideration.*

CAPITAL BUDGET

Project Description	Total Amount Authorized	Additions/ (Deletions) to Project	Project as Adjusted	$ Expended from Inception of Project	Estimated Amount Required Next Three Years		
					19X4	19X5	19X6
Computer Installation	$1,700,000	($300,000)[a]	$1,400,000	$1,000,000[b]	$400,000[b]		
Warehouse Improvements[c]	3,000,000		3,000,000				2,450,000
						550,000	
Office Furniture	100,000		100,000				
						100,000	
Salesmen's Vans & Showrooms[d]	1,450,000	100,000	1,550,000				550,000
					$400,000	$650,000	$3,000,00

[a] Price drop in minicomputers
[b] Phase I & II of project completed in 19X3, final phase complete in 19X4
[c] Total project expected to be completed in two years
[d] Preliminary bid was $1,450,000. Price increase anticipates additional cost of $100,000.

Design First's
Business Plan
Appendix
(Exhibits referred to
Under "Administration/Operating Controls")

DESIGNS FIRST LTD

Financial Highlight Report

Exhibit A

DATE PREPARED/INITIAL

MONTH OF _____ 19 ____

MONTH								YEAR TO DATE					
Original (Revised) Goal		Actual		Actual Last Year				Original Goal		Actual		Actual Last Year	
$	%	$	%	$	%			$	%	$	%	$	%
////		////		////		Gross Bookings							
						NET SHIPMENTS OR REVENUES (1)							
						GROSS PROFIT							
						MARKETING EXPENSE							
						INVENTORY HANDLING							
						GENER'L & ADMINISTRATIVE EXPENSE							
						TOTAL EXPENSES							
						Other Income/(Expense)							
						Net Operating Income							
						Net Income Before Taxes							
						NET INCOME AFTER TAXES							
						ORDER BACKLOG							
////		////		////		TRADE RECEIVABLES END OF MONTH		////		////		////	
////		////		////		INVENTORY-END OF MONTH		////		////		////	
////		////		////		TRADE ACCOUNTS PAYABLE END OF MONTH		////		////		////	
////		////		////		SHORT-TERM LOAN BALANCE END OF MONTH		////		////		////	
////		////		////		RECEIVABLES-AVERAGE DAYS OUTSTANDING		////		////		////	
////		////		////		RECEIVABLES-PAST DUE 90 DAYS & OVER (2)		////		////		////	
////		////		////		INVENTORY TURN INDEX (3)		////		////		////	
						WORKING CAPITAL RATIO							
						DEBT/EQUITY RATIO							
						Returns (4)							
						CANCELLATIONS (4)							

(right margin, vertical: STATEMENT · BALANCE SHEET AND RATIOS · CONTROL INFORMATION)

(1) After Return, Allowances and Discounts.
(2) % Column = Percent of Total Receivables   (3) 12 Mos. Cost/Sales Divided by Average of 12 Prior Mos. Inventory
(4) PERCENT OF GROSS SHIPMENTS

DESIGNS FIRST LTD.
Order/Booking Data
July 1, 19X3 to July 7, 19X3

Page 1

STYLE #	SIZE RANGE 4	6	8	10	12	14	TOTAL UNITS	COLOR #	DOLLAR VALUE THIS WEEK	SEASON TO DATE	ORIGINAL SEASON TARGET	% OF TARGET ACHIEVED	# WEEKS TO END OF SEASON
2104	2	6	12	14	4	1	39	18	$ 740	$1540	—		
2104	1	8	17	19	7	2	54	24	1790	2133	—		
2104	4	16	22	28	14	3	87	35	1870	3436	—		
2104	16	22	36	38	15	2	129	41	1923	5095	—	—	—
TOTAL STYLE	23	52	87	99	40	8	309	—	6323	12204	21000	58%	4
2206	6	8	14	16	9	2	55	18	610	2722			
2206	7	10	18	20	11	5	71	24	512	3514			
2206	9	12	15	17	13	7	73	35	910	3613			
2206	12	14	19	8	10	8	71	41	1271	3514			
2206	5	7	10	14	12	4	52	47	890	2574	—	—	—
TOTAL STYLE	39	51	76	75	55	26	322	—	4193	15937	33,900	47%	4

Exhibit B

Page 1

DESIGNS FIRST LTD.
Order Backlog Summary
July 1, 19X3 to July 7, 19X3

			TOTAL UNITS	INVENTORY		
STYLE #	COLOR	SIZE	UNSHIPPED	FINISHED GOODS	IN PROCESS	TOTAL
2104	18	4	2	12	—	12
2104	18	6	6	18	—	18
2104	18	8	12	24	—	24
2104	18	10	14	24	—	24
2104	18	12	4	18	—	18
2104	18	14	1	12	—	12
TOTAL			39	108	—	108
2104	24	4	1	24	12	36
2104	24	6	8	36	18	54
2104	24	8	17	48	24	72
2104	24	10	19	48	24	72
2104	24	12	7	36	18	54
2104	24	14	2	24	12	36
TOTAL			54	216	108	324

Exhibit C

DESIGNS FIRST LTD.
Sales Forecast
Through the Week of July 7, 19X3

STYLE #	ORDERS SHIPPED SEASON TO DATE	DOLLARS BOOKED SEASON TO DATE	% OF TARGET	ORIGINAL SEASON TARGET	REVISED FORECAST
2104	5095	$12204	58	21000	30,000
2206	14850	15937	47	33900	33,900
2708	3572	8931	71	12500	75,500
3107	5929	16933	45	38000	32,000
4150	9509	31213	42	75000	75,000
4236	9509	34912	47	75000	75,000
5190	9509	36120	42	86000	86,000
6713	10503	32409	36	90000	80,000
6842	10503	23650	43	55000	55,000
7090	12911	24503	35	70000	60,000
8041	11201	13120	41	32000	30,000
8290	7501	8662	55	15750	20,790
8395	8655	10640	28	38000	30,000
8680	7512	8360	22	38000	30,000
8712	35810	42755	57	75000	87,000
8941	40922	51600	60	86000	95,000
8955		1875	15	12500	0
9015	7500	9831	29	33900	20,000
9022	30910	34500	46	75000	75,000

Exhibit D

DESIGNS FIRST LTD.
Cash Forecast
For the Period Through July 15, 19X3

WEEK OF	ORIGINAL FORECAST			ACTUAL COLLECTION & DISBURSEMENTS			REVISED FORECAST		
	CASH IN	CASH OUT	BAL	CASH IN	CASH OUT	BAL	CASH IN	CASH OUT	BAL
Cash on Hand— Beg. of Period—Actual			175,500			175,500			175,500
July 1–7	80,000	50,000	205,500	64,513	56,512	183,501	64,513	56,512	183,501
July 8–15	56,000	74,000	187,500	83,778	92,895	174,384	83,778	92,895	174,384
July 16–22	273,000	248,000	212,500				275,000	250,000	199,384
July 23–29	136,000	124,000	224,500				95,000	125,000	169,384
Sub-Total	545,000	496,000					518,291	524,407	
Cash on Hand— End of Period			224,500						169,354

Exhibit E

DESIGNS FIRST LTD
Purchase Order Report
Through the Week of July 7, 19X3

STYLE #	REVISED SALES FORECAST AS OF JULY 7, 19X3		GOODS RECEIVED TO DATE	SCHEDULED DELIVERIES	ADD'L GARMENTS REQUIRED OR (CANCELLATIONS)	TOTAL PLAN
	SALES	SALES CONVTD. TO GOODS REQD				
2104	30000	19200	8000	14000	(3000)	19000
2206	33900	21700	12500	6000	3200	21700
2708	15500	9900	4100	5000	—	9100
3107	32000	20500	10200	5000	5000	20200
4150	75000	48000	6000	32000	10000	48000
4236	75000	48000	18000	10000	20000	48000
5190	86000	55000	22000	12000	21000	55000
6713	80000	51200	11200	20000	20000	51200
6842	55000	35200	20000	20000	(5000)	35000
7090	60000	38400	40000	10000	(10000)	40000
8041	30000	19200	15000	5000	—	20000
8290	20790	13300	7000	15000	(10000)	12000
8395	30000	19200	8000	10000	—	18000
8680	30000	19200	6200	10000	3000	19200
8712	87000	55700	25000	3000	—	55000
8941	95000	60800	30000	30000	—	60000
9015	20000	12800	6000	10000	(3000)	13000
9022	75000	48000	28000	15000	5000	48000

Exhibit F

DESIGNS FIRST LTD

Accounts Receivable Aging

Page **1**
Date **07/15/X3**

CUSTOMER No / Name	INV NO	INVOICE DATE	TRANS CODE	CURRENT	31–60 DAYS	61–90 DAYS	OVER 90 DAYS
1404 Arata Fashions	00132	05/31/X3	INV			9,000.00	
	00227	07/20/X3	INV	3,500.00			
Total 1404 Arata Fashions		12,500.00		3,500.00		9,000.00	
Percentage		100.0		28.0		72.0	
6000 Comstock Modes	00001	04/01/X3	INV				350.00
	00119	05/12/X3	INV			175.00	
	00134	05/31/X3	INV			950.00	
Total 6000 Comstock Modes		1,475.00				1,125.00	350.00
Percentage		100.00				76.3	23.7
6200 Bernsteins Dept.	00180	06/25/X3	INV		400.00		
	00180	07/27/X3	REC		400.00 –		
Total 6200 Bernsteins Dept.		0.00					
Percentage		100.0		100.0			
7800 Dede's Shoppe	00214	06/30/X3	INV		1,750.00		
	00214	07/29/X3	REC		1,750.00 –		
Total 7800 Dede's Shoppe		0.00					
Percentage		100.0		100.0			
Total Page 1		13,975.00		3,500.00		10,125.00	350.00

Exhibit G

DESIGNS FIRST LTD
Accounts Payable Aging

Page 1
Date 07/15/X3

No	VENDOR Name	DATE	CURRENT	31–60 DAYS	61–90 DAYS	OVER 90 DAYS
21020	Hong Kong Trading	6/12/X3	10,200			
		6/14/X3	8,900			
	Total 21020 Hong Kong Trading	19,100	19,100			
32035	Far East Exports	5/05/X3		6,897		
		5/07/X3		12,953		
		6/08/X3	14,050	——		
	Total 32035 Far East Exports	33,900	14,050	19,850		
40075	ABC Freight Forwarders	7/01/X3	5,250			
		7/10/X3	4,500			
		7/10/X3	6,280			
	Total 40075 ABC Freight Frds.	16,030	16,030			
	Total Page 1	69,030	49,180	19,850		

Exhibit H

DESIGNS FIRST LTD
Daily Management Report
Date July 7, 19X3

	CASH		ACCOUNTS RECEIVABLE		ACCOUNTS PAYABLE	
	This Yr.	Last Yr.	This Yr.	Last Yr.	This Yr.	Last Yr.
Opening Balance	185,700	90,259	979,000	632,000	932,475	845,000
Cash Receipts	25,250	17,300	(25,250)	(17,300)	XXXXX	XXXXX
Cash Disbursements	(5,540)	(12,975)	XXXXXX	XXXXXX	(5,450)	(12,975)
New Purchases	XXXXXX	XXXXXX	XXXXXX	XXXXXX	38,700	55,250
Sales	XXXXXX	XXXXXX	48,000	35,000	XXXXXX	XXXXXX
Ending Balance	205,500	94,584	1,001,750	649,700	965,725	887,275

	BOOKINGS			SHIPMENTS		
	Mo. to Dte This Yr.	Target This Mo.	Last Yr. This Mo.	This Yr.	Target This Mo.	Last Yr. This Mo.
Opening Balance	32,000			26,900		
New Orders/Shipments	58,000			48,000		
Cancellations/Reruns	(5,690)			—		
Ending Balance	84,310	612,000	360,000	74,900	585,000	327,000

Exhibit I

Appendix B

How to Prepare an Operating Budget

The operating budget is represented in summary form as the first column of projections on the profit or loss or income statement. As such, it is not only an important statement to be shown to a potential lender or investor; it is also an indispensable tool with which to control one's business.

An operating budget has four elements—sales, cost of sales, selling and general and administrative expenses, and taxes. Compilation of each can be involved.

FORMULATING THE SALES FIGURES

Purpose of the Sales Forecast

Of the four procedures in the operating budget, the sales figures are the most uncertain and the most difficult to project. Because sales represent income (with cost of sales, selling and general and administrative expenses, and taxes representing outgo), sales are the *basis* of the operating budget, and all other components are developed after it has been forecasted.

The first step in formulating a sales forecast is to focus on its purpose, or goal; it is not unusual to prepare separate forecasts for different purposes. For example, in developing a forecast for your sales staff, you would approach the task more "bullishly" than in developing a (sales) target for your banker. Similarly, if you're starting a new business, you might want to use a conservative approach before venturing forth with a new investment. If you plan to generate two different sales goals simultaneously, review each plan separately. Then the goals may be integrated, perhaps into a third plan, so that sales targets are coordinated among departments. When the forecast is completed, explain any deviations to each department, thereby providing an understanding of each one's performance.

Evaluation of the Sales Effort

Because the sale of a product or service represents a culmination of the efforts of all organization members, evaluation of sales should consider the effect of four different segments of the (sales) process: *product, marketing, inventory,* and *general policies and outside forces* (for example, the economy, foreign policies, ecology, and new technology).

1. Product
   a. Competitiveness of the product
   b. Recognition of the stages in the product life cycle (for example, product development, market testing, introduction to the market, growth, peaking out, and decline)

2. Marketing
   a. Who the customer is
   b. Share of the market (Estimate the total market and determine what you company's reasonable share might be.)
   c. Distribution network (Assess your sales force and consider enlarging it or employing new outside agents.)
   d. Promotional campaigns
   e. Backlog (Consider your company's current backlog in the forecasting procedure.)
   f. Historical performance (previous experience)

3. Inventory
   a. Availability of product (Current inventory positions must be considered before sales can be forecasted.)
   b. Company's capacity to manufacture a product
   c. Inventory storage (Warehouse capacity must be evaluated. If it is not sufficient, consider better methods of inventory control and improved purchasing techniques.)

4. General policies and outside forces
   a. Pricing (How competitive is your company?)
   b. Import programs (Determine the effect on your product and your share of the market.)
   c. Strategy (Define objectives on introducing new lines and creating new approaches.)

d. The economy and the environment (How will economic and environmental factors affect sales? Is your product recession proof? How will it fare in the environment in which you're attempting to sell?)

Selection of the Sales Forecasting Method

Sales forecasting techniques fall into two basic categories—formal and informal. Formal techniques are generally very costly, requiring in-depth mathematical and statistical resources. These sophisticated approaches are generally employed by giant companies, which are not as flexible as the smaller to medium-sized company. For example, because the larger business must maintain an adequate inventory well in advance of a sales campaign, it may have to build a plant, employ a large staff of additional personnel, or order materials to realize its goals.

The smaller company can change plans more rapidly. Thus if sales do not materialize, it can reduce costs quickly—a tremendous advantage and one that most entrepreneurs must employ repeatedly, adjusting their sales forecasts accordingly. The small to medium-sized company therefore usually avails itself of informal (forecasting) techniques, often referred to as "educated guess forecasting."

In preparing such a forecast, it is customary to utilize any of several data sources and then compile the results, referring to the evaluation checklists just provided. We recommend you use at least two of the following approaches and then compare the results.

Sales Forecast by Salespersons   In accumulating forecasting data, it is helpful to start with one's sales force, asking that each member provide an estimate of total units to be sold. Such a request forces the salesperson to make a commitment regarding his or her performance and provides you with the information you need as well. You must evaluate each estimate in light of the salesperson's optimism. Then, by combining home office accounts with the total forecasts of your sales force, you should have a reasonably good idea of projected sales for the company.

Sales Forecast by Customer   An evaluation of your company's customer list—at least for major accounts—combined with an estimate of other customers served provides a basis for comparing your sales force's projected goals with your own estimates.

Sales Forecast by Department   Sales forecasting by department is an approach used for the most part by retailers. Retailers sometimes also prepare forecasts by major product areas, such as television sets, sewing machines, or better dresses.

Sales Forecast by Product   Manufacturers and retailers frequently employ this technique. It is particularly helpful to companies with limited production facilities because it identifies the production potential. In such cases, an analysis of past performance may be the starting point. If there is more than one product involved, prepare a schedule for each one. If you are considering a new product, you may utilize the manufacturer's experience in handling a similar product for the forecast.

Tabulation of the Sales Forecast (By Salesperson, Customer, Department, and Product)

The form in Figure B.1, which allows comparison after tabulating the results by more than one method, will be useful in contrasting the current year's forecast with last year's achievement.

Monthly Forecasts

Once you are satisfied with the sales forecasts, separate them into monthly segments, a task that may be facilitated by use of the form in Figure B.2. Because this schedule is usually prepared prior to the end of the fiscal year, you may have to estimate the last two months in the "actual" column.

Utilization of the Sales Forecast

Once you have established your sales goals, review them. Are they realistic? For example, significant variations between time frames should be noted

Salesman, Customer Department or Product	Sales Forecast Table—19X1			
	Forecast 19X1	Actual 19X0	Increase (Decrease)	
			$	%
Totals				

Figure B.1   Format for comparing tabulated results

	Actual Results 19X0				Forecast 19X1			
	Monthly Achievement		Year to Date Achievement		Monthly Achievement		Year to Date Achievement	
	$	%	$	%	$	%	$	%
Jan.								
Feb.								
Mar.								
Apr.								
May								
June								
July								
July								
August								
Sept.								
Oct.								
Nov.								
Dec.								
Total								

Figure B.2   Format separating sales forecasts into monthly segments

and forecasts adjusted when necessary. Factors mentioned earlier, such as the general economic climate, addition of new products, or a major promotional campaign, should also be reviewed again and evaluated in connection with goals.

DETERMINING COST OF SALES
For the Manufacturer and Distributor

Regardless of whether a company is manufacturing or just distributing a product, knowing its cost is essential if you are to control your business. However, determining cost can be a complicated procedure, not only for a trading company or distributor but also for a manufacturer, whose cost covers many components. In both cases, the most efficient way to proceed is to prepare a **cost card** for every item being sold. Shown in Figure B.3, the cost card is a detailed document listing all the components of a particular product.

The following checklist of component costs may help you complete the cost card. Designed for a manufacturer, it is more inclusive than would

```
┌─────────────────────────────────────────────────────────┐
│  Product _____       │
│  Estimated Selling Price _____        │
│  Estimated Gross Profit _____        │
├─────────────────────────────────────────────────────────┤
│                                                           │
│                                                           │
│  Costs                          XX                        │
│     Raw Materials               XX                        │
│                                 XX                        │
│                                 XX              XX        │
│                                                           │
│                                                           │
│                                                           │
│  Labor                                                    │
│     Direct Labor                XX                        │
│     Fringes                     XX              XX        │
│                                                           │
│                                                           │
│  Manufacturing Cost                             XX        │
│     (Overhead % × Labor)                                  │
│                                                           │
│                                                           │
│  Total                                         XXX        │
│                                                           │
│                                                           │
│                                                           │
│                                                           │
└─────────────────────────────────────────────────────────┘
```

Figure B.3   A cost card

be necessary for a distributor because a manufacturer must consider materials, labor, and overhead. The distributor need only contend with the cost of materials.

1. Materials

    • Base cost of raw materials

    • Purchasing department costs allocated to product

    • Freight to bring material to manufacturing plant

    • Cost of accessories or subassembly components

    • Custom duties on imported materials

2. Labor

    - Direct labor costs allocated to product
    - Payroll tax costs
    - Other fringe benefits distributed to labor, such as pension costs
    - Allocable portion of vacation and sick pay
    - Cost of "down" time on machinery

3. Manufacturing costs (allocated costs of the following)

    - Depreciation of machinery and plant
    - Supervision of labor force
    - Factory supplies
    - Factory rent (if plant is not owned)
    - Property taxes
    - Miscellaneous cost of materials and labor not covered elsewhere

For the Retailer

The cost of sales in retailing businesses is actually arrived at through the computation of markup. For example, most retailers utilize either a 100 percent markup over cost or a 50 percent gross profit on the product selling price. One might, however, use something higher or lower. In that case, first compute the average markup (and in so doing consider the cost of markdowns; see "Knowing Your Company's Quirks" in Chapter 1). Once you've determined the average markup, apply the figure to projected sales as follows:

$$\text{Net markup} \times \text{projected sales} = \text{gross profit}$$

Conversely,

$$\text{Projected sales} - \text{gross profit} = \text{cost of sales}$$

Assuming sales of $1 million and an average net markup of 49 percent, apply the above formulas as follows:

$$.49 \times 1,000,000 = \$490,000$$
$$\$1,000,000 - 490,000 = \$510,000$$

Thus cost of sales is $510,000.

	Gross Profit Forecast 19X1			Actual Results 19X0			Increase (Decrease)	
Product or Department	Projected # of Units to be Sold	Cost per Unit	Cost of Sales	# of Units Sold (mfg. only)	Cost of Sales		$	%

Figure B.4   Worksheet for tabulating cost cards to derive total cost of sales

Total Cost of Sales

Once you've computed a cost card or average markup (whichever is applicable) for every department or product, compute the total cost of sales by multiplying the projected sales of each product by its cost. A worksheet such as the one in Figure B.4 will help you tabulate the various cost cards in order to arrive at total cost of sales.

Contingent Costs

We recommend establishing a small reserve for contingent costs. This amount is often arbitrary or arrived at through trial and error. Once you decide what it will be, you can begin compiling a profit worksheet, using a format such as the one in Figure B.5.

Profit Worksheet		$	%
Sales (after discounts & returns)			100[a]
Cost of Sales			
Reserve for Contingent Costs			
Total Cost of Sales			
Gross Profit			

[a]All percentages are usually measured from the net sales figure. Thus this line item is sometimes referred to as the budget base.

Figure B.5   Profit worksheet—beginning

Sales and Costs of Sales Reevaluation

Before going on to the next procedure in preparing your operating budget, evaluate sales, costs of sales, and gross profit on your profit worksheet (see Figure B.5). If they are not up to par (refer to previous performance and industry averages), now is the time to make some adjustments. Proceed with the compilation of overhead or selling and general and administrative expenses only if you show a reasonable gross profit.

COMPILING SELLING AND GENERAL AND ADMINISTRATIVE EXPENSES (OVERHEAD)

Preplanning the Profit Route

After you've established a basic strategy in terms of sales, costs of sales, and gross profit, you should focus on what kind of pretax profit picture you want to have before deciding how much you can spend on selling and general and administrative expenses. Do this by using a fixed target, that is, a predetermined amount such as your **pretax profit** (net profit before taxes), which is usually computed as a percentage of sales. For example, if you assume that your sales target is $1 million, with costs established at 62 percent of sales, you are left with a gross profit of 38 percent or $380,000. If you aim for pretax profits of 10 percent, or $100,000, you can compute what you can afford in selling and general and administrative expenses like this:

	$	%
Sales	1,000,000	100
Cost of Sales	620,000	62
Gross Profit	380,000	38
Pretax Profit	100,000	10
Selling and General and Administrative Expenses		
should not exceed	280,000	28

Will the amount you are left with be sufficient? Because all components of your profit objective must be attainable and compatible with all other elements of the budget, you may have to review your sales strategy or gross profit policies in order to make that happen. Knowing where you are heading is the first step in getting there. Thus it is essential that you preplan your route.

Cutting Up Your Expenses

In determining selling and general and administrative expenses, we suggest an overall allocation of that budget before you establish each line item of expense. For example, you may wish to allow 50 percent of the total overhead budget for selling expenses and 20 percent for general expenses, with the balance allocated to administrative costs. We strongly recommend this procedure, particularly if each department prepares its own operating budget, because this approach generally ensures that each department conforms with the total plan.

Expense Worksheet

The next step is to break down expenses. If you have been in business for a while and can rely on previous experience, an analysis of past operating expenses is a good starting point. If yours is a new business, operating statistics for a similar business are available from sources such as Robert Morris, *RMA Annual Statement Studies.* Or you may choose to seek the aid of a CPA who has handled similar businesses.

In the worksheet in Figure B.6, we have allowed for the classification of fixed, variable, and **semivariable expenses.**

By comparing the forecasted expense with the preceding year, you should be able to determine whether a particular expense is realistic. A word of caution, however: Every line item *should* be justified. The typical bureaucratic approach of exceeding the previous year's allotment on general principles must be avoided at all costs because it represents a lack of fiscal responsibility and a senseless misuse of funds.

Major Expense Categories

Having found that certain items (such as salaries, advertising, and travel) make up the bulk of your overhead expenses, use worksheets to help you budget these expenses. We strongly recommend that you submit detailed supports for those line items that represent a significant portion of your overhead.

Salary   The salary expense form, such as that in Figure B.7, forces you to evaluate each member of your staff when projecting a salary increase.

Travel   In developing travel expense budgets, a brief description of the purpose of the proposed trip eliminates a lot of inessential travel. When

SELLING AND GENERAL AND ADMINISTRATIVE (Overhead) EXPENSE WORKSHEET—19X1

Acct. #	Description	Actual Expenses 19X0	Forecasted Expenses—19X1			
			Variable	Semi-Variable	Fixed	Total
847	Office Expense					
849	Office Salaries[a]					
875	Telephone					
877	Travel[a]					
879	Utilities					
	Totals					

[a]Detailed worksheet

Figure B.6. Overhead expense worksheet

SALARY EXPENSE FORM

Employee	1	2	3	4	5
	Present Salary Per Month	Per Month	# Months of Raise	Total Raise	Total Col. 1 + Col. 4

Figure B.7   Salary expense form.

TRAVEL EXPENSE FORM

Employee	1	2	3	4	5	6
	Number of Days Estimated for Trip	Daily Living Expense Rate	Total Living Expense (Col. 1 × Col. 2)	Fare—Air/Auto/Rail	Local Expenses	Total (Add Cols. 3, 4 & 5)
Itinerary of trip and/or purpose (attach further description if not sufficient room)						

Figure B.8   Travel expense form

FORECASTED SELLING, GENERAL, AND ADMINISTRATIVE (OVERHEAD) EXPENSES —BY MONTH	Total	JAN	FEB	MAR	APR	MAY	JUN	JUL	AUG	SEP	OCT	NOV	DEC
Sales													
Sales Department													
Variable													
Commissions													
Total													
Fixed													
Salaries													
Travel													
Advertising													
Supplies													
Total													
Total Sales Dept.													
General													
Fixed													
Salaries													
Rent													
Semi-Fixed													
Shipping Labor													

Figure B.9   Form for compiling monthly targets

a trip is made for sales reasons, this portion of the budget should coordinate with your company's sales forecasts. Use a form like the one in Figure B.8 to help control travel expenses.

Breaking Down Your Annual Projections

Once you've formulated your operating budget, break down your projections for both sales and expenses into monthly allotments so you can measure your targets on a monthly basis, thereby better controlling your business. The worksheet in Figure B.9 provides a format for compiling these monthly targets.

Note that you may insert the sales projections (that is, net sales) on this worksheet to simplify the preparation of the variable and semivariable expense computations. For expenses that have wide seasonality, such as advertising costs, a separate worksheet may be necessary in order to allocate that annual target.

Winding Up the Operating Budget

At this point, we suggest you tally where you stand before going on to the final procedure—determining your tax bill. Picking up where you left off when you began to compile a profit worksheet (Figure B.5), take time now to summarize your profit and expense results, as shown in Figure B.10.

Is your pretax profit in line with your goal? If so, you can go on to the next phase. If not, you'd better backtrack and make some revisions. Perhaps you need only adjust certain expense budgets. It may be that you need to generate a higher gross profit or make your sales targets more ambitious. And don't forget to compare the percentage relationships to industry ratios; a potential lender or investor certainly will.

Profit Worksheet	$	%
Sales (After Discounts & Returns)		100
Cost of Sales		
Reserve for Contingent Costs		
Total Cost of Sales		
Gross Profit		
Selling Expense		
General & Administrative Expense		
Total Expenses		
Pretax Profit		

Figure B.10   Profit worksheet—conclusion

CALCULATING YOUR TAXES

Once you are satisfied with your pretax profit, computing taxes is simply a matter of complying with a rate structure established by local, state, and federal authorities. If a rate book is not available, ask your CPA to provide you with the necessary tax rates because you will want to make adequate provisions in your budget for this line item. Remember to include local and state taxes if applicable.

Appendix C

How to Prepare a Capital Budget

As an expansion of one line item on the cash statement (fixed asset expenditures), the capital budget elaborates on long-term investments in which your company will be engaging. Because most companies do not have unlimited funds, thoroughly evaluate and compare *each* potential investment before you commit yourself and your company to the expenditure. Consider the cost to your company (that cost may require financing), the return on investment, and the advantages of purchasing (over leasing) the equipment or facility.

This appendix focuses on evaluating alternatives in a potential expenditure. Once you've completed the evaluation, the decision on whether to make an investment (and add it to your budget) should be relatively simple. The methods used to make this decision are extremely technical and there are constantly changing tax ramifications to be considered; so we divide this effort into two responsibilities.

One is the job of the entrepreneur, and your task is that of fact finder, assumption formulator, and ultimate decision maker. To assist you in the first two endeavors, we have provided a checklist to guide you. Your accountant then must take your facts and assumptions and prepare the calculations that enable you to evaluate a potential investment and decide whether or not to buy or invest.

ENTREPRENEUR'S CHECKLIST FOR CAPITAL BUDGET CONSIDERATIONS

    A. Purchasing facts and assumptions (if equipment or facility is not leased)
        1. Purchase price to acquire the asset (the result of bids acquired from various contractors or vendors)—a fact

255

2. Sales price of old asset (if replacement is a consideration)—an assumption
3. Residual value or proceeds on sale of new asset at the end of its life—an assumption
4. Costs for financing (if applicable, it may be appropriate to get some bids or estimates from potential lenders or investors)—could be fact or assumption

B. Operating assumptions
1. Estimated life of new asset to be acquired
2. Cash forecast on the new asset
   a. Cash inflow
      (1) Consider any receipt of cash or revenue generated by the new asset
      (2) Consider the reduction of costs or overhead for labor-saving devices, such as personnel costs, payroll taxes on personnel, inventory taxes on reduced inventory requirements, a more efficient method of handling a job
      (3) Are any of your costs to be passed on to customer?
   b. Cash outflow
      (1) Leasing costs (if equipment or facility is not purchased)
         (a) Lease rate
         (b) Residual values
         (c) Handling of investment tax credit—passed on or
         (d) Termination costs of lease
         (e) Up-front costs
      (2) Operating cash outflows
         (a) Personnel and attendant overhead costs to operate the asset
         (b) Utilities, fuel, repairs, and maintenance to operate the asset
         (c) State or local property taxes

Having accumulated the appropriate facts and assumptions, turn them over to your accountant, who will then consider tax regulations on **depreciation** (a calculation allocating the cost of a fixed asset over a period of years) and **investment tax credits** (an arbitrary mechanism allowed by the Internal Revenue Service to encourage investment in capital assets), along with various methods of computing your return on your investment. From this input, he or she will produce a set of alternatives enabling you to decide on the contemplated expenditure or investment. It is your responsibility to study the alternatives and choose the one that appears most profitable. If you are to assess your options intelligently, you should understand the various methods available for calculating and evaluating the investment.

EVALUATING A CAPITAL INVESTMENT

Basically, there are two approaches. The first is a simple one in which time is *not* considered. The second and more complicated approach takes time into account. Although there are numerous methods that do not consider time as an evaluation factor, we shall review only two, the **cash payback method** and the **accounting rate of return.**

Cash Payback Method

The cash payback method of evaluation considers only the number of years required to recover (or pay back) the initial investment being contemplated with the payback obtained from the amount of **net cash flow** (after taxes) generated by the capital asset. To illustrate, let's look at a cash flow setup for four alternative investments (Table C.1).

Because the payback method does not consider the importance of earnings generated after the initial investment is recouped, all four alternatives would be evaluated equally. In every case the investment is recovered by 19X2. Under this method, you would also fail to rate alternative X a better investment than the others, even though X offers the opportunity to recover the bulk of your investment faster and therefore reinvest the proceeds somewhere else.

Accounting Rate of Return

Sometimes called the **average rate of return** or the **financial statement method,** the accounting rate of return calculates the ratio of average annual earnings (over the life of the investment and after depreciation and

Table C.1   Cash Flows for Investment Alternatives

| Investment | Initial Purchase Price | Cash Flow Generated by the Investment | | | | |
		19X1	19X2	19X3	19X4	19X5
W	$5,000	$1,000	$4,000	$ 500	$500	$2,000
X	5,000	4,000	1,000	2,000	500	500
Y	5,000	2,500	2,500	—	—	—
Z	5,000	2,500	2,500	500	500	—

Table C.2   Cash flows for four projects

Year	Project W	Project X	Project Y	Project Z
1	$1,000	$4,000	$2,500	$2,500
2	4,000	1,000	2,500	2,500
3	500	2,000	—	500
4	500	500	—	500
5	$2,000	500	—	—
5 Yr. Total	8,000	8,000	5,000	6,000
Average Cash Flow	$1,600	$1,600	$1,000	$1,200

taxes) to initial outlay. (Initial outlay is equal to the purchase price of the asset.)

Using the same cash flow figures as in the payback example, let's evaluate the criteria presented in Table C.2. Assuming an initial investment of $5,000, the accounting rate of return method considers the five-year cash flow in the evaluation. However, it too ignores the concept of "the sooner the better." The calculation for each investment would be as follows:

	Alternative W	Alternative X	Alternative Y	Alternative Z
Avg. Cash Flow / Initial Outlay	$\dfrac{1600}{5000} = 32\%$	$\dfrac{1600}{5000} = 32\%$	$\dfrac{1000}{5000} = 20\%$	$\dfrac{1200}{5000} = 24\%$
	(Return on Investment)	(ROI)	(ROI)	(ROI)

Alternatives W and X would be evaluated equally, overlooking the fact that alternative X offers substantial returns faster than alternative Y.

Discounted Cash Flow Measures

Money may be worked every day, twenty-four hours a day. Nothing can be employed more fully than money. As long as it has an earning capacity, money will be considered a valuable commodity. And because time is an element of its earning power, it has an inherent value and cannot be ignored. Thus in contrast with the cash payback method and the accounting rate of return, an approach that considers the importance of time is much more valid in providing a tool to evaluate an investment.

Although there are many such approaches available, we will examine only two of them. Both are **discounted cash flow methods.** The first is called the **net present value method.** Net present value is determined by computing the difference between the present value of future receipts and the present value of future disbursements, both of which are accounted for in your cash flow. The other method is called the **rate of return,** also referred to as the **discounted rate of return, time adjusted return, rate of return on the investment, investment yield,** the **rate of growth of the return,** or the **internal rate of return.**

Net Present Value Method   To illustrate the net present value method, let's look at the four alternatives (with their cash flows) used to illustrate cash payback and accounting rate of return and see how they compare when the factor of time is taken into account (Table C.3).

You will also need to refer to a **present value** table like Table C.4. (Table C.7, at the end of this appendix, is an expanded present value table.)

For the sake of simplicity, let's assume money is worth 10 percent today (that is, it would cost, on the average, 10 percent to borrow). Let's see how alternatives W and X compare if we discount, or determine the net present value of, their cash flows (Table C.5).

Note that even though both alternatives W and X are profitable, X is almost 40 percent more profitable than W. Thus we know that even if we pay 10 percent for cash to finance the expenditure or investment, it will still be profitable.

Now, let's use the same approach with alternatives Y and Z (Table C6).

Here we see that alternative Z is marginally profitable if money is worth 10 percent (but Y would give you no profit at all). If you were to pay less than 10 percent for financing and could borrow for the expenditure along with borrowing for the more profitable ventures, perhaps you should consider this investment. Out of the four possibilities, three are profitable—W, X, and Z. However, alternative X is the *most* profitable.

Table C.3   Assumed Cash Flow on Alternative Investments

| Alternatives | Initial Purchase Price | Cash Flow Generated by the Investment | | | | |
		19X1	19X2	19X3	19X4	19X5
W	$5,000	$1,000	$4,000	$ 500	$500	$2,000
X	5,000	4,000	1,000	2,000	500	500
Y	5,000	2,500	2,500	—	—	—
Z	5,000	2,500	2,500	500	—	—

Table C.4   Present Value of $1

Period	4%	8%	10%	12%	28%
1	.962	.926	.909	.893	.781
2	.925	.857	.826	.797	.610
3	.889	.794	.752	.712	.477
4	.855	.735	.683	.636	.372
5	.822	.681	.621	.567	.291

Table C.5   Alternatives W and X, with Discounted Cash Flows

Alternative	Cash Flow	Present Value Table at 10%	Net Present Value of Cash Flow
W			
19X1	$1,000	.909	$ 909
19X2	4,000	.826	3,304
19X3	500	.752	376
19X4	500	.683	342
19X5	2,000	.621	1,242
	8,000		
			6,173
		Initial Investment	5,000
		Profit on Investment	1,173
X			
19X1	$4,000	.909	$3,636
19X2	1,000	.826	826
19X3	2,000	.752	1,504
19X4	500	.683	342
19X5	500	.621	310
			6,618
		Initial Investment	5,000
		Profit on Investment	1,618

Table C.6   Alternatives Y and Z, with Discounted Cash Flows

Alternative	Cash Flow	Present Value Table at 10%	Net Present Value of Cash Flow
Y			
19X1	$2,500	.909	$2,272
19X2	2,500	.826	2,065
19X3	—	—	—
19X4	—	—	—
19X5	—	—	—
			4,337
		Initial Investment	5,000
		Loss on Investment	663
Z			
19X1	$2,500	.909	$2,272
19X2	2,500	.826	2,065
19X3	500	.752	376
19X4	500	.683	341
19X5	—	—	—
			5,054
		Initial Investment	5,000
		Profit on Investment	54

Rate of Return   Rate of return is another system using a discounted cash flow. This approach to the evaluation of capital expenditure proposals is used to project an annual rate of return on an investment. In other words, the rate of return may be defined as the interest rate equivalent to the income that the investment will yield in addition to the return of the original expenditure. In the evaluation process, you may compare this yield with the cost of financing. If the yield is greater than the cost (of financing), you would have an investment worth consideration. If the yield is less, you should not consider the investment.

Although it may be used by itself or as a reinforcement of the net present value approach, the rate of return becomes more technically difficult to calculate. It, too, uses the present value table, but there is a lot of guesswork involved before you can actually determine the yield. Thus we leave the fine points of this approach to the accountants, although it is *essential* that you are aware of this frequently used method. Whenever your accountant prepares calculations on a projected investment or leasing arrangement, it is your responsibility to make sure he or she uses at least one of the discounting methods available so that you will have a realistic evaluation tool.

Weighing Alternatives

If you understand these tools (approaches to evaluation), you can give your accountant a potential investment and the facts and assumptions you have compiled, which will enable your accountant to do his or her job.

Let's assume that you are in the garment business and you are contemplating warehouse improvements in the neighborhood of $3 million. You must have this facility in order to operate efficiently. Should you buy or should you lease? Let's look at the calculations your accountant comes up with. Those in Figure C.1 enable you to evaluate a purchase through net present value. The calculations in Figure C.2 show the net present value of cash flow if you were to lease.

Both calculations are the result of facts and assumptions you have supplied. They are only as good as the data you provide. Though each alternative involves risk, one may appear more advantageous than the other. However, an evaluation of the assumptions may provide you with additional insight in making your decision.

You should also ask yourself whether the investment is worth the risk to you and your company. Can you invest the funds to better advantage elsewhere? Can the investment improve employee relations or enhance your company's standing in the community? If so, is the latter important? Moreover, a note of caution is in order. Because the forecasted cash flows on the

	PROJECTED STREAM OF CASH FLOW					DISCOUNTED CASH FLOW
	(1)	(2)	(3) = (1) − (2)	(4) = (3) × 48%	(5) = (1) − (4)	(6)
Year	Projected Reduction of Warehouse Expenses (A)	Depreciation (B)	Taxable Income	Income Tax (C)	Net Cash Flow After Taxes	Present Value of Net Cash at 16% (D)
1	$178,900	200,000	(21,100)	(10,100)	189,000	162,918
2	446,200	200,000	246,200	118,200	328,000	243,704
3	504,900	200,000	304,900	146,400	358,500	229,798
4	474,600	200,000	274,600	131,800	342,800	189,225
5	442,900	200,000	242,900	116,600	326,300	155,318
6	420,750	200,000	220,750	106,000	314,750	129,047
7	420,750	200,000	220,750	106,000	314,750	111,421
8	420,750	200,000	220,750	106,000	314,750	95,998
9	420,750	200,000	220,750	106,000	314,750	82,779
10	420,750	200,000	220,750	106,000	314,750	71,448
11	420,750	200,000	220,750	106,000	314,750	61,376
12	420,750	200,000	220,750	106,000	314,750	52,878
13	420,750	200,000	220,750	106,000	314,750	45,639
14	420,750	200,000	220,750	106,000	314,750	39,343
15	420,750	200,000	220,750	106,000	314,750	33,993

Net present value of operational results   (E). $1,704,885

Residual value of warehouse   1,300,000

Total cash inflow   3,004,885

Less discounted value of stream of cash outflow on purchase and financing of warehouse project   (F)   2,033,837

Net present value of warehouse project   (G) $ 971,048

Figure C.1   Net present value of proposed purchase of warehouse and warehouse improvements

(continued below)

Key Assumptions

(A) Projected Reduction of Warehouse Expenses—It is estimated that the company will save approximately $.45 per garment over the projected useful life of the warehouse. This will include storage, handling, payroll and inventory taxes, easier access to product, increased shipping ability and hence increased inventory turnover.

(B) Depreciation—15 year straight line.

(C) Effective incremental tax rate is estimated to be 48%.

(D) Assumes present cost of money at 16% for short-term funds.

(E) Property is expected to increase in value at the rate of 10% per annum. At the end of the 15th year, it is expected that it may require $500,000 of renovations. The residual value has been discounted at 16%.

(F) Assumes cost of money at 14% for long-term funds. Total purchase price $3,000,000, 20% down payment, 15-year amortization schedule.

Conclusions

(G) Purchasing the facility generates a net present value (NPV) of more than twice the NPV of leasing the facility.

Please Note: *The rate of return* or the interest that is equal to the operating income that the investment will yield *plus* the increased value of the property at the end of 15 years *plus* returning the original cost of the investment is slightly more than 20%. Thus if funds presently cost 16% the investment is worthy of consideration.

Fig. C.1 *(continued)*

	PROJECTED STREAM OF CASH FLOW					DISCOUNTED CASH FLOW
Year	(1) Projected Reduction of Warehouse Expenses (A)	(2) Lease Rent (B)	(3) = (1) − (2) Taxable Income	(4) = (3) × 48% Income Tax (C)	(5) = (3) − (4) Net Cash Flow After Taxes	(6) Present Value of Net Cash at 16%
1	$178,900	$300,000	$(121,100)	$(58,100)	$(63,000)	$(54,306)
2	446,200	300,000	146,200	70,200	76,000	56,468
3	504,900	300,000	204,900	98,300	106,600	68,331
4	474,600	300,000	174,600	83,800	90,800	50,121
5	442,900	300,000	142,900	68,600	74,300	35,367
6	420,750	300,000	120,750	58,000	62,750	25,727
7	420,750	300,000	120,750	58,000	62,750	22,151
8	420,750	300,000	120,750	58,000	62,750	19,138
9	420,750	300,000	120,750	58,000	62,750	16,503
10	420,750	300,000	120,750	58,000	62,750	14,182
11	420,750	300,000	120,750	58,000	62,750	12,236
12	420,750	300,000	120,750	58,000	62,750	10,542
13	420,750	300,000	120,750	58,000	62,750	9,098
14	420,750	300,000	120,750	58,000	62,750	7,844
15	420,750	300,000	120,750	58,000	62,750	6,777

NET PRESENT VALUE $300,179 (D)

Figure C.2   Net present value of proposed lease of warehouse and warehouse improvements.

(continued below)

Key Assumptions

(A) Projected Reduction of Warehouse Expenses—It is estimated that the company will save approximately $.45 per garment over the projected useful life of the warehouse. This will include storage, handling, payroll and inventory taxes, easier access to product, increased shipping ability and hence increased inventory turnover.

(B) Lease Rent—Net, Net Lease at $25,000/month 15 year lock in. Right to negotiate with landlord at the end of 15 year term. No residual values at termination of lease.

(C) Effective incremental tax rate is estimated to be 48%.

Conclusions

(D) Although leasing the property is lucrative, it appears that purchasing the property will provide more than twice the return. See evaluation of purchase and the assumptions stated therein.

Fig. C.2 *(continued)*

Table C.7 The Present Value of $1

Period	1%	2%	4%	6%	7%	8%	9%	10%	11%	12%	14%	16%	20%
1	.990	.980	.962	.943	.935	.926	.917	.909	.901	.893	.878	.862	.833
2	.980	.961	.925	.890	.873	.857	.842	.826	.812	.797	.771	.743	.694
3	.971	.942	.889	.840	.816	.794	.772	.751	.731	.712	.677	.641	.579
4	.961	.924	.855	.792	.763	.735	.708	.683	.659	.636	.594	.552	.482
5	.951	.906	.822	.747	.713	.681	.650	.621	.593	.567	.522	.476	.402
6	.942	.888	.790	.705	.666	.630	.596	.564	.535	.507	.458	.410	.335
7	.933	.871	.760	.665	.623	.583	.547	.513	.482	.452	.402	.354	.279
8	.923	.853	.731	.627	.582	.540	.502	.467	.434	.404	.353	.305	.233
9	.914	.837	.703	.592	.544	.500	.460	.424	.391	.361	.310	.263	.194
10	.905	.820	.676	.558	.508	.463	.422	.386	.352	.322	.272	.227	.162
11	.896	.804	.650	.527	.475	.429	.388	.350	.317	.287	.239	.195	.135
12	.887	.788	.625	.497	.444	.397	.356	.319	.286	.257	.210	.168	.112
13	.879	.773	.601	.469	.415	.368	.326	.290	.258	.229	.184	.145	.093
14	.870	.758	.577	.442	.388	.340	.299	.263	.232	.205	.162	.125	.078
15	.861	.743	.555	.417	.362	.315	.275	.239	.209	.183	.142	.108	.065
16	.853	.728	.534	.394	.339	.292	.252	.218	.188	.163	.125	.093	.054
17	.844	.714	.513	.371	.317	.270	.231	.198	.170	.146	.109	.080	.045
18	.836	.700	.494	.350	.296	.250	.212	.180	.153	.130	.096	.069	.038
19	.828	.686	.475	.331	.277	.232	.194	.164	.138	.116	.084	.060	.031
20	.820	.673	.456	.312	.258	.215	.178	.149	.124	.104	.074	.051	.026
25	.780	.610	.375	.233	.184	.146	.116	.092	.074	.059	.039	.024	.010
30	.742	.552	.308	.174	.131	.099	.075	.057	.044	.033	.020	.012	.004

investment are merely a projection, *not* an actual accomplishment, your conclusions must be enhanced by additional considerations (for example, assessing past performance if your company has been around for a while). As part of that process, you should note any possible variance from past capital budgets, taking stock of similar expenditures that missed the mark. Ask yourself such questions as the following: Did the investment cost more than it should have? Did it earn as much as it should have? This evaluation can help you discern pitfalls to avoid in the future. Over the long run, it also tests the accuracy of your forecasting ability.

Once you've completed all the evaluations, you can make your decision on the investment. If you're going to go with the expenditure, you add it to your capital budget. As part of this process, you've undoubtedly determined how you will finance the asset; so in the final step, you have only to determine to which year of budget projection it will be assigned—next year, the following, or three years hence. To facilitate that task, you might ask yourself the following questions: When does the company need the asset? When will it be ready for it? Can management supervise the installation of the project in the time designated? Will there be sufficient personnel to staff and/or use it?

Appendix D

How to Prepare a Cash Forecast

The purpose of a cash forecast is to allow you to be comfortable while you're efficiently operating your business. Because it tells you when to borrow more funds or seek additional investment, it would be financial suicide not to have some idea of when the cash will be coming in and at what rate it is going out. Thus most entrepreneurs constantly work with some kind of informal cash flow, and when they need evidence of this control to present to a third party, they prepare a formal cash forecast.

Essentially, there are two parts to a cash forecast—cash receipts and cash disbursements. Each component is made up of several elements relevant to the nature and size of the business. Here we deal with receipts and disbursements that are representative of most businesses and focus on businesses that operate on an accounts receivable basis, rather than on companies generating cash sales exclusively. We also examine the three concluding procedures to cash forecasting: determining cash positions, compiling the cash forecast, and evaluating the forecast.

FORECASTING CASH RECEIPTS

There are two methods of forecasting cash receipts from the sale of your product: using daily cash collections or your past experience in average collections. The latter method is available only to companies that have been in business for a while (and thus have accumulated some collections experience), but the first method may be used by older businesses as well as by younger companies that don't yet have this resource. They need only avail themselves of the information provided through industry ratios (for example, Robert Morris and Associates).

268

Using Daily Cash Collections

This method of forecasting cash receipts requires that a ratio be established between total cash collected and total sales dollars (which have been adjusted for year-end sales figures). Once you have determined the ratio, you can apply it to the total amount of forecasted sales, thereby enabling you to compute the total amount of forecasted collections. By dividing forecasted collections by the number of business days in the year, you may determine the average amount collected per day. The final step is to allocate the average daily collection to the applicable month. Figure D.1 illustrates this procedure.

Facts:

Terms of sale—net 30 days	$340,000
Total cash collected in 19X1	425,000
Less total December sales, 19X1	25,000
Add December sales from 19X0 (prior year)	30,000
Adjusted sales figures to correspond with cash collected	$430,000

Computations:

Ratio: $\dfrac{\text{Cash Collected}}{\text{Adjusted Sales}} =$ $\dfrac{340,000}{430,000} = 79\%$

Forecasted sales: 510,000

Computed collections: $510,000 \times 79\% = \$403,000$

Business days in the year (excluding holidays): 248

Daily cash collection: $\dfrac{403,000}{248} = \$1,625/\text{day}$

Allocation of Cash Receipts:

Month	# Bus. Days	Forecasted Collections (# Days × $1,625)
JAN	22	$ 35,750
FEB	19	30,875
MAR	22	35,750
APR	21	34,125
MAY	22	35,750
JUN	20	32,560
JUL	21	34,125
AUG	23	37,375
SEP	19	30,875
OCT	19	30,875
NOV	21	34,125
DEC	19	30,875
Total	248	$403,000

Figure D.1   Forecasting cash receipts from daily cash collections

Any special terms offered to customers during the course of the year must be considered and computed into the forecast. For example, if you offer special discount terms to encourage sales for the pre-Christmas selling season (such as ninety-day terms in October, compared with the usual thirty-day terms), you should forecast sales generated by the special promotion as collectible in January rather than in November.

Using the Average Collection Method

Forecasting receipts through average collections involves using an accounts receivable aged trial balance, which enables you to discern historical patterns of "on time" and "past due" collections. However, because the method requires previous experience within your business, it can be used only by companies that have been in business for a minimum of two years. The information in Table D.1 illustrates this method of cash receipt forecasting.

Half the accounts receivable (the current receivables of $3,000 divided by $6,000 of your total receivables of $6,000) falls within the current position. Assuming that thirty-day terms represent the normal selling terms in your business, $1,500, or 25 percent, falls in the thirty-day column; $750, or 12.5 percent, represents accounts that are sixty and ninety days past due. By reviewing more than one aged trial balance, you can determine whether the percentages in each position (thirty, sixty, ninety or over ninety days) remain relatively the same. Once you have analyzed the data, you can apply the percentages to the sales forecast (covered in Appendix B). For example, if you are forecasting sales of $30,000 in September, you may assume, providing your terms of sale have not changed dramatically, that you will collect those sales as shown in Table D.2.

After completing your sales forecast and determining the collections average your business has experienced, you may use the worksheet in Figure D.2 to forecast collections by period.

Table D.1 Accounts Receivable Aged Trial Balance

Customer	Total	Current	30 Days	60 Days	90 Days/Over
ABC Co.	$1,000	$ 500	$ 250	$ 250	
DEF Co.	2,000	1,000	500	500	
GHI Co.	3,000	1,500	750		750
	$6,000	$3,000	$1,500	$ 750	$ 750
	100%	50%	25%	12.5%	12.5%

Table D.2   Average Collection Experience

Oct	50%	$15,000
Nov	25%	7,500
Dec	12.5%	3,750
Jan	12.5%	$ 3,750
	100%	$30,000

Forecasting Receipts of Miscellaneous Items

In addition to collections on the sale of the company's product, most businesses have other cash collections resulting from the sale of miscellaneous assets, capital equipment, rental of space, or the sale of scrap.

If there is a clearly defined pattern in your business and/or if the amounts are significant, we recommend that you incorporate the funds into your cash forecast. However, if you cannot project these items with any degree of accuracy, we suggest that you withhold collections from the forecast and classify the collections from miscellaneous sources as a reserve.

FORECASTING CASH DISBURSEMENTS

The sales forecast developed in Appendix B forms the basis of not only the operating budget and the cash receipts forecast but also for many items of cash disbursements, such as raw materials, labor, and variable overhead expenses.

Raw Materials

In order to comply with a sales forecast such as that outlined in Appendix B, it is essential that adequate levels of inventory be on hand at a specific time. This requires extensive planning in ordering as well as in having an adequate supply of cash available with which to pay bills. The best device to meet this situation is the **reverse timetable,** which helps you estimate how time and funds will be expended prior to an anticipated sale. For example, if you plan to ship $500,000 of sales in April, you had best have the appropriate merchandise on hand in March in order to meet your projected sales figures.

Assume that the estimated lead time from the date the order was placed to the receipt of goods is two months. If you are manufacturing the goods, you must also consider the production cycle. Therefore let's assume one month for production. Another required factor is knowing what per-

ASSUMED AVERAGE COLLECTION CYCLE—50%—25%—12.5%—12.5%

Sales Actual (A) & Forecasted (F)	Jan	Feb	Mar	Apr	May	Jun	Jul	Aug	Sep	Oct	Nov	Dec
Sep 800,000 (A)	100,000											
Oct 400,000 (A)	50,000	50,000										
Nov 100,000 (A)	25,000	12,500	12,500									
Dec 200,000 (A)	100,000	25,000	12,500	12,500								
Jan 400,000 (F)		200,000	100,000	50,000	50,000							
Feb 500,000 (F)			250,000	125,000	62,500	62,500						
Mar 600,000 (F)				300,000	150,000	75,000	75,000					
Apr 700,000 (F)					350,000	175,000	87,500	87,500				
May etc.												
Jun												
Jul												
Aug												
Sep												
Oct												
Nov												
TOT												

Figure D.2 Worksheet for forecasting collections by period

centage of sales you must reserve to pay for raw materials. You may determine this figure from analyzing your cost cards or historical financial data. The final data required concerns the terms of purchase for raw materials. Table D.3 schedules the information you will need as a basis for preparing a cash disbursements forecast of raw materials.

Having completed the schedule, you can plot the effect of forecasting $500,000 of sales in April. (In Table D.4, we have purposely omitted data for the other months so you can see what must be accomplished with respect to inventory planning and its corresponding effect on the cash disbursements cycle.)

As the table illustrates, an April sales forecast of $500,000 translates into a May payment of $100,000 for goods that must be on hand in January in order to meet the forecasted sales.

Table D.3   Data Required to Complete Cash Disbursements Forecasts for Raw Materials

Facts or Assumptions Required	Data	Source of Data
1—Sales forecast	$500,000 in April	Assumption
2—Raw materials required	20% of sales	A historical statistic or a cost card allocation
3—Conversion of sales to raw materials required	$500,000 × 20% = $100,000	Computation
4—Est. lead times: receipt of goods from time order of raw materials	Two months	Historical statistic
Production cycle	One month	Historical statistic
5—Purchase terms	60 days after receipt of goods	Terms to be negotiated with supplier

Table D.4   Reverse Timetable (Conversion of Projected Sales Forecast > to Raw Materials Requirements > to Payment of Raw Materials)

Month	Sales Forecast	Placement of Order for Raw Materials	Receipt of Goods for Production	Payment of Goods
Jan.		$100,000[a]		
Feb.				
Mar.			$100,000	
Apr.	$500,000			
May				$100,000
Jun.				
Jul.				
etc.				

[a]20% × $500,000

Direct Labor

Similarly, **direct labor** (labor used in the manufacture of a product) expenses are often handled in the same way as cash disbursements for raw materials, with a separate schedule prepared for each expenditure. The usual procedure is to start with a fact sheet, which is converted to a disbursement schedule (see Table D.5).

Having compiled the information in Table D.5, you can complete the payment schedule for direct labor expenses (Table D.6).

Thus you see how the aforementioned April sales forecast of $500,000 necessitates a March payment of $103,700 for labor to produce (or distribute) the goods sold in April.

Table D.5   Data Required to Complete Cash Disbursements Forecast for Direct Labor

Facts or Assumptions Required	Data	Source of Data
Sales forecast	$500,000 in April	Assumption
Direct labor requirements	17% of sales	Historical statistic (cost card allowance)
Fringe benefits	22% × direct labor	Federal/state regulations & union contract
Conversion of sales to direct labor requirements	$500,000 × 17% = $85,000[a] $ 85,000 × 22% = 18,000 103,700	Computation
Estimated lead time	One month	Historical fact
Payment terms	Month worked	Historical fact

[a]Or a factor of sales may be computed as follows:

$$\frac{103,700}{500,000} = 20.74\%$$

Proof: .2074 × 500,000 = $103,700

Table D.6   Reverse Timetable for Payment of Direct Labor Expenses

Month	Sales Forecast	Direct Labor Expended	Payment for Direct Labor
Jan.			
Feb.			
Mar.		$103,700	$103,700
Apr.	$500,000		
May			
Jun.			
Jul.			
etc.			

Variable and Semivariable Expenses

Most of the groundwork for forecasting cash disbursements of other variable and semivariable expenses (such as sales commissions or factoring fees) was completed when the expense budget was prepared, as shown in Figure B.6 (the overhead expense worksheet). Figure D.3 may be used to convert the data from Figure B.6 into a cash forecast by month.

Because variable and semivariable expenses have already been computed into a percentage of sales, you need only apply that percentage to the forecasted sales figures. Typically, payment of variable and semivariable expenses follows the forecasted sales by one month (regardless of whether you have collected payment on those sales). Therefore if sales of $500,000 are generated in April and variable and semivariable expenses total 10 percent of sales, $50,000 will be expended in May. Table D.7, another reverse timetable, will help you forecast these expenses.

Fixed Expenses

The typical procedure in forecasting cash disbursements for fixed expenses is to total the expenses for the number of months budgeted and divide by the number of months within that period. For example, if fixed expenses total $240,000 for a twelve-month period, a provision for $20,000 per month should be estimated for the cash disbursements forecast.

However, you may have some fixed expenses, such as advertising, shipping, taxes (federal and state), interest, bonuses, and contributions to pension or profit-sharing trusts, that create a major fluctuation of cash disbursements during the period covered. In other words, these expenses might necessitate a cash disbursement of $20,000 one month and $50,000 the next. When this is the case, a separate schedule for each major expenditure will facilitate cash forecasting.

Capital Expenditures

Once you have decided to spend money for a capital item (machinery, equipment, improvements on a building, or whatever), the best way to

Table D.7 Reverse Timetable for Payment of Variable and Semivariable Expenses

Month	Sales Forecasted	Payment of Variable/ Semivariable Expense
Jan.		
Feb.		
Mar.		
Apr.	$500,000	
May		$50,000
Jun.		
etc.		

FORECASTED SELLING, GENERAL, AND ADMINISTRATIVE (OVERHEAD) EXPENSES—BY MONTH													
	Total	Jan.	Feb.	Mar.	Apr.	May	Jun.	Jul.	Aug.	Sep.	Oct.	Nov.	Dec.
Sales Department													
Variable													
Commissions													
Total													
Fixed													
Salaries													
Travel													
Advertising													
Supplies													
Total													
Total Sales Dept.													
General													
Fixed													
Salaries													
Rent													
Semi-Fixed													
Shipping Labor													

Figure D.3   Worksheet for preparing overhead expenses—cash forecast

forecast expenditures is to get competitive bids for the undertaking and then schedule it the way we have indicated for all other expenditures.

DETERMINING CASH POSITIONS

The starting point in putting together a cash forecast is the actual cash position of your company at the beginning of the period under scrutiny. However, in order to measure the amount of cash you need to borrow or seek from investors, you must be able to predict the amount of cash you need to operate your business efficiently. For example, assume you determine you should have a five-day supply of cash on hand. You might then assume that for a particular twenty-two day month you need $132,000 or $6,000 a day. Thus you should keep $30,000 of cash on hand at all times for that month (5 × $6,000 = $30,000).

In computing your cash position, you may also determine that your average amount of cash on hand satisfies the anticipated compensating balance requirements. If you're presenting the forecast to a banker, it is essential to compute that requirement into the ending cash position, a procedure that may be accomplished as follows.

Suppose a cash forecast indicates that you need approximately $250,000 in loans. If you're contemplating a bank loan and you're aware that many banks have, say, a 15 percent compensating balance requirement, the ending cash balance in the forecast should be stated as $37,500 (15% × $250,000) less any **cash float** (the amount in outstanding checks—written but not cleared—at any given time). To obtain the cash float, you average the amount of outstanding checks for a year by reviewing bank reconciliations during that time frame.

To complete our example, assume that cash float averages $5,000. Subtracting $5,000 from your compensating balance requirement of $37,500 would leave you with a balance of $32,500. Therefore you would have to add $2,500 to your daily cash requirements to maintain the proper cash balance to meet cash needs and satisfy the bank's requirements. Table D.8 schedules the aforementioned data.

Table D.8 Guidelines for Determining Minimum Cash Balances

Minimum cash balance required (5 days × $6,000)	$30,000
Compensating balance requirement ($250,000 × 15%)	37,500
Minus cash float	5,000
Net compensating balance	32,500
Additional cash required	2,500
Total cash requirement (Minimum cash—$30,000 plus additional cash required—$2,500)	$32,500

CASH COMPILATION SCHEDULE

Description	Jan.	Feb.	Mar.	Apr.	May	Jun.	Jul.	Aug.	Sep.	Oct.	Nov.	Dec.	Total
Cash on Hand—Beginning of Period													
CASH COLLECTIONS													
Accounts Receivable													
Other													
Total Collected													
CASH DISBURSED													
Raw Materials													
Direct Labor													
Other Mfg. Expenses													
Variable & Semi-Variable Expenses													
Fixed Expenses													
Capital Items													
Total Disbursed													

Figure D.4   Cash compilation schedule
(Continued below)

Excess or (Shortage) of Receipts over Disbursements									
Cumulative Cash Position									
Before Borrowing or Additional Equity									
Additional Cash Requirements									
Cash on Hand—End of Period									

Figure D.4   *(Continued)*

COMPILING THE CASH FORECAST

Once you've determined your cash position, you're ready to put all your elements together into a cash forecast. We suggest the format shown in Figure D.4, which will enable you to accumulate all the components of cash receipts and cash disbursements.

EVALUATING THE FORECAST

After your forecast is completed, you may evaluate it by asking yourself the following questions:

1. Are these requirements realistic?
2. How do they stack up with the operating budget?
3. Can I reduce my requirements by running a more efficient operation?

The following internal factors could be reevaluated to determine whether you might reduce cash requirements:

1. Can certain accounts receivable be revised in order to speed up collections?
2. Could inventory turn be increased or cost of goods reduced?
3. Should there be any budget cuts in overhead?
4. Can the price of the product be increased?
5. Is an increase in production feasible?

Once you are satisfied that all these bases have been covered, a brainstorm session with your staff and your outside advisory team will help you determine the best way to approach your potential lender/investor. It is inevitable that your advisory group will ask for your reevaluation of your cash forecast—and what you have done to reduce requirements—before they respond to the problem regarding the feasibility of financing of additional cash requirements.

Appendix E

How to Prepare a Long-Term Forecast

To understand long-term forecasting, you must differentiate between planning and forecasting. **Planning** is the process through which you determine what you want for your company in the future and decide how to get it. Long-term forecasting enables you to formulate a picture of what the future may look like once you get there.

Long-term forecasting is expressed through all of the projections (beyond the current year) on your financial statements: the profit or loss or income statement, the cash statement and capital budget summary, and the balance sheet. As a technique used to calculate the financial impact of your long-range plans, it provides the answers to such questions as the following:

1. How much will the company earn? (answered through the projections on the profit or loss or income statement)

2. How much financing will the company need? (answered through the projections on the cash statement)

3. How much will fixed asset expenditures cost? (answered through the projections on the capital budget summary)

4. What will the company's financial condition be if we pursue the plans established? (answered through the projections on the balance sheet)

This appendix deals only with long-term forecasting for the profit or loss or income statement and for the cash statement. Because long-term forecasting for capital expenditures (the capital budget) is an integral part of cash forecasting, we refer you to Appendix C and to "Capital Expenditures" in Appendix D. As for the balance sheet, because the preparation for this is very technical, we suggest that if you don't have someone on your staff to handle the job, have your CPA or financial adviser assist you with it.

HOW TO PREPARE THE LONG-TERM PROFIT OR LOSS FORECAST

The long-term (beyond one year) profit or loss projections, like those for the operating budget (the current year on the profit or loss statement—described in Appendix B) apply to four components: sales, cost of sales, selling and general and administrative expenses, and taxes. However, unlike the projections compiled for the operating budget, long-term forecasts are prepared with little or no attention to detail.

Formulating and Evaluating the Sales Forecast

The key to long-term forecasting, just as with the operating budget, is sales. Yet such particulars as sales rep's units or geographical goals need not be calculated. Instead, evaluate sales strategy and respond to it for the longer term (see the checklist in "Evaluation of the Sales Effort" in Appendix B).

To illustrate, one way to determine your sales goal is to assign a percentage to your sales plan in terms of growth. That is, what growth rate per year is realistic for your company—5, 10, 15 percent or more? Or you might ask what sales volume the company should have, say, three years from now. Whichever approach you use, you will have to evaluate whether your company can attain that goal and if it can do so through internal growth or whether a merger or acquisition is in order.

The process is reminiscent of the chicken and egg puzzle. After you decide on a growth rate for your company, you will have to review the strategy for getting there in order to determine whether it is realistic. (Can your company handle the growth without too much burden?) You should then confirm your estimated growth rate or counter with another. It is a constant back and forth process and you must be comfortable with the objectives you set. Figure E.1 should help you visualize the procedure.

Table E.1 shows computations for the years succeeding the base year (that is, the operating budget) but deals exclusively with projections based on internal growth. (A merger or acquisition has too many variables and must be tailored to the specific needs of a particular company.) Thus we'll assume that your sales goal is $1 million, with a projected growth rate of 15 percent.

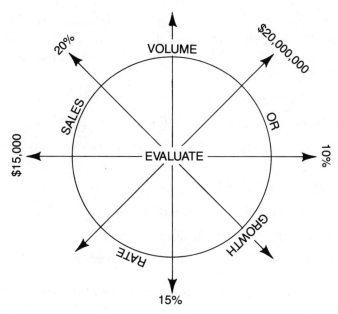

Figure E.1   How to conceive and evaluate your sales forecast

Table E.1   Sales Computations for Three Projected Years

	Growth	Sales (Rounded to)	Source
Base year		$1,000,000	Operating budget
1st projected year of long-term forecast	150,000	1,150,000	Computation
2nd projected year of long-term forecast	172,500	1,322,500	Computation
3rd projected year of long-term forecast	198,375	1,520,875	Computation

Computing Cost of Sales

Once you've completed your long-term sales forecast, computing the cost of sales is your next priority. Again, there is a difference between computing cost of sales for the operating budget and cost of sales for long-term profit or loss projections. Although the operating budget is geared to detail, an extension of a cost card analysis according to product, the long-term forecast focuses on strategy or a plan and then reduces that strategy to financial terms.

Any techniques you use to evaluate costs of sale should include a comparison of the company's actual experience with that of the competition (information available through Robert Morris Associates, *RMA Annual Statement Studies*, as well as Dun and Bradstreet). The following checklists should serve as a guide for this procedure. If you're a manufacturer, consider the following:

- Technical advances in manufacturing equipment
- More efficient manufacturing methods
- Subcontracting the more difficult or more costly components of your product
- Improving quality control
- Hiring a more technically oriented staff
- Better utilization of waste product
- Incorporating waste product into a new product

If you're a manufacturer, a distributor, or a retailer, consider the following:

- New sources of supply of product or raw materials
- Negotiating better terms with suppliers
- Volume buying for a larger discount
- Compare selling price with competitors (if selling price is substantially lower, cost must be also)

After you have reviewed alternatives in reducing costs, develop a method for monitoring performance and determine realistic goals for cost of sales—65, 60, 57.5 percent. How does this compare with your competition (see Robert Morris or Dun and Bradstreet)? After you have translated your goals into a percentage, you may chart your forecasts as shown in Table E.2, which is based on the assumption that you have decided on a 65 percent cost of sales. This will give you a 35 percent gross profit. Remember, gross profit equals sales minus cost of sales.

Now stop and evaluate your forecast. Can you reduce the cost of sales in the time frame you've set for yourself? Are the methods you contemplate

Table E.2   Charting a Gross Profit Forecast

Year	Sales	Gross Profit
Base year	$1,000,000	$350,000
1st projected year	1,150,000	402,500
2nd projected year	1,350,000	472,500
3rd projected year	1,500,000	525,000

feasible? Do you have or can you acquire the equipment and staff that will enable you to accomplish your goals? If your answers to these questions are positive, go ahead. If your answers are negative, some revisions are in order.

After you have forecasted sales, cost of sales, and gross profit, you must project your pretax profit. You might want to refer to "Preplanning the Profit Route" in Appendix B to see how it's done for the operating budget. For the long-term forecast, the method is comparable, again utilizing a percentage of sales, but on projected sales figures for the second, third, fourth, and so on years *after* the current year, or operating budget.

Determining Selling and General and Administrative Expenses (Overhead)

Once you determine your pretax profit, you will know how much is available for overhead (see computation in "Preplanning the Profit Route" in Appendix B). You should then evaluate whether that figure is realistic in relation to sales volume.

The following checklist may be helpful in completing such an evaluation:

1. Personnel (Should we retain current staff or add to it? How much of an additional support system would be needed to service sales? How much would it cost?)
2. Facilities (Will we need new quarters or equipment? What is the cost?)
3. Auxiliary services (What attendant auxiliary services will we need: fringe benefits, telephone services, or secretarial service? What will they cost?)

The answers to these questions will help determine whether your overhead projection is sufficient for the base year (or operating budget). To extend the forecast for the long term, you will need to separate your overhead into fixed and variable expenses (for example, see Chapter 3), because all overhead expenses do not increase in the same proportion to sales. Variable expenses, for example, tend to increase with each sales dollar. In contrast, some fixed expenses remain stationary; others are incremental (they tend to rise as the company moves into successive levels of sales volume).

To show you how an **incremental expense** (semivariable) increases, let's assume that you need one bookkeeper to handle your business until sales reach a volume of $500,000. Thereafter, you will need two bookkeepers to handle company affairs until sales reach a level of $1,750,000. Theoretically, then, whether your volume is $501,000 or $1,750,000, your need for two bookkeepers will be the same.

Table E.3 shows how the various overhead expenses relate to one another and to sales. We are assuming that variable expenses will cost 10 percent of every sales dollar and that incremental expenses will rise at the rate of $12,500 for every $500,000 in sales.

During the last increase in sales volume, when the projection went from $1,500,000 to $1,600,000, an incremental overhead expense of $12,500 had to be added, along with a variable expense of $10,000, giving you a total increase in overhead of $22,500.

Now evaluate your pretax profit in comparison with your overhead. Is it realistic or do you need to make some adjustments? At this point, when you have completed the long-term forecasts for all the components of your profit or loss statement, assemble them and evaluate the whole picture (Table E.4).

Do all the components—sales, cost of sales, and overhead expenses—form a cohesive plan? Does the pretax profit meet your objectives? Will you have the size business you want three years from now? After you have satisfied yourself with respect to these questions, prepare a computation for the Internal Revenue Service and state and local tax authorities.

Table E.3 Relationship of Overhead Expenses to Sales

Total Sales	Sales Increment Over 1,000,000	Overhead Expenses			
		Fixed	Incremental Fixed	Variable	Total
1,000,000	—0—	100,000	—0—	100,000	200,000
1,150,000	150,000	100,000	12,500	115,000	227,500
1,350,000	350,000	100,000	12,500	135,000	247,500
1,500,000	500,000	100,000	12,500	150,000	262,500
1,600,000	600,000	100,000	25,000	160,000	285,000

Table E.4 Compilation of Long-Term Forecasts

	Base Year	%	1st Proj. Year	%	2nd Proj. Year	%	3rd Proj. Year	%
Sales	1,000,000	100	1,150,000	100	1,350,000	100	1,500,000	100
Cost of sale	650,000	65	747,500	65	877,500	65	975,000	65
Gross prof.	350,000	35	402,500	35	472,500	35	525,000	35
Overhead ex.	200,000	20	227,500	20	247,500	18	262,500	18
Pretax prof.	150,000	15	175,000	15	225,000	17	262,500	17

Table E.5 Hypothetical Projections

	Base Year	1st Proj. Year	2nd Proj. Year	3rd Proj. Year
Pretax prof.	150,000	175,000	225,000	262,500
Income tax	71,250	83,125	106,875	125,000
Net profit	78,750	91,875	118,125	137,500

Computing Income Tax

Your income tax rate is statutory, but an *overall* effective rate may be computed for all three of the tax branches—federal, state, and local. Once again, we advise you to consult your professionals before deciding on a percentage. To illustrate, if we assume the rate has been computed at 47 percent of pretax profit, your projections would look like those in Table E.5.

Thus you can complete your long-term forecast for your profit or loss or income statement.

THE LONG-TERM CASH FORECAST STRATEGY

Because a long-term cash forecast tells you how much cash you will receive and expend over a period, it enables you to determine how much financing—if any—you will require in order to accomplish long-range goals. In order to provide an adequate picture of your company's cash situation, however, you must translate the long-term projections for sales, cost of sales, and overhead into cash requirements. Responding to questions such as the following will help you accomplish this task.

- Will I have to introduce and test-market a new product?

- Must I increase my sales force? If so, will training be required?

- How much advertising will I have to do?

- Must I establish new territories?

- Will new facilities or new equipment be required?

- How much must I expend for research and development of the product(s)?

- Will I have to hire a new technical staff?

- If I must make staff additions, what auxiliary services must I furnish?

Whenever you answer yes to one of the questions, you must also ask yourself: At what cost?

As you assess cash needs, you must also concern yourself with conserving cash. For example, the major areas in which you might effect savings are in inventory and accounts receivable. Can inventory turnover be improved? If so, how long will it take? It might be wise to compute what cash savings you can expect by increasing your turn from, say, three to four or four to five (see "Inventory" in Chapter 7 for the computation). Or you might consider decreasing accounts receivable. Should you be charging interest? Are there other ways you can improve on your credit policy for more effective control?

Formulating strategy is crucial to long-term cash forecasting. Once it is defined, the procedures outlined in Appendix D for forecasting cash receipts and cash disbursements may be employed. Appendix D focuses on monthly timing requirements, but substituting a year for a month will solve the timing problems for the long-term forecast. When you've completed that, compare cash receipts with cash disbursements. If disbursements exceed receipts and you've used every saving strategy you can think of, you know you are going to need to raise cash. But because this is the long-term forecast, you should have plenty of time to assemble a convincing proposal.

APPENDIX F

SBA Field Office Addresses

Boston	Massachusetts 02114, 150 Causeway Street
Holyoke	Massachusetts 01040, 312 High Street
Augusta	Maine 04330, 40 Western Avenue, Room 512
Concord	New Hampshire 03301, 55 Pleasant Street
Hartford	Connecticut 06103, One Financial Plaza
Montpelier	Vermont 05602, 87 State Street, P.O. Box 605
Providence	Rhode Island 02903, 57 Eddy Street

New York	New York 10007, 26 Federal Plaza, Room 3214
Albany	New York 12207, Twin Towers Building, Room 922
Elmira	New York 14904, 180 State Street, Room 412
Hato Rey	Puerto Rico 00918, Federal Office Building, Carlos Chardon Avenue
Newark	New Jersey 07102, 970 Broad Street, Room 1635
Camden	New Jersey 08104, East Davis Street
Syracuse	New York 13202, 100 South Clinton Street, Room 1073
Buffalo	New York 14202, 111 West Huron Street
St. Thomas	Virgin Islands 00801, Franklin Building

Philadelphia	Bala Cynwyd, Pennsylvania 19004, One Bala Cynwyd Plaza
Harrisburg	Pennsylvania 17108, 1500 North Second Street
Wilkes-Barre	Pennsylvania 18702, 20 North Pennsylvania Avenue
Baltimore	Towson, Maryland 21204, 7800 York Road
Wilmington	Delaware 19801, 844 King Street

Clarksburg	West Virginia 26301, 109 N. 3rd Street
Charleston	West Virginia 25301, Charleston National Plaza, Suite 628
Pittsburgh	Pennsylvania 15222, 1000 Liberty Avenue
Richmond	Virginia 23240, 400 N. 8th Street, Room 3015
Washington	D.C. 20417, 1030 15th Street, N.W., Suite 250
Atlanta	Georgia 30309, 1720 Peachtree Road, N.W., Suite 600
Biloxi	Mississippi 39530, 111 Fred Haise Boulevard
Birmingham	Alabama 35205, 908 South 20th Street
Charlotte	North Carolina 28202, 230 South Tryon Street, Suite 700
Greenville	North Carolina 27834, 215 South Evans Street
Columbia	South Carolina 29201, 1801 Assembly Street
Coral Gables	Florida 33134, 2222 Ponce de Leon Boulevard
Jackson	Mississippi 39201, 200 East Pascagoula Street
Jacksonville	Florida 32202, 400 W. Bay Street
West Palm Beach	Florida 33402, 701 Clematis Street
Tampa	Florida 33607, 1802 North Trask Street, Suite 203
Louisville	Kentucky 40202, 600 Federal Place, Room 188
Nashville	Tennessee 37219, 404 James Robertson Parkway, Suite 1012
Knoxville	Tennessee 37902, 502 South Gay Street, Room 307
Memphis	Tennessee 38103, 167 North Main Street
Chicago	Illinois 60604, 219 South Dearborn Street
Springfield	Illinois 62701, 1 North Old State Capitol Plaza
Cleveland	Ohio 44199, 1240 East 9th Street, Room 317
Columbus	Ohio 43215, 85 Marconi Boulevard
Cincinnati	Ohio 45202, 550 Main Street, Room 5524
Detroit	Michigan 48226, 477 Michigan Avenue
Marquette	Michigan 49885, 540 West Kaye Avenue
Indianapolis	Indiana 46204, 575 North Pennsylvania Street
Madison	Wisconsin 53703, 122 West Washington Avenue, Room 713
Milwaukee	Wisconsin 53233, 735 West Wisconsin Avenue
Eau Claire	Wisconsin 54701, 500 South Barstow Street, Room B9AA
Minneapolis	Minnesota 55402, 12 South Sixth Street
Dallas	Texas 75202, 1100 Commerce Street
Albuquerque	New Mexico 87110, 5000 Marble Avenue, N.E.

Houston	Texas 77002, 1 Allen Center, Suite 705
Little Rock	Arkansas 72201, 611 Gaines Street, P.O. Box 1401
Lubbock	Texas 79401, 1205 Texas Avenue
El Paso	Texas 79902, 4100 Rio Bravo, Suite 300
Grande Valley	Harlingen, Texas 78550, 222 East Van Buren, Suite 500
Corpus Christi	Texas 78408, 3105 Leopard Street, P.O. Box 9253
Marshall	Texas 75670, 100 South Washington Street, Room G12
New Orleans	Louisiana 70113, 1001 Howard Avenue
Shreveport	Louisiana 71163, 500 Fannin Street
Oklahoma City	Oklahoma 73102, 200 N.W. 5th Street
San Antonio	Texas 78206, 727 East Durango, Room A–513
Kansas City	Missouri 64106, 1150 Grand Avenue
Des Moines	Iowa 50309, 210 Walnut Street
Omaha	Nebraska 68102, Nineteenth and Farnam Streets
St. Louis	Missouri 63101, Mercantile Tower, Suite 2500
Wichita	Kansas 67202, 110 East Waterman Street
Denver	Colorado 80202, 721 19th Street, Room 407
Casper	Wyoming 82601, 100 East B Street, Room 4001
Fargo	North Dakota 58102, 653 2nd Avenue, North, Room 218
Helena	Montana 59601, 613 Helena Avenue, P.O. Box 1690
Salt Lake City	Utah 84138, 125 South State Street, Room 2237
Rapid City	South Dakota 57701, 515 9th Street
Sioux Falls	South Dakota 57102, 8th and Main Avenue
San Francisco	California 94105, 211 Main Street
Fresno	California 93721, 1229 N Street
Sacramento	California 95825, 2800 Cottage Way
Honolulu	Hawaii 96813, 1149 Bethel Street, Room 402
Agana	Guam 96910, Ada Plaza Center Building, P.O. Box 927
Los Angeles	California 90071, 350 South Figueroa Street
Las Vegas	Nevada 89101, 301 East Stewart
Reno	Nevada 89504, 300 Booth Street
Phoenix	Arizona 85004, 112 North Central Avenue
San Diego	California 92188, 880 Front Street
Seattle	Washington 98174, 915 Second Avenue
Anchorage	Alaska 99501, 1016 West Sixth Avenue, Suite 200
Fairbanks	Alaska 99701, 501½ Second Avenue
Boise	Idaho 83701, 216 North 8th Street, P.O. Box 2618

| Portland | Oregon 97204, 1220 South West Third Avenue |
| Spokane | Washington 99120, Courthouse Bldg., Room 651, P.O. Box 2167 |

REFERENCES

Belew, Richard C. *How to Negotiate a Business Loan.* New York: Van Nostrand Reinhold, 1973.

Bierman, Harold, Jr., and Smidt, Seymour. *The Capital Budgeting Decision.* New York: Macmillan, 1975.

Bluestone, Morton D. *Accounting, A Self-Instruction Guide to Procedures and Theory.* New York: Collier Books, 1973.

Brightly, Donald S. *Complete Guide to Financial Management for Small to Medium Sized Companies.* Englewood Cliffs, NJ: Prentice-Hall, 1980.

Cohn, Jules A., and McKinney, Catherine Scott. *How to Computerize Your Small Business.* Englewood Cliffs, NJ: Prentice-Hall, 1980.

Danco, Leon A. "A Rasputin As Your Business Advisor." *The Music Trades*, October 1977, pp. 39–42.

Danco, Leon A. "Business Mule Syndrome." *The Music Trades*, August 1977, pp. 28–94.

Danco, Leon A. "The Fine Art of Using Advisors." *The Music Trades*, December 1977, pp. 89–94.

Danco, Leon A. "Hometown Advice Is Best." *The Music Trades*, November 1977, pp. 56–62.

Danco, Leon A. "Learning to Perpetuate the Firm." *The Music Trades*, September 1977, pp. 74–79.

Danco, Leon A. "Like Mules, One Man Business Heads Don't Reproduce Well." *The Music Trades*, June 1977, pp. 36–39.

D'Anna, John P. *Inventory and Profit, the Balance of Power in Buying and Selling.* New York: American Management Association, 1966.

Drones, William G. *Finance and Accounting for Nonfinancial Managers.* Reading, MA: Addison Wesley, 1979.

Fields, Louis W. *Bookkeeping Made Simple.* New York: Doubleday, 1956.

Follett, Robert. *How to Keep Score in Business, Accounting and Financial Analysis for the Non-Accountant.* New York: New American Library, 1978.

Goodman, Sam R., and Reece, James S., Eds. *Controller's Handbook.* Homewood, IL.: Dow Jones-Irwin, 1978.

Halacy, D.S., Jr. *Computers—The Machines We Think With.* New York: Harper & Row, 1962.

Harwood, Gordon B., and Harmonson, Roger H. "Lease or Buy Decisions." *Journal of Accountancy*, September 1976, pp. 83–87.

Hayes, Rick Stephan, and Howell, John Cotton. *How to Finance Your Small Business with Government Money: SBA Loans.* New York: Wiley, 1980.

Heckert, J. Brooks, and Kerrigan, Harry D. *Accounting Systems, Design and Installation.* New York: Ronald Press, 1953.

J. K. Lasser Tax Institute. *How to Run a Small Business*, 4th edition. New York: McGraw-Hill, 1950.

Johnson, Robert W. *Capital Budgeting.* Belmont, CA: Wadsworth, 1970.

Kryszak, Wayne D. *The Small Business Index.* Metuchen, NJ: Scarecrow Press, 1978.

Lavine, A. Lincoln. *Manual on Commercial Law*, 2nd ed. Englewood Cliffs, NJ: Prentice-Hall, 1958.

Mathes, Sorrell M. *The Smaller Company's Board of Directors.* New York: National Industrial Conference Board, 1967.

Meyer, John N. *Accounting for Non-Accountants.* New York: Hawthorne Books, 1967.

Nierenberg, Gerard I. *The Art of Negotiating.* New York: Cornerstone Library, 1968.

Randle, Paul A., and Swenson, Philip R. *Managing Your Money.* Belmont, CA: Lifetime Learning Publications, 1979, chaps. 2 and 3.

Robert Morris Associates. *RMA Annual Statement Studies.* Philadelphia: Robert Morris Associates, annual.

Silver, Gerald A. *Small Computer Systems for Business.* New York: McGraw Hill, 1978.

Simini, Joseph Peter. *Accounting Made Simple.* Garden City, NY: Doubleday, 1967.

Sweeney, Allen. *Accounting Fundamentals for Nonfinancial Executives.* New York: Amacom, 1972.

Sweeney, Allen, and Wisner, John N., Jr. *Budgeting Fundamentals for Nonfinancial Executives.* New York: Amacom, 1975.

Thomson, Thomas W., Berry, Leonard L., and Davidson, Philip H. *Banking Tomorrow, Managing Markets through Planning.* New York: Van Nostrand Reinhold, 1978.

Tracy, John A. *How to Read a Financial Report.* New York: Wiley, 1980.

Tucker, Spencer A. *The Break-Even System, A Tool for Profit Planning.* Englewood Cliffs, NJ: 1963.

Wasserman, Paul; Olive, Betsy Ann; Allen, Eleanor; George, Charlotte; and Way, James. *Encyclopedia of Business Information Sources*, Vol. 1. Detroit, MI: Gale Research Company, 1970.

Glossary

ACCOUNTS PAYABLE The sums of money a business owes its creditors

ACCOUNTS RECEIVABLE The sums of money customers or clients owe a business

ACCOUNTING RATE OF RETURN (METHOD) An approach to evaluating an investment through which one calculates the ratio of average annual earnings (over the life of the investment and after depreciation and taxes) to initial outlay. Also called the average rate of return or the financial statement method

ACID TEST RATIO See quick acid ratio

AGED ACCOUNTS RECEIVABLE See aged trial balance

AGED INVENTORY A listing of all merchandise showing the length of time the business has held each product

AGED TRIAL BALANCE The (accounts receivable) figures showing the amounts owed to the business and the length of time each segment has been outstanding. An expansion of a schedule of accounts receivable. Also called aged accounts receivable

AMOUNT See loan amount

ANNUAL CLEANUP A process through which the borrower with a line of credit pays up all loans

ASSETS Whatever the business possesses that can be measured in dollars

ASSIGNMENT The awarding of a business share or interest to a third party

AUDIT TRAIL Notations or references in the books of account that enable anyone to trace entries to the original source document

AUDITED STATEMENTS Financial statements prepared by a CPA following an intensive examination of original documents (invoices, shipping reports, bank statements). A study of inventory, a confirmation of accounts receivable, and a third party's verification of an asset or an accounts payable

AVERAGE RATE OF RETURN See accounting rate of return

BACKLOG Orders that have not been shipped

BALANCE SHEET A statement what records assets in relation to liabilities and equity

BOOKS OF ACCOUNT The ledgers and books of original entry

BOOKS OF ORIGINAL ENTRY See journals

BOOKS OF SECONDARY ENTRY See ledgers

BREAKEVEN The sales point at which the business will have covered expenses but at which there is neither profit nor loss

BRIDGE LOAN An interim, short-term loan before one obtains long-term or alternative financing

BUDGET See operating budget

BUDGETED BALANCE SHEET See projected balance sheet

CALL A LOAN To ask for immediate payment of a loan in its entirety

CAPITAL Money

CAPITAL BASE The money an owner and investors inject into a business that becomes a permanent investment in the business

CAPITAL BUDGET A projection of funds to be used for expenditures—usually equipment, land, or buildings—that generate benefits extending beyond one year

CAPITAL INVESTMENT An expenditure of funds for a long-term asset, such as equipment, land, or a building

CASH FLOAT The amount of money in outstanding checks—written but not cleared

CASH FLOW The process of cash entering and leaving a business

CASH FORECAST A projection of the amount of cash available (through receipts, revenues, and a reduction of expenses) and the amount of cash required for expenses, overhead, equipment, and taxes. Also called a statement of projected cash

CASH PAYBACK METHOD An approach to the evaluation of an investment whereby one considers only the number of years required to recover the initial investment with the payback obtained from the amount of net cash flow (after taxes) generated by the capital asset to be purchased

CASH POSITION STATEMENT See cash statement

CASH STATEMENT A record of a company's receipts and disbursements. Also called a cash position statement or a statement of cash receipts and cash disbursements

CHARACTER LOAN A loan in which the reputation of a company's owner serves as security

CHART OF ACCOUNTS A list of all the classifications to be "controlled" by an accountant or bookkeeper—that is, current assets, fixed assets, liabilities, capital, income, and expenses

CIRCULAR OFFERING A brochure used to sell a limited partnership or stock interest that does not require the approval of the Securities Exchange Commission

CLOSELY HELD CORPORATION A corporation that does not have widely distributed stock or stock that is traded publicly. Sometimes called a family corporation

COLLATERAL The asset with which a loan is secured or guaranteed (may be accounts receivable, inventory, equipment, or real property)

COMMON STOCK Stock whose owners are not entitled to preferential treatment with regard to dividends or to the distribution of assets in the event of liquidation, although the owners do have voting privileges

COMPENSATING BALANCE A minimum amount (usually a percentage of the loan) that should be retained in the bank at all times during the life of a loan

COMPILATION (REPORT) A presentation by an accountant or CPA of financial information in standard reports to be used solely for management's benefit

CONTROL ACCOUNT An item listed in the general ledger in condensed, summarized form

CONTROLLABLE EXPENSES Expenses one may increase or decrease by choice

CONVERTIBLE DEBENTURE A certificate that, in return for a loan, entitles the bearer to accept either repayment of the loan in cash or its conversion into a predetermined amount of common stock

CONVERTIBLE FEATURES The right of stockholders to transfer stock from common to preferred, vice versa, or into a loan. The feature may also be applied to a loan, enabling the lender to convert the loan to stock. See convertible debenture

CORPORATION A fictitious body adopted as a device wherein an individual or group of individuals may act only through directors, who are elected by owners or shareholders and who guide its policies and elect its officers

COST CARD A detailed document listing all component costs of a product

COVENANTS (OF A LOAN PACKAGE) Conditions and stipulations of the basic loan agreement

CREDITOR Anyone to whom a business owes money

CURRENT RATIO The relationship between current assets and current liabilities. Also called the working capital ratio

DATING PROGRAM An arrangement with suppliers enabling a business to purchase goods on extended terms, usually with no interest rates

DEBT-EQUITY RATIO The relationship between the amount a business owes and its combined capital and retained earnings

DEBT SERVICING The amount of money (principal and interest) a business can afford to pay back comfortably

DEPRECIATION An accounting or tax calculation allocating the cost of a fixed asset over a period of years, the number of which is usually related to the type and life of an asset

DETAILED ANNUAL STATEMENT A report made up of three components—a balance sheet, a profit or loss statement, and often a cash statement—that provide a full description of assets, liabilities, and expenses. Same as the financial statements, but more detailed

DIRECT COSTING The process of accumulating expenses (or costs) attributable only to a division or segment of a business under evaluation

DIRECT COSTS The dollar amount expended in manufacturing a product for such basics as raw materials and labor

DIRECT LABOR Labor used in the manufacture of a product

DIRECT LOAN A loan granted directly by the Small Business Administration (an agency of the federal government) without bank involvement

DISCOUNTED CASH FLOW METHODS Procedures used to evaluate an investment that consider the effect of time and interest rates on investment yield. The most common uses of this approach are the net present value method and the rate of return method

DISCOUNTED RATE OF RETURN See rate of return method

DISCOUNTING When it relates to a method of evaluating an investment, it refers to a determination of what a potential investment is currently worth rather than its value in the future (the same as a determination of present value)

DISSOLUTION Termination or extinction of a business arrangement

EARNINGS STATEMENT See profit or loss statement

EQUITY The amount invested in a business by the entrepreneur and/or other investors plus the amount of money eared and retained by the business since its inception. Thus it is made up of two components: capital and retained earnings

FACTORING OPERATION An organization that provides financing by purchasing accounts receivable at a negotiated discount rather than make a loan

FAMILY CORPORATION See closely held corporation

FINANCE COMPANY An organization that lends money, usually with accounts receivable or inventory as security

FINANCIAL CONTROLS Procedures and data utilized by management to regulate and evaluate a company's profit effectiveness

FINANCIAL STATEMENTS Reports in the form of numbers that record a company's financial status. They include a profit or loss (or income) statement, a balance sheet, and often a cash statement

FINANCIAL STATEMENT METHOD See the accounting rate of return method

FIXED EXPENSES Expenses that are constant

FORECASTING A projection in a particular area, such as sales, profits, or expenses

FRANCHISE An arrangement in which the originator of a business sells the use of the name (and sometimes other services) and the products to a third party who runs the business

GENERAL LEDGER A book of secondary entry in which summarized transactions from the journals are posted. It lists each item in the chart of accounts

GENERAL PARTNERSHIP A business relationship created by two or more persons who actively participate in the business and whose liability is unlimited

GROSS PROFIT The difference between sales and costs of sales

GUARANTEED LOAN A loan guaranteed or supported by a third person

HALF-AUDIT See review (report)

HIDDEN EXPENSE An expense that may be unforeseen and thus not considered, such as the cost of markdowns

INCOME PLAN See operating budget

INCOME STATEMENT See profit or loss statement

INCREMENTAL EXPENSES See semivariable expenses

INDIRECT COST An expense that may be considered a direct cost when one product is involved but, in the case of more than one product, becomes an allocated cost to each one. Examples are manufacturing costs, supplies, rent, utilities, and supervisory services

INTEREST The amount paid for the use of money

INTERIM LOAN See bridge loan

INTERNAL RATE OF RETURN See rate of return and rate of return method

INVENTORY TURN The number of times stock or merchandise is sold within a specified period

INVESTMENT TAX CREDIT An arbitrary mechanism allowed by the federal government (Internal Revenue Service) to encourage investment in capital assets. The amount of the investment and the life of the asset are the criteria used in calculating the credit against the tax imposed

INVESTMENT YIELD See rate of return

INVOICE SKIPPING Payment of an invoice out of chronological sequence

JOINT VENTURE Co-ownership of an enterprise for a given, limited purpose, usually for a specified time, without the powers, duties, and responsibilities that accompany a partnership

JOURNALS Books of original entry in which all transactions are listed chronologically before they are recorded elsewhere, such as in the ledgers

LEDGERS Books of secondary entry that record a detailed summary of specific accounts (such as accounts payable, accounts receivable, fixed assets, and so forth) in the general ledger. Also called secondary or subsidiary ledgers. Ledger in the singular usually refers to the general ledger

LIABILITIES Debts or the amount, in dollars, owed by a business

LIMITED PARTNERSHIP A business relationship created by two or more persons in which the powers, authority, and liability of each are limited

LINE OF CREDIT An agreement to make monies available in increments up to an agreed-upon maximum

LIQUID ASSETS Assets that may be readily converted to cash

LIQUIDITY The determination of how readily an asset, or other investment, may be converted to cash

LOAN AMOUNT The dollar figure to be borrowed

LOAN GUARANTEE A pledge by a third person to secure a loan

LOAN RATE The price or interest paid for a loan

LOAN TERMS The conditions (such as length of time and type of loan) under which one borrows money

LOAN WITH WARRANT An arrangement whereby, in return for cash or other investment, the recipient issues a certificate authorizing the lender to purchase common stock at a special price during a specified period of time

LONG-TERM FORECAST A projection of costs, sales, gross profit, cash, accounts receivable, or inventory as they affect a business beyond the period of one year

LONG-TERM LOAN A loan due and payable sometime after one year

MARKDOWN The amount to which merchandise has been marked after it fails to sell at the original price

MARKUP The amount a seller adds to the cost of a product, or the difference between the selling price and the cost of a product

NET CASH FLOW The difference between cash in and cash out

NET INCOME The amount remaining from sales after paying all expenses, including income taxes

NET PRESENT VALUE METHOD A process of evaluating an investment by computing the current value of all cash inflows minus the current value of all cash outflows using an assumed rate of interest

NONCONTROLLABLE EXPENSES Expenses that cannot be changed, such as utilities or rent set by a lease

OPEN TO BUY A term used (usually in the retail business) for an inventory budget

OPERATING BUDGET A projection of a company's sales and expenses and the resulting net income over the short term. Also called a budget, a projected profit or loss plan, or income plan

OPERATING LEASE An agreement entitling one to use facilities, equipment, or vehicles for a specific price during a designated period of time

OPERATING PROFIT The difference between gross profit and operating expenses (selling, general, and administrative expenses—overhead)

OVERHEAD The cost of keeping the doors open. It is made up of selling, general, and administrative expenses

PARTICIPATION (LOAN) A situation in which two or more lenders pool funds under the same agreement

PARTNERSHIP See general and limited partnerships

PERPETUAL INVENTORY (CONTROL) The continual maintenance, through records, of the amount of inventory on hand without having to count it physically

PLANNING The process through which a company establishes goals and the methods of accomplishing them

POINTS A percentage of the loan, paid as a fee at the loan's onset, in addition to interest

PREPAYMENT PENALTY An amount over and above the amount owed that the borrower pays after deciding to settle the loan earlier than the agreed-upon date

PREFERRED STOCK Stock whose owners receive preferential treatment with regard to dividends. It also provides preferential treatment to stockholders on the distribution of assets in the event of the company's liquidation

PRESENT VALUE The current rather than the future value of an asset. See net present value method

PRETAX PROFIT Earnings before taxes

PRIME RATE The rate of interest granted to a bank's most credit-worthy customers

PROFIT OR LOSS STATEMENT That part of the financial statements that discloses the amount of money earned, or lost, within a specified period, usually a month, a quarter, or a year. Also referred to as the income statement, statement of earnings, or the P & L. It should not be confused with the projected profit or loss or income *plan*, which are other names for the operating budget

PROJECTED BALANCE SHEET A statement summarizing results of the operating budget and the cash forecast. Also called a budgeted balance sheet

PROJECTED PROFIT OR LOSS (PLAN) See operating budget

PUBLICLY HELD COMPANY A business organization whose shares are actively traded in a public marketplace, such as the New York, the American, or the Pacific Stock Exchange, or over the counter

QUICK ASSET RATIO The sum of cash and accounts receivable in relation to current obligations. Also called an acid test ratio

RATE See loan rate

RATE OF GROWTH OF THE RETURN See rate of return method

RATE OF RETURN The yield of an investment (which may be interest earned, rental income, or dividends) in relation to the investment (which could be cash, equipment, or securities). Also called rate of return on the investment, internal rate of return, investment yield

RATE OF RETURN METHOD A procedure for evaluating an investment whereby a projected yield is compared with a contemplated investment. Also called the discounted rate of return, internal rate of return, time adjusted return, rate of return on the investment, investment yield, or the rate of growth of the return

RATE OF RETURN ON THE INVESTMENT See rate of return and rate of return method

RECEIVABLES See accounts receivable

RESERVES Funds put aside for potential losses

RETAINED EARNINGS The money a company earns and keeps in the business

REVERSE TIMETABLE A planning device whereby one works backward from a final deadline (for shipping or whatever) to estimate the required intermediary deadlines and/ or funding

REVIEW (REPORT) An unaudited financial statement (prepared by an accountant or a CPA) in which the professional analyzes those accounts that make it possible to assure a third party that no material changes are necessary in the financial statements in order for them to conform to generally accepted accounting principles. Also called a half-audit

SCHEDULE (OF ACCOUNTS RECEIVABLE) A listing showing the total owed by each customer or client

SECONDARY OR SUBSIDIARY LEDGER See ledgers

SECURED LOAN A loan backed by collateral

SECURITY OR PLEDGE AGREEMENT A pact between borrower and lender in which the borrower promises certain assets in the event of default on the loan

SEGMENTATION A method of grouping (by product, geographical area, or sales rep, for example) in order to determine contribution to the company's overall profits

SEMIVARIABLE EXPENSES A combination of fixed and variable expenses represented by an expense such as shipping labor. Also called an incremental expense

SHORT-TERM FORECAST A projection of sales costs, gross profit, accounts receivable, expenses, or inventory for periods of less than one year.

SHORT-TERM LOAN A loan due and payable within one year

SPECIFIC IDENTIFICATION A method of computing gross profit through which the cost of every sale is calculated

SPLIT BORROWING A situation in which a business borrows from two or more lenders without letting one know about the other

STANDARD COST OF GOODS SOLD The sum of all costs, both direct and indirect, that are allocable to a product

STANDBY FEE A price paid to a lender to make funds available in the event that they are needed. It is paid whether or not funds are used

STATEMENT OF ASSETS AND LIABILITIES See balance sheet

STATEMENT OF ASSETS, LIABILITIES, AND CAPITAL See balance sheet

STATEMENT OF CASH RECEIPTS AND CASH DISBURSEMENTS See cash statement

STATEMENT OF EARNINGS See profit or loss statement

STATEMENT OF FINANCIAL POSITION See balance sheet

STATEMENT OF PROJECTED CASH See cash forecast

SUBCHAPTER S CORPORATION An organization in which shareholders elect to have the corporation assume the tax status of either a proprietorship or a partnership, thereby altering the federal tax position for each shareholder

SUBORDINATED DEBT A debt that takes second place in a company's obligations (typically an officer's or shareholder's loan to the company). It may be viewed as equity by another lender or outside analyst, which may be to the advantage of the borrower

TERMS See loan terms

TIME ADJUSTED RETURN See rate of return method

TRANSFER To shift ownership from one party to another

UNAUDITED STATEMENTS Financial statements prepared by a CPA but without an examination of the material summarized therein in the same detail that would be used in an audited statement

UNSECURED LOAN A loan not backed by collateral

VARIABLE EXPENSES Expenses that rise and fall in relation to sales volume

VENTURE CAPITALIST A company or individual that lends or invests capital in somewhat risky businesses

WORKING CAPITAL RATIO See current ratio

Index

Terms are defined on page numbers indicated in bold face.